"Masterful storytelling! Readers won't be able to put (it) down."

DIANE JOHNSON, *ROMANTIC TIMES*

"Diane Noble spins stories with vivid characters in rich settings that touch both the heart and the spirit. Challenging and always satisfying."

ANNIE JONES, BESTSELLING AUTHOR

"From California wine country to exotic Granada, Diane Noble takes the reader into wonderfully authentic settings with real people living their faith. Awesome!"

LYNN BULOCK, BESTSELLING AUTHOR

Distant Bells

DIANE NOBLE

DISTANT BELLS
published by Alabaster Books
a division of Multnomah Publishers, Inc.

International Standard Book Number: 1-59052-522-1
Previously 1-57673-400-5

Cover photo courtesy of Diane Noble
Design by Brenda McGee

Scripture quotations are from: *The Holy Bible,* New International Version (NIV)
©1973, 1984 by International Bible Society, used by permission of
Zondervan Publishing House

Alabaster is a trademark of Multnomah Publishers, Inc.
and is registered in the U.S. Patent and Trademark Office.
The Alabaster colophon is a trademark of Multnomah Publishers, Inc.

Printed in the United States of America

For information:
MULTNOMAH PUBLISHERS, INC.•POST OFFICE BOX 1720•SISTERS, OREGON 97759

Library of Congress Cataloging-in-Publication Data

Noble, Diane. 1945—
Distant bells / by Diane Noble.
p. cm.
ISBN 1-59052-522-1
ISBN 1-57673-400-5 (alk. paper)
I. Title.
PS3563.A317976505 1999
813'.54—dc21 99-37047
CIP

05 06 07 08 09 10 — 10 9 8 7 6 5 4 3 2

PROLOGUE

At a remote farmhouse in Western Spain

"IT IS AS YOU SUSPECTED."

Julian watched Raúl Chávez turn away from the computer monitor to look up at him. As usual, the younger man's face was a mask, devoid of emotion. No passion for the Tres Equis cause. No thrill of discovery. Just a man doing his job. Americans would call him a computer genius. Or a geek.

If Raúl didn't have the gifts Julian needed for the operations of Tres Equis to succeed, he would be expendable. But for now, the younger man held the fate of the organization in his hands. He was anything but dispensable. A fact Julian needed to remedy.

Soon.

Raúl was still peering into Julian's face, almost as if trying to read his mind. Julian let his gaze drift to the computer screen.

"Tell me what you have found."

"Our security has been breached, more than once."

"Show me." Julian leaned forward as Raúl opened another electronic file.

"The first instance is dated May 13 of last year. The latest, three days ago." He scrolled down the graphs on the site counter, pointing out the identical server and system numbers. "The frequencies of the visits also have increased. Sometimes the sites are hit several times in one day."

"By the same individual?"

"Or individuals using the same computer."

"What information was downloaded?"

"At first it was historical data."

"And then?" Julian clenched his jaw as he waited to hear how much damage might have been done to Tres Equis.

"And then it gets more specific."

"Such as?"

"The medieval link to the organization. Key words for the search included *cults in Spain*, both historical and modern."

"Those alone do not necessarily lead the inquiries to us."

Raúl nodded absently. "True. But he then targets our exact locale—Castilla y León Province, then Western Spain." He glanced up at Julian, eyes somber, brows arched. "Finally Salamanca."

"I see." Julian studied the younger man. He'd known him for years, and at one time considered him his protégé. It had been Raúl's idea to break into the internal systems of the thousands of possible links to Tres Equis and set up monitoring systems that were impossible to detect.

But Raúl's greatest contribution was Chaos.

That little treasure would make millennium bugs pale in comparison. The Chaos bug would set into motion events such as Spain and its pitifully weak leadership had never seen before.

Beside the keyboard someone in Raúl's cell subgroup had placed—in an act of whimsy, Julian supposed—a brass paperweight shaped like a cockroach. They named it Chaos. Julian lightly stroked the bug's head as he leaned closer to the monitor screen.

Raúl clicked the mouse. "Take a look at this, Julian." He scrolled to another list, dated just days ago. "The search engine was following another key word. Here it is. *Insurrection.*"

Julian's fingers paused in midair above the roach's antennae. "Insurrection?"

"And *fascism in Spain today.*"

Julian stood back. "That still does not mean the search will lead specifically to us."

Raúl turned again, his expression grave. "I have created a profile on this individual. His personal and professional history tells us that he is not one to search out of idle curiosity. I believe he has the capability to make that final link to Tres Equis."

Julian pulled up a chair and settled wearily into it. "We are too close to change our plans now. Tell me what you know about this *researcher*—" the word rolled off his tongue with sarcasm—"and we will decide how best to stop him. Quietly. We need no attention brought our direction now. The time is too close. As you are aware, an investigation might cause...difficulties. Extreme difficulties."

Raúl turned again in his chair and clicked on to another file. "We traced his search engine back to his e-mail address. This is what I have discovered." And he began to read down a detailed list. "He resides in the United States. California. He is in law enforcement."

Julian let out an irritated breath. "What kind of law enforcement?"

"He's a sheriff. Small town in Northern California."

"What else? The list looks long."

Raúl nodded. "He has a history of going after criminals linked to cults. Has made it his life's work, it appears."

"If he thinks Tres Equis is a cult, then we have nothing to worry about." Perhaps Raúl was jumping to conclusions.

"There is something else."

"What is that?"

"He has recently purchased two British Airways tickets."

"To—?"

"San Francisco to Madrid, two weeks before Easter."

Julian waited to hear more. He had always relied on instincts. One did not survive in politics without them. And now these instincts were telling him this *intruder* was more dangerous than even Raúl suspected. "His name?"

"Elliot Gavin. Sheriff Elliot Gavin."

"You said two tickets?"

"Yes."

"Do you have the name of his companion?"

"Katherine Cassandra 'K.C.' Keegan."

"I want you to get every detail you can find about these two."

Raúl nodded. "I've already begun."

"I want to know everything about them, from the brand of toothpaste they use to their favorite breakfast cereal. Everything."

"I understand."

"I want to know exactly where they are heading and for how long. And especially why."

"I have been working on their file."

"You know whom to contact in the States."

"I will make the call immediately."

"Then we wait. Until they leave U.S. soil—" anticipation glittered in his eyes—"and they are in our hands."

Raúl turned back to the computer and clicked to a new site. "There's one more item of interest. Something I just discovered this morning."

Julian peered over his shoulder as the new file came into view.

"It seems that Elliot Gavin and Katherine Keegan have applied for a marriage license. They have asked for special permission to be married in Spain."

Julian smiled for the first time since entering the room. "Spain, you say?"

"Yes, Granada."

Now he chuckled. A plan was formulating. A perfect plan. "Granada is lovely in the spring." He laughed again. "Very lovely indeed."

ONE

KATHERINE CASSANDRA KEEGAN—WHO NEARLY ALWAYS PREFERRED to be called K.C.—noticed the American couple before Elliot Gavin, her fiancé, did. She spotted them as she and Gav entered the small, family-run hotel in Granada, Spain.

The Americans stood out, like surfers in the Sahara. Aleuts in Ecuador. Gauche among the graceful. Poised halfway up a steep, wooden staircase, they coolly observed those milling beneath them—as if they all were *truly* beneath them. It was off-season for tourists in Granada, and though there were other guests about, they were mostly European.

K.C. swallowed her annoyance and tried to catch their gaze with a smile and a nod. After all, she and Gav and their American *cousins* were in a foreign country, thousands of miles from home. Displaced patriots should stick together, shouldn't they?

But the aloof couple let their gazes drift idly, their expressions bored. Purposely bored. Midfifties, K.C. surmised as she wheeled her indestructible TravelPro toward the front desk. The tourists were both dressed in black denim and pricey western boots. She, in a long, broomstick-pleated skirt. He, in designer jeans. Dripping with silver jewelry. A touch of turquoise here and there. Long, dark, gray-streaked, wavy hair. Au naturel. Both of them.

K.C. stopped to push her eyeglasses up on her nose—it seemed they were forever scooting down at the most inopportune time—and exchanged a glance with Gav.

He lifted an amused brow. "Fellow Americans?" he whispered as he dragged his own suitcase closer to hers.

"How'd you guess," she muttered as her luggage wheels once again bumped across the tile floor.

He groaned softly. "Maybe we ought to claim a different country of origin. Or at least make it clear we're not from a nearby state."

She chuckled. "We don't know what part of the country they're from. Though I can guess...."

"Santa Fe," they said in unison, then snickered quietly as they moved below the couple to the check-in desk, just behind the staircase.

Gav stepped up to the old-fashioned wooden desk. A pleasant-looking man looked up from running a credit card through the scanner.

"*Señor...señora*? May I assist you?"

"It's señorita," K.C. corrected quickly. "At least for another few days." She couldn't hide her smile or the blush that warmed her face. "Actually, make that two days, two hours, and fifteen minutes."

"And we've booked two rooms," Gav added. "For two nights, then—"

The man behind the counter laughed, a big, robust, and thoroughly delightful sound. "Ah, my friends! You must be our expected guests." He looked at K.C. "Señorita Keegan, your aunt mentioned that we would recognize you by the flame color of your hair."

K.C. gave him a self-conscious grin as she tucked a strand behind one ear. Her aunt never failed to rave about K.C.'s red-gold hair—mostly because it matched her own. But K.C. saw nothing to rave about in the ordinary, stick-straight, chin-length look of it. And after their hours of traveling she was sure it was a disheveled flame-colored mess. She brushed her bangs with her fingertips, and gave him another smile.

The proprietor laughed again. "Our friends—your aunt Theodora and Father Max—spoke fondly of you both." He pronounced their names with an almost musical Spanish accent....

He stuck out his hand to Gav, then stepped from behind the desk and kissed K.C. on both cheeks.

K.C. grinned up at the innkeeper at the mention of her beloved great-aunt Theodora and Father Max, the retired rector of K.C.'s home church in Pelican Cove. Newlyweds at age seventy-something, they'd spent their honeymoon here at the eighteenth-century country inn, the Santa Cristina, less than one year before. It was at their recommendation that K.C. and Gav decided to head to Granada for their own wedding.

"And you must be Alfredo," Gav was saying. "Theo and Max have told us about you and your beautiful wife, Marta."

Alfredo's smile stretched even broader, his even teeth showing white against his olive skin. "And, as you Americans say, how are Theo and Max? You have seen them very recently, yes?"

"Oh yes," K.C. broke in. "They drove us to the San Francisco airport yesterday—"

"Excuse me," purred a deep female voice at K.C.'s elbow. "Señor, I thought you were readying our room. You said it would be only a moment. My husband and I prefer not to wait any longer." Coolly insistent. Quietly tenacious. Unmistakably American.

K.C. knew before looking that it was the woman she'd noticed earlier, and for an instant an assessing gaze met hers before turning back to the innkeeper.

Alfredo gave the woman a pleasant nod. "You may wait in the lobby if you would like." He nodded toward the small, exquisitely furnished lobby with its rich carpet, fire crackling in the fireplace, antique tables and chairs conveniently placed nearby, the strum of a Spanish guitar playing soft and low from a hidden stereo system. "There is no need to remain on the stairs."

After their long day of travel by train from Madrid and their flight from the U.S. the day before, K.C. would have been glad to collapse in the welcoming parlor, given half the chance. She couldn't understand why the couple didn't simply sit down and await their rooms.

But the woman standing beside her obviously didn't agree. "We have had a terribly long day and we wish to relax anywhere but in a public room." Her words were perfectly enunciated, as though Alfredo were hard of hearing. She fixed a stare on Alfredo's face, apparently unwilling to look away, or even to blink, until she got her way.

By now the woman's husband was standing beside her. Both were tall, in perfect command of their personal space. *And everyone else's,* K.C. noted.

She exchanged a glance with Gav. His face was slightly

flushed; he was having a difficult time not putting the two Americans in their place. But he stood his ground and reached to pull K.C. nearer in one swift, gentlemanly and protective motion.

"Please..." Alfredo, once again standing behind his desk, gestured to the lobby. "If you will be so kind as to step into the parlor, I will personally see to your room as soon as I help the others who are waiting."

"It won't do much good to check them in if they can't get into their rooms..." the woman grumbled, but her husband had now taken her arm in his and led her from where she'd planted herself by the front desk. Their boots clicked across the tile floor, and with heads held high, the two settled quietly onto a small jacquard sofa near the fireplace.

"Now—" Alfredo gave a heavy sigh and a slight smile—"where were we?"

K.C. wanted to apologize for the rude behavior of their fellow Americans, but something in Alfredo's eyes told her it was unnecessary. She gave him an understanding smile. "We were about to tell you that we'd just seen Theo and Father Max. They send their love."

He scanned their credit card through a small machine and filled out the necessary paperwork. "We must talk later." He handed them their keys. "Will you join us for supper?"

"We'll be delighted to," Gav said after a questioning glance toward K.C.

"I'm looking forward to meeting Marta," K.C. added. "For weeks Theo talked of nothing but her sweet spirit and delicious cooking."

"She is in the kitchen preparing our meal now." Alfredo glanced at a room off the center patio, just beyond the lobby. "And our supper will be served at nine o'clock in the dining room." He smiled gently. "I am glad you will be joining us. We can only serve twelve guests, and your table is the only one available.

"Perhaps you will join us for a glass of our special Spanish sherry after dinner. We can speak privately then, about Theo and Max and about your wedding plans."

Another taxicab pulled to the outer doorway, unloading more guests, and K.C. and Gav pulled their suitcases out of the way to make room.

"You may wait there by the fire for your room to be ready." Alfredo gestured to the parlor, and K.C. thought he winked, but she couldn't be sure.

With a smile fixed on her face, she wheeled her suitcase toward the Americans. Gav's suitcase wheels clattered behind her.

The couple looked up but didn't speak as K.C. and Gav settled into two nearby chairs. By now, some of the other guests were standing and talking as they awaited their own rooms.

K.C. decided it wouldn't hurt to be friendly. "Hard to be the only Americans in a Spanish-speaking world."

The woman gave her a cool, appraising look. "Actually, the languages you hear aren't Spanish. For instance, the couple standing by the doorway—" she nodded pointedly—"are speaking Portuguese. And the man near the terrace window is French. You might say this is quite a cosmopolitan meeting place."

"You speak French and Portuguese?" K.C. asked politely, already knowing the answer.

"I'm fluent in seven languages." She touched her hair with her fingertips and tilted her chin slightly.

"I'm impressed." K.C. meant it. "I took two years of Spanish in high school, another two of German in college, but can't remember much of either."

Gav leaned toward the couple. His tone was friendly when he spoke. "We're from California. This is my fiancée, K.C. Keegan, and I'm Elliot Gavin."

The tall man stood to shake Gav's hand. "Glad to meet you. This is my wife, Arabella, and I'm Wyatt. We're the Sterns, hailing from New Mexico."

"New Mexico," Gav mused blandly as he sat down again. "Is that right?"

"Ah, New Mexico." K.C. didn't dare look at Gav.

"Santa Fe," Arabella said.

K.C. swallowed hard to suppress her giggle.

"What brings you to Spain?" Arabella sounded bored.

K.C. met Gav's gaze and, just as she did each time their wedding was mentioned, felt a blush creep across her face. "We're to be married. The day after tomorrow."

"Married!" Arabella actually looked excited. "Why, how wonderfully romantic! Isn't it, Wyatt?"

Her husband nodded as he stroked his well-groomed beard. "It is." The beard and mustache gave him an aristocratic yet artistic look. "You'll be married here, in Granada?" He didn't seem surprised.

"In a private garden inside the Alhambra." Gav's tone was tender, and, though he was speaking to the Sterns, he didn't take his eyes off K.C. She sighed, barely listening to his words, delighting instead in the look of this man who would soon be her husband. His kind face, bronzed by the wind and sun, framed by a shock of unruly dark hair. The deep brown warmth of his eyes. The set of his chin that hinted at a stubborn streak. The touches of humor at the corners of his mouth. She sighed again as her heart did a quick somersault. How she loved him!

"It's fenced by a hedge," he was saying. "Has more bushes

and fountains per square foot than any other rose garden on earth. At least that's what we've been told." He chuckled, breaking K.C.'s reverie. She blinked and looked back to the Sterns as Gav added, "We'll of course see it for ourselves tomorrow."

Arabella let out a sigh, and her features softened. "That's even more romantic," she murmured, giving Wyatt a loving look. "A wedding inside that beautiful, ancient fortress. Surrounded by roses and lilies and lilacs, ponds and waterfalls. Oh, think of it!"

"There's no more glorious place on earth," Wyatt agreed. His expression said he was an authority.

Gav reached for K.C.'s hand. "The day after tomorrow. At two in the afternoon."

K.C. frowned slightly, wishing Gav hadn't told them the time. There was something about the couple that made her uncomfortable. Perhaps it was simply their boorish behavior.

"Will you be in Spain long?" Arabella locked her hazel-eyed gaze on K.C.

"Not as long as we'd like." K.C. was content to give them no more information.

But Gav seemed suddenly to have lost his law-enforcement reticence, perhaps because the Wyatts were fellow Americans. "K.C. will be teaching a one-week course in Salamanca week after next. After the wedding we plan to spend some time in Barcelona, then head back for a few days in Madrid, then on to Salamanca by train."

"Salamanca is a beautiful city," Wyatt said. "One of the best-preserved medieval cities in Europe."

"You've been there?" K.C. asked the question more out of courtesy than any real desire to know.

"Many times," Arabella said to K.C., then murmured something in Spanish to her husband. She spoke too rapidly for K.C. to translate, but there was amusement in her eyes. Rude amusement.

Her husband laughed softly, then turned to K.C. and Gav. "I must apologize. My wife sometimes slips into the language of the region we're discussing. She prides herself on speaking Castilian Spanish, the purest version on earth. Found in Salamanca, as you may know."

"Yes, I know." K.C. swallowed an irritated sigh.

Gav cleared his throat. "We'll be in Salamanca during Holy Week. We hear it's something to see."

Arabella lifted a brow. "Holy Week, you say?"

Gav gave the woman a quizzical look. "Yes."

If he'd been sitting closer, K.C. would have given him a poke in the ribs, but instead she nodded, keeping a bland smile pasted on her face.

"Perhaps we'll see you there." Wyatt's brilliant smile flashed, white teeth against tanned skin.

His pleasant look caused K.C. to breathe easier, and it occurred to her that jet lag must surely be turning her mind to Jell-O. This couple was simply being friendly. Her return smile was warmer. "We'll be staying in the medieval quarter, though we don't know exactly where."

Arabella looked concerned. "During Holy Week hotel accommodations are hard to come by. If you don't have anything booked by now..." She flicked her long fingers dramatically and shook her head.

"We don't need to worry." Gav's smile was confident. "Our arrangements are being made by the university where K.C. will be teaching."

"Ah...the university..." Wyatt leaned back with a sigh, looking wise and familiar with the school. "You'll be teaching U.S.

students through a study abroad program, am I right?"

K.C. drummed her fingers on the arm of her chair. The couple's myriad questions were growing increasingly irritating. "How did you know?"

Arabella and Wyatt exchanged another amused look. "You obviously don't speak Spanish." Arabella tilted her chin. "It would be difficult, would it not, to teach Salamancan students in their native language." She laughed.

Before K.C. could blurt out a reply she'd be sorry for later, Alfredo stepped to the parlor doorway, speaking first in Spanish, then repeating his words in English: "Your rooms are ready."

The four Americans stood. "Will we see you at supper?" K.C. could have kicked her dear fiancé for the question.

"Oh, dear..." Arabella gave her husband an accusing look. "I believe we forgot to reserve a table. Darling, I think you should speak to the proprietor. Arrange for us to sit with our new friends."

Wyatt's face seemed to darken. "If you hadn't been so dead set on getting into our room before the maids had it ready, I wouldn't have been so distracted."

"Good to talk to you." Gav stuck out his hand as if to forestall the simmering ill will.

"Yes, yes." Wyatt let his gaze drift from his wife to Gav. "I'm sure we'll see you again." He smiled.

"Yes, of course," K.C. added, forcing a pleasant tone. She nodded toward Arabella who was now standing with her hands planted on her slim hips.

The woman seemed rather distraught. *Over dinner reservations?* K.C. laughed to herself and reached for her luggage. Soon she and Gav were rattling their suitcases across the floor toward the staircase.

But as they mounted the stairs, pulling the awkward bundles on wheels behind them, she had the prickly sensation she was being watched. At the first landing, she turned. Arabella stood in the parlor, her face lifted toward them.

K.C. shivered as the hazel-eyed gaze drifted nonchalantly to Wyatt, now in the middle of a passionate tirade in Spanish, directed toward Alfredo. Over dinner, no doubt.

Shaking off her unease, K.C. followed Gav up the stairs, hoping against hope that their table was already full.

Two

The next morning at dawn, K.C. headed down the stairs to meet Gav in the lobby. He was in his running clothes and grinned up at her as she descended. Her heart skipped a beat at the boyish, mussed-haired, all-American look of him. Scuffed Nikes with reflectors. Running shorts that showed off his great legs—an attribute she loved to tease him about. Ah yes, this same man who always caused her head to spin and her heart to skip would be her husband in a little more than twenty-four hours.

She reached up, stroked his cheek with the backs of her fingers, and smiled into his eyes. "Good morning, my love."

His expression said he wanted to gather her into his arms and kiss her soundly. But with other early-rising guests moving about the lobby awaiting breakfast, he merely smiled and stepped back to look her up and down.

She saw the glimmer in his eyes and turned a small pirouette, grinning as she circled. "You like?" She'd purchased her own running outfit at home, complete with air-bubble running shoes, just for the trip. A fluorescent headband framed her ponytail, complementing her green shorts and bright yellow pullover top. It wasn't until they landed in Madrid and saw that Spaniards had a penchant for dark and somber colors that K.C. realized her mistake.

But it didn't seem to matter to Gav. "I like." He arched a brow, his approval evident. "A lot!" Then he stooped to retie his shoe. "You ready?"

They trotted out the door, stopping to stretch for a minute just outside the inn. Then they jogged down the main street leading to the *Alcazaba*, or citadel, just a mile or so away.

A scant ten minutes later they halted at the thick walls, breathless. "I didn't realize I'd be so out of shape," K.C. panted.

"We're still getting over jet lag." Gav's breathing was heavy too as he placed one foot against the citadel wall to stretch out a hamstring.

The sun was just rising and reflected off the morning haze that covered Granada, stretching out a thousand feet or so below their lofty viewpoint. The city's whitewashed, tile-roofed buildings and cottages rose through the rapidly clearing mist.

K.C. leaned over the wall, looked straight down, and gasped. She stepped back, heart pounding, knees weak. Even her toes seemed to melt with fear inside her running shoes. A years-old phobia of heights washed over her, and she swallowed hard.

Gav didn't notice her distress. He quit massaging his calf and stepped closer to peer into the deep ravine. "This was built to protect the Moors from invasion. I can see why it stood through the centuries—no one had the guts to come against them."

K.C. tried to keep her voice from shaking. "If the forty-five degree climb didn't get the invaders, the boiling oil poured over the side by the Moors would." She laughed nervously.

Gav chuckled and turned to lean against the wall, facing the upper gardens of the Alhambra. K.C. noticed his eyes narrowed and, puzzled, she turned to face the same direction.

Strolling down the path were Arabella and Wyatt Stern. They seemed surprised to see Gav and K.C., but waved and headed toward them.

Gav groaned. "Shall we do the polite thing and wait for a quick hello?"

"Actually, I'd prefer to give them a polite wave as we sprint by." But it was too late. The couple had quickened their pace.

Arabella gave them a wide smile once they were standing in front of K.C. and Gav. "Ah, if it isn't our bride and bridegroom! Tomorrow's the grand day, yes?"

Wyatt assumed a bored pose at his wife's side. As they had been the night before, both were dressed in black.

"Good morning." K.C. managed. She had the sudden, awful feeling they might ask to be included among the wedding guests. "How are our fellow Americans today?"

She wasn't far from wrong. Arabella was obviously not to be sidetracked. "And how are the plans coming, sweetie?" Her look was calculating. *Girls understand these things,* it said.

"Our plans aren't extensive—the guest list is small. Private."

K.C. and Gav exchanged a glance, and he added, "Virtually nonexistent. Bride, groom, minister—and our friends, the Aznars—"

"Oh?" Wyatt broke in, leaning forward. "The innkeepers are friends of yours?"

"New friends," K.C. said without missing a beat. She wasn't about to tell the nosy couple anything more.

But Arabella didn't seem to notice. She sighed. "I still say this is the most romantic of wedding places and plans. We couldn't stop talking about it last night, isn't that right, dear?" She arched a plucked brow toward her husband.

Wyatt assumed another look of artistic boredom. "Yes. Romantic indeed." At his lack of emotion K.C. felt a surprising ripple of sympathy for Arabella.

Gav cleared his throat. "We really must be on our way."

"Must finish our run." K.C. began jogging in place to prove her point. "Today's going to be a busy day. A lot to do." She adjusted her headband, gave the couple a smile, then headed after Gav as he jogged down a path leading away from the ancient fortress.

The path dropped at a rapid rate, zigzagging in switchbacks to the base of the tree-covered ravine. The air smelled of decaying leaves and loamy soil warmed by shafts of sunlight. K.C. breathed in the fragrance as her feet beat the ground in tandem with Gav's. She brushed away any darkness the Sterns' presence had brought and let herself feel the exhilaration of the run. A lacy tangle of new growth from trees she couldn't identify shaded the path. The sounds of equally unknown morning birds and the toll of distant church bells flooded her senses.

As her feet thudded the path, happiness washed over her, and she couldn't keep the grin from her face. *Lord, you are so good to me!* The man she loved was before her, the glory of God's creation was all around her, and the sense of the Creator's presence sang within her.

Could any day be more perfect or blessed?

A half hour later, they crossed a rickety wood-plank footbridge then halted on the far side of the ravine.

K.C. was panting harder than before, and walked slowly to let her body cool and her heart rate slow. After a moment she was breathing easier. "This one thing I know, my love—" hands on hips and still breathing hard, her gaze took in the Alhambra, its palaces, gardens, and fortress walls, towering above them, golden in the morning sun—"There's no way I will jog back up that incline."

Gav jingled a few pesetas in his shorts pocket. "Do I hear the word *taxi* about to be uttered?"

She glanced around. "You read my mind. But I don't see a single person or car. Let alone a cab."

"They hovered like bees around a hive yesterday."

"That was in town—and around the Alhambra, not here." They were now walking along a narrow cobbled street, leading to a centuries-old *Albaicín* district, heart of the original Moorish settlement. K.C. recognized the whitewashed houses clinging to the hillside from the pictures in their guidebook. She chuckled.

"What's funny?"

"I remember reading that the streets in this section all begin with *Cuesta*. Now I know why."

He grinned. "Means *slope?*"

"No question." She stooped to tie her shoe. "I'm being a good sport, Gav, but I'm getting hungry. Plus we said we'd meet the Aznars and the minister at nine. It's already eight, and I don't think I can make it back up to the inn in an hour, let alone eat breakfast and shower."

"You get grumpy when you're hungry." Gav reached to help her stand. He smiled into her eyes, his expression telling her he loved her, grumps and all. He held on to her hand as they started walking back toward the bridge they'd just crossed. Suddenly Gav stopped. "I've got an idea. You stay here. I'll head back, get a taxi—or Alfredo—to bring me back over to get you."

She shook her head. "Nope. Whither thou goest—and all that." She smiled into his eyes. "I'll be fine. Lead the way, great hunter." She gave him a gentle shove.

He began to jog again, and, laughing, she took off after him. "Hey, my love! Wait for me—"

Just then her toe caught—on what, she couldn't tell—but she felt a sharp pain. Then a snap somewhere near her ankle. She toppled forward, arms akimbo, and hit the ground as a *whoosh* was pushed from her lungs.

She wailed in pain and curled sideways to grab her foot. Gav spun around and sprinted toward her.

"Oh, sweetheart—" He knelt and gathered her into his arms.

She rubbed her ankle and winced. She drew in a deep breath, made a valiant effort to stand, then settled back in tears. That was when it hit her.

"Oh, Gav! What if I can't walk? Our wedding! How will I get down the aisle tomorrow?"

"I'm more concerned with you walking at all. Let's just take it a step at a time—"

She smiled through her tears at the pun, but Gav didn't seem to get the humor. "Let me try to get up—" She braced herself against him with a moan, and he struggled to help her to her feet. Finally, she was upright, but by now her foot was throbbing and already starting to swell. She looked up at Gav helplessly.

"I'll have to leave you here, Kace. I'll run for help. Be back as fast as I can."

This time she had to agree. She nodded, swallowing hard.

"First we have to find a safe place for you to wait." He

glanced around. "Can you make it across the bridge?"

"I'll try." She drew in a deep breath, her eyes closed. Then hopping on her right foot and clinging to Gav, she made her way across the arched wooden structure.

He nodded to a stone bench under a canopy of branches. "You'll be safe here. Off the beaten path."

She nodded mutely, feeling sorry for herself. He helped her ease onto the bench and elevate her left foot. Then with deft and gentle fingers, he unlaced the running shoe and pulled it from her foot. "How's that?"

She gave him a weak smile. "Okay." She pulled off her sock. Already, the swelling had doubled her ankle's size.

"Oh, honey, I'm so sorry."

"It's okay," she repeated. "Please, just go. Hurry."

"I promise." He seemed reluctant to leave her.

"Just go, Gav. I'll be fine."

He stooped, gave her a kiss, then sprinted away.

For a moment K.C. sat with her eyes closed, gulping deep breaths to ease the pain and praying to ease her discomfort at being left alone. She didn't even know the language, for heaven's sake. Then she chuckled. As if she would have to explain what had happened. Anyone could see her foot was nearly twice the size it should be.

She looked across the bridge to the Albaicín, wondering again why no one was on the streets. The tour book hadn't said that the Albaicín was a ghetto or a place to avoid because of crime. But then it wouldn't. She'd heard tourists were seldom warned of dangers in any region throughout Europe. The host country didn't want to scare off those who brought them revenue.

Still...she wondered at the whereabouts of the children, the strolling mothers pushing baby carriages. Or women hanging wash on lines out their windows. Men on their way to work. The taxis and buses and automobiles. Even bicycles.

Her gaze moved to the path where she fell. She squinted, pushing up her glasses on her nose as she peered at the ground. She probably should have worn her contacts for her run, but she hadn't thought of it.

She frowned. What had she tripped on? There didn't seem to be any uneven stones in the place.

She was still studying the path when a dark car crept up the narrow, cobbled street on the opposite side of the ravine. It slowed, and K.C. had the impression the driver was looking for someone. She started to wave, thinking it might be Gav miraculously back already, then thought better of it and kept her hand in her lap.

The car started forward, then backed up, and K.C. had the strange sense that she'd been spotted. Her heart skittered. A silly reaction. What did she have to fear?

Then the passenger side window lowered.

She blinked in surprise. It was Arabella Stern, and, K.C. supposed, Wyatt in the driver's seat.

Arabella had obviously spotted K.C. She turned to say something to the driver, then waved at K.C. "We'll be right there," she called, and the window rose again.

Wyatt pulled to the side of the road, and the couple hurried across the bridge to K.C.

She smiled when they reached her. "You must have intercepted Gav—"

Arabella and Wyatt exchanged an odd look, then turned again to K.C. "No, we haven't seen him," Wyatt said. "We assumed he was with you."

"How did you know—?" K.C. frowned. "I just fell a few

minutes ago. And suddenly, here you are."

Arabella laughed, a musical sound, like tinkling bells. "When you left us this morning, we stayed to watch the sunrise and absorb the glorious Alhambra as it was struck by the morning sun. Of course we saw the two of you jog down from the fortress, across the bridge—over to the Albaicín."

"We were looking for the Albaicín gypsy caves when we saw you fall," Wyatt added, patting the small binoculars hanging by a strap around his neck. "Wanted to help. That is, if you'd like help."

K.C. laughed at her earlier apprehension. "Of course. Gav's on his way back to the inn, but if we hurry maybe we can intercept him before he sends out a search and rescue team."

Wyatt looked amused. "You'd better let us be your crutches, young lady."

"You don't know what you're asking for," K.C. said with a chuckle.

Arabella stood on her right, Wyatt on her left, and supported K.C. as they slowly moved back across the bridge. Within minutes, she was tucked into the backseat of the dark sedan.

Wyatt touched his foot to the accelerator, and Arabella turned to smile at K.C. "I can imagine how distressed you are about the wedding—"

"Perhaps we should take you directly to an infirmary," Wyatt broke in. "The sooner you get this looked at, the sooner it will begin to heal."

"No, no. Really. I'd rather get back to the inn. Gav will be worried if he goes for me, and I'm not there."

"Dear, I agree with Wyatt. I think we should take you to the infirmary. We know of one near the cathedral. We can be there in a zip. The doctor there is an acquaintance of ours. He's only open until ten on Sundays. If there's a wait, we really should get there now." She glanced at her watch.

"I don't have my passport or ID," K.C. protested. "Really, I'd rather go back to the inn first. Then I can gather my things and go with Gav to see a doctor."

"It's up to you," Wyatt said absently. He was now guiding the car through the narrow, cobbled streets, and it struck K.C. that he seemed to know exactly where he was headed.

A taxi appeared in front of them, and K.C. hoped for an instant that it might be Gav in the passenger seat. It wasn't. The cabby reached through his open window to pull in his driver's side mirror, and Wyatt did the same. When the vehicles passed, K.C. held her breath. There wasn't an inch to spare.

"You won't find most doctors available today." Arabella had turned in her seat again and looked at K.C. with a worried frown.

"Oh, dear. With our travel schedule, I completely forgot what day it is." K.C. looked out the window at the empty streets. Of course. That explained it. Everyone was in church. She felt strangely bereft.

Wyatt guided the sedan to a stop at an intersection near the turnoff for the Alhambra; the hills of the Albaicín were behind them and the outskirts of Granada before them. K.C. could see the towers of the cathedral rising in the distance.

She assessed the situation. If doctors were truly unavailable today, it would be wise to go with the Sterns. But then Gav would be worried sick. She couldn't do that to him.

"Might make the difference between walking down the aisle tomorrow or postponing the wedding," Arabella said as if sensing K.C.'s dilemma. "Really. We don't mind. We'd love to help make tomorrow a special day—"

Wyatt glanced over his shoulder. "Why don't I drop you two off at the infirmary. Then I'll head back to the inn, or even to the place we found you, to find Gav. I'll explain and bring your young man back with me." He turned toward the city without waiting for K.C.'s answer.

K.C. let out a sigh. Her foot was throbbing with pain, and she leaned her head against the seat with her eyes closed. They were right. It was the wisest thing to do under the circumstances. "Take me there," she said finally. "But are you sure I can get assistance without ID?"

"We know Doc Rafael. It will be fine." Arabella laughed. "He actually prefers to be called Doc. He watches *Gunsmoke* reruns, fancies himself a throwback to the old American West."

For some reason the only image that came to her mind was that of Doc Holliday, cohort of outlaws. She shivered, wondering at her too vivid imagination…and her recent penchant toward paranoia whenever the Wyatts crossed her path.

K.C. was surprised and impressed with the modern facility. Within an hour, her foot had been poked and probed and x-rayed. Doc Rafael was a somber, round-faced man of fifty or so. He was bald, though he'd combed a long strand of dark hair across his head in an attempt to hide his scrubbed and shiny scalp. His mustache sported more hair than did the rest of his head.

He spoke English when explaining her injury, much to K.C.'s gratitude. When he spoke to Arabella, however, he used Spanish. And though she couldn't understand the conversation, K.C. noticed he used the soft, elegant intonations of the pure Castilian Spanish rather than the local dialect.

After he wrapped her foot in a snug elastic bandage, she remained sitting on the side of the examination table. He sat opposite her on a rolling stool. He glanced at his notes on her chart and looked up.

"You have a soft-tissue sprain."

"I didn't break anything, then?" Relief flooded over her. Maybe she would walk down the aisle after all.

"No. Your bones are strong. But you must keep this foot—how do you say?—ah, elevated. And, of course, ice. You must use ice. Many hours today. Fewer tomorrow."

She nodded.

And he smiled quite suddenly. "You are to be wed tomorrow, yes?"

"Yes." She looked at her foot and sighed.

"You are young. You will heal quickly." He absently tugged at his mustache. "Something to remember about your wedding day. To tell your children and grandchildren, yes?"

"Yes."

"I have medicine for your pain." He rolled his stool across the room to a cabinet.

But K.C. shook her head before he stood to open it. "No. I'd rather not. I don't need anything. Thank you."

"I insist." He moved back across the room to stand over her. "Injuries such as this can be very painful. Sometimes later, after the trauma is over, the discomfort is greater. You need to be prepared." He met her gaze and smiled as he pressed a round plastic bottle into her hand. "Perhaps if you begin taking them today, by tomorrow you will be able to make your way down the aisle after all."

She nodded and accepted the medicine.

He seated himself again, then rolled his stool back across the room. After making a few more notes, he handed K.C. a pamphlet on caring for her foot and explained in greater detail about the snug bandage and the need for ice. Finally, he handed her some papers to sign. They were in Spanish, and he briefly explained any terminology she couldn't understand.

His voice was pleasant as he told her he was certain the Sterns—because of their fluency with the language—would take care of any red tape involving the Spanish government's health care services.

He helped her stand. "Your—how do you say?—your fiancé is waiting. He and Señor Stern arrived while you were in the laboratory."

Gav.

K.C.'s relief was almost overwhelming. "Thank you. I'd like for him to help me. Can you ask him to come in?"

"Of course, of course. I was about to ask him myself." Doc Rafael stepped to the door and called to Gav.

And then Gav was by her side, looking frantic and worried. "Are you all right?"

"She will be dancing the flamenco before you know it." He snapped his fingers to one side and smiled. "Your bride-to-be is young and strong. She will heal fast."

K.C. nodded mutely, so glad to see Gav she could weep. He wrapped one arm around her, and she leaned against him to hobble to the door.

"I have a wheelchair to get you to the sedan, if you would prefer," the doctor called after them.

"I prefer my fiancé," K.C. murmured to Gav. "Always."

Less than five minutes later, they were waiting in Wyatt and Arabella's car, while the older couple remained inside with the doctor, presumably to take care of whatever paperwork needed to be filled out.

K.C.'s foot ached and her stomach growled. She sighed as Gav rested his cheek against the top of her head. She could hear the thud of his heart, and another sigh whispered through her lips. She wanted to be close enough to hear his heartbeat forever.

"Penny for your thoughts."

She smiled. "Hmm. Just thinking how much I love you."

He gave her a gentle squeeze.

"And I was thinking about tomorrow."

He kissed the top of her head. "And all our tomorrows to come," he said, his voice husky.

Arabella settled into the thick leather chair across from Doc's polished mahogany desk. Her husband sat next to her, his gaze also intent on the doctor.

"We did as you asked."

Arabella smiled slightly. Wyatt's Spanish was impeccable.

"We set up her fall. Then brought her here. Did you get what you needed from her?"

Doc Rafael nodded. "It is as it should have been."

"I sense they distrust us," Arabella said.

The doctor laughed. A short, brittle sound. "You are all Americans. I would think they would trust you implicitly." Then he shook his head. "You forget, trust is not necessary for our plans. Our motive is simply to remove the obstacles. *All* obstacles. Nothing more."

"We understand." Arabella leaned back in her chair, studying her hands.

"Yes, I am certain you do."

She felt the doctor's gaze and looked up to meet it. She knew what he was thinking—she could see it in his eyes. He was thinking of her past.

His expression softened. "Your experience from years ago will help you."

Arabella didn't have to glance at Wyatt to know he was scowling in disapproval. She could feel it. As always when her past was mentioned.

Doc removed his glasses and wiped them slowly with a handkerchief. He replaced them and gave Wyatt a hard look, as though he too sensed his irritation. "Take care of this woman—your *wife*. She is a tribute to the memory of Franco. To all of us who worked for him in those days."

He kept staring, his eyes magnified by the thick lenses. Finally he stood and gave them a nod of dismissal. "I am sure they are wondering where you are, what you are doing in here." He rummaged through some papers on his desk, then handed a small stack to Arabella. "Have the woman fill these out. Tell her you will return them. That should answer any unasked questions."

Arabella nodded and accepted the forms. She stood with Wyatt, and they turned to go.

"One more thing." She turned back to find Doc Rafael absently pulling at his mustache.

"What is that?"

"Julian sent word that all is ready. We must protect our plans at all costs."

Arabella swallowed hard as she nodded.

Julian. Yes, Julian. His image almost shimmered in her mind, along with the memories that she couldn't stop...memories of another young leader so like him...another mission...another life.

She shook the thoughts away as Doc went on.

"Good. Then we will proceed, beginning with the young people who await you."

With that, he ushered the couple to the door.

Three

K.C. AND GAV RETURNED TO THE INN A FEW MINUTES PAST NOON. Though the kitchen was closed until the midday meal at three o'clock, Marta Aznar—a delicate woman with golden skin and silver hair—served a fresh-baked loaf of bread, a pot of regional cheese, three kinds of olives, and a basket of fruit to the starving bride- and groom-to-be.

K.C. sighed and slid into a chair in the cozy dining room, and Gav scooted another chair into place so she could elevate her left leg. Marta fussed around, looking for an ice bag. She brought it a few minutes later and laid it gently atop K.C.'s bandaged foot.

After placing on the table a silver pot of espresso and a small pitcher of warm milk for *café con leche,* Marta settled into the chair opposite K.C., and Gav took the seat at her right. Between bites of the sumptuous, impromptu meal, the two began the tale of their adventure.

As they talked, K.C. poured herself a cup of coffee, then reached for a slice of crusty bread.

Gav had just done the same when the lace-curtained French door opened, and Alfredo entered the dining room. He brightened when he saw the group, and he strode to the table, smiling—until he saw K.C.'s bound foot.

"Tell me what happened." His brow was creased with worry.

K.C. went through it again, giving them the details, complete with the fortuitous arrival of the Sterns and her visit to the doctor. Through the telling, Marta clucked sympathetically, and Alfredo's frown remained in place.

When K.C. finished speaking, Marta leaned forward. "And what about the wedding?" She glanced at the foot. "Will you be able to walk to the garden?"

The older women looked so sad that K.C. reached for her hand. "Of course." She grinned at Gav. "Even if the groom has to carry me there himself."

The group chuckled.

K.C. handed a few sections of a peeled orange to Gav, then delighted in the fragrance and flavor of the section she popped into her mouth.

Alfredo looked at his watch then back to K.C. and Gav. "Did you know that today is Sunday?"

"We found out this morning," K.C. said. "We'd truly forgotten, with jet lag and all."

"I know how stressful travel can be in that regard—that is why I asked. But if you would like to join us," Alfredo continued, "we have invited Duncan MacGowan, our friend from Porto, Portugal, to hold services this afternoon in the Alhambra garden. Since he will officiate at the wedding, it will give you a chance to meet him and discuss the ceremony. If you are not too tired."

"That's wonderful—" Gav began, then glanced at K.C. "But are you feeling up to it, Kace?"

Marta giggled softly at the endearment, and K.C. gave her a quick smile before turning back to Gav. "I'll be fine..." Then she considered her running clothes and remembered the state of her hair. "Oh, dear. I would like to freshen up. Change into something a bit more appropriate."

"You're beautiful just as you are." Gav looked into K.C.'s eyes, and a thrill coursed through her at the tenderness she saw there. Suddenly it was as if no one else was in the room. Marta sighed.

K.C. felt her cheeks color and quirked a brow to remind Gav they weren't alone. He cleared his throat and began again. "I'll carry you up to your room when you're ready..."

She grinned at him and reached over to pat his cheek. "I was kidding earlier about carrying me to the garden. But now we're talking two flights of stairs—" She winked at Marta and Alfredo. "Is this love or what?" They laughed and she popped another olive into her mouth, savoring its rich smoky flavor.

They spoke a few more minutes about the wedding plans, and Alfredo explained that early the following morning he would drive them into the city to pick up the legal paperwork for the marriage from the consulate.

K.C. was ready to excuse herself, feeling the fatigue of the morning settling in, but Marta leaned forward. "We would like to speak with you about some things while we are alone." She glanced about the small room, eyeing the doors and windows with a cautious glint in her eyes.

K.C. forgot her throbbing foot, her weariness, and leaned forward. "What is it?"

Alfredo cleared his throat. "Some of what we are about to tell you, your aunt and her husband already know."

Gav inclined his head, looking at Marta. "This is about your background..."

"Yes," she said. "Something that happened a long time ago."

"Theo and Max told us what happened during the Franco years. About your—" K.C. hesitated—"your troubles."

"Troubles...yes." Alfredo spoke slowly. "A good word for a very bad time."

"They told us that you opposed Franco's dictatorship," Gav said. "That you spent years in prison for helping lead an underground movement to depose him." He paused, looking at Alfredo. "That took a lot of courage."

The older man's eyes were filled with pain. "The cost was great. Too great."

Marta reached for his hand. "You did what you had to do, my husband."

Dropping his head, Alfredo fell quiet for a moment before going on. "There is something that we did not tell your aunt and her husband about those years...something we need to tell you. But what you are about to hear must be kept in the utmost confidence."

"Yes, of course," K.C. said with a small frown.

"We do not talk much about this anymore," Alfredo said. "Sometimes it seems as though our hearts might break if we dwell on the past, on what we cannot change about the present, or the future."

Marta let out a long sigh, and touched her husband's hand as though to comfort him. "We need your help. That is the only reason we share our pain. For years we have carried this secret. We have trusted few to bear this burden with us, especially in the early years. And now?" She looked into her husband's eyes. "Now, we feel it is time at last to ask for help." She turned back to K.C. and Gav. "And you will understand after you hear our story, why we are asking you."

K.C. nodded. "Please, go on."

Marta began to speak, her voice low. "We were betrayed by those we thought were our friends, those who worked in the movement with us. The atrocities committed by Franco are too horrible to speak of now, but at the time—nearly twenty-five years ago now—we bravely told all. We wanted others to join our work to free our country from this cruelest of men."

Alfredo broke in. "We believed in the power of the written word. At the time, I was working for a newspaper that was government owned, government controlled. I wrote what I was told to write." A look of shame crossed his face, then disappeared. "That was how I earned a living for my family."

Family. K.C. hadn't known that they had children.

"But he worked all night in our attic, running a printing press of another kind," Marta said, pride lighting her golden face. "Papers that told the truth about Franco and the corruption that surrounded him."

"We distributed the papers to hundreds each week, though no one knew their source."

"Except those who called themselves our friends." A moment of silence followed Marta's statement, then she whispered, "They came for us in the night. They went straight to the attic and found our work, our press, the papers that Alfredo had written." Tears filled her eyes. "They took both of us away."

"Arrested you both?" K.C. felt the sting of tears behind her own eyes.

Marta nodded. "Yes."

Alfredo's face seemed carved in granite, so hard was he working to keep his composure. "We had two young children...they were asleep in bed. They slept through the commotion, though I have no idea how."

Tears were spilling down Marta's cheeks now, and she reached into her pocket for a tissue. "Our babies—" she began, then couldn't go on.

Alfredo reached for her hand, taking it in both of his own, giving it a gentle squeeze. Apparently that gave her the strength she needed, and she continued. "I was kept in prison for weeks without a trial. Finally, Alfredo confessed so that I might be released."

Marta's expression as she looked at her husband told K.C. clearly that the cost for this confession had been dear.

Alfredo's voice as he took up the tale was devoid of emotion, as stoic as his granite face. "By then our children had been placed in a foster home. We were never allowed to see them again."

He paused for a moment before continuing. "I was forced to labor in the caves behind what is today known as Franco's Folly—the monument that he had built for himself. It is carved into a mountain of pure granite. Men were killed, some standing right beside me.

"There were explosions, cave-ins, but nothing stopped his prisoners from carrying on. I worked in a labyrinth of secret passageways deep in the bowels of the mountain. Many of the rooms we carved out were the same later used to imprison us.

"He turned the beautiful mountain into a graveyard of sorrow. Political prisoners built it and died for it. Died for Franco's Folly."

K.C. felt ready to choke with sorrow. "But Franco's out of power now, has been for several years. Your children should have been released, sent home to you!"

"They were so young, I am certain they do not remember their real names. We were told they were sent to live with a family that was close to Franco."

K.C. could scarcely take in what she was hearing. "How old were they when you last saw them?"

Marta's face softened. "It has been more than twenty-five years since our troubles began. María was three, almost four, and José, only two years old."

K.C. swallowed the lump that had formed in her throat. "I can't imagine the pain...the loss..." She couldn't go on.

Alfredo drew a deep breath. "Through the years we spent every peseta we could spare to find them." He shook his head. "All of these years we thought they had simply vanished without a trace."

"The Franco administration destroyed every record of our children," Marta said. "All our photographs, birth certificates, medical records. Everything."

For a moment no one spoke, then Gav said, "Why did you decide to tell us now?"

But K.C. had noticed a different inflection in Alfredo's voice. "You said all these years you *thought* they had vanished." She frowned. "But now? Do you know something more?"

Alfredo's granite face softened again. "Yes, that is why we need your help. Why we have chosen to tell you our story."

Before Alfredo could go on, there was a rap at the French doors. The innkeeper gave all three of them an apologetic look and stood to answer it.

K.C. stifled a groan when it turned out to be the Sterns.

"There you are!" Arabella hurried to K.C. and Gav, rushing past Alfredo who was still holding the door open.

Wyatt trailed behind her. The couple had changed from their earlier outfits and were now dressed in their signature black denim. Arabella wore a heavy squash blossom necklace, each petal inlaid with turquoise. Wyatt sported tooled western boots, while Arabella's were made of a buttery-soft black leather. A cloud of his-and-hers Chanel arrived with them at the table.

"Darling girl!" Arabella was positively gushing. "We've been *so* worried. We looked everywhere. We even tried your room." She rattled a small bottle of herbal tablets. "These work so well for pain. I get migraines, and there is no greater relief in the world than these can provide." She thrust the bottle into K.C.'s hand. "You must try these. Immediately." She paused, then added, "Marta, dear, please fetch us some water."

Beside her Wyatt chuckled and shook his head. "You must forgive my wife." He glanced at the others at the table. "She tends to be a mother hen. Even toward me." He laughed again and reached for two chairs from a nearby table. "Do you mind if we join you?" Without awaiting an answer he pulled the chairs across the tile floor.

Marta was standing, her dismay apparent, but K.C. reached for the older woman's hand. "Please, don't worry about the water. I'll get some myself in my room." She removed the ice pack from her foot and swung her left leg to the floor, wincing in pain.

Gav stood to help her. "We really must be going. It's been wonderful talking with you," he added smoothly to Alfredo. "We'll have to get together again later."

The corners of Arabella's mouth tightened, and K.C. had the oddest impression the woman was disappointed. But then, K.C. thought, with her pain and fatigue and jet lag all combined, it was probably just her imagination.

By two o'clock K.C. had managed to get through her shower (by standing like a stork on one leg), and had attempted a short nap with her foot perched atop two fluffy pillows. But the pain kept her from sleeping.

Finally, she hobbled to the bathroom sink and, after a

moment of studying Doc Rafael's bottle of pain medication, she popped a couple of capsules into her mouth, rinsing them down with a glass of water. Surprisingly, it took only a few minutes for a sweet blush of well-being to overtake her and remove the edge of pain.

She felt well enough to pull a brush through her hair and tie it back with a fresh ribbon. Next she donned a two-piece linen traveling outfit, though because a brisk wind had kicked up and was now rattling the windows, she added a turtleneck sweater under the jacket. She hobbled to the mirror, pushed up her glasses, and had a look.

It was hard to suppress a light-headed giggle. Very chic. Except for the walking sandals. With Velcro straps, they were the only shoes that would fit over her swollen, bandaged left foot.

A knock sounded at her door. When she opened it, Gav stood there, and the light in his eyes said she looked glorious. He didn't seem to even notice the rugged-looking sandals paired with the classy skirt and top. In fact, he was staring into her eyes with such intensity that she knew he hadn't even noticed her outfit.

"Have I told you today how much I love you?" He stood there, so handsome it made her throat ache. And when he moved toward her he walked with the easy grace that she'd always loved about him.

Grace and virility in a most striking mix. And sturdy beyond words. That was her Gav. Sturdy in body, soul, and spirit. Though not an exceptionally tall man, he nonetheless seemed as big and sturdy as the trunk of an oak tree. Maybe a giant redwood. She sighed, drinking in the sight of him.

Her Gav.

How close they'd come to losing each other just two years before. Misunderstandings, immaturity…even God's perfect timing had drawn them apart. Just as growing up, falling in love all over again, and God's perfect timing had brought them back together.

He was standing directly in front of her now, staring at her with eyes that seemed ready to melt into hers.

"I don't remember." She smiled into his devastating eyes. "I believe you'll need to tell me you love me again. Maybe more than once."

He stepped closer and lifted her chin with gentle fingertips. K.C.'s heart skittered, then skipped, then danced. "I love you, Kace. I believe I always have. And I know I always will."

She sighed again. Deeply. Then swallowed the sting in her throat. "That's once," she murmured. "How about a dozen or two, maybe three dozen times..."

He nodded, looking at her lips. "I love you..." He couldn't seem to stop gazing at her lips.

"Would you like to kiss me, Gav? I think I'd like that even better."

He grinned. "I thought you'd never ask."

"Since when did I have to as—" But her words were lost as Gav's lips pressed against hers. She leaned into his embrace.

A searing pain shot up her leg, and K.C. yelped and sprang back, only to yelp again. Now she was hopping on her right foot, arms waving, trying desperately to regain her balance without dropping her left foot to the floor.

Gav's face flooded with dismay. "Oh, honey. Oh, I'm so sorry." He gathered her into his arms to support her weight and steady her movement. After a moment she felt his chest shake.

He was laughing!

She pressed away from him. "You can't possibly think this is funny."

His expression was a blend of compassion and amusement.

"K.C., you've been as graceful as a ballerina all your life—even during your tomboy years when you could beat every boy in the neighborhood at climbing trees or playing football. You might have been skinny, strong, and full of spunk. But you were always graceful—" he quirked a brow—"until now." He chuckled again, then stepped away from her to give a quick imitation of her stork dance.

She feigned annoyance, then laughed with him. "You're gonna pay, Elliot Gavin." She narrowed her eyes. "I don't know when. I don't know how. But you're gonna pay."

He grinned. "I can't wait."

A few minutes later, they were heading to the garden where the wedding would be held the following afternoon. Alfredo had arranged for a gardener to transport the two of them in a small electric cart.

They wound along a tree-lined gravel path, through wild gardens and formal gardens, through thickets of eucalyptus and woods of cedar and oak, around cascading fountains and reflecting pools, climbing upward into the most beautiful gardens in the Alhambra, the *Generalife*.

So filled with foliage and flowers were the gardens that they seemed to spill over the cliffs, a thousand feet or so above the citadel, as if the beauty was too great to be contained in its allotted space.

K.C. remained silent and perfectly still as they drove through the gardens. Her early light-headedness had settled into a foggy drowsiness, causing the beautiful gardens to appear somehow otherworldly. Even menacing. Shivering, she glanced up at Gav to see if he noticed the change. But he seemed lost in his silence and sense of awe.

Finally, the driver pulled to a smooth stop. Gav hopped down and reached for K.C., easing her to the ground. She grabbed hold of him as the world seemed to tilt off its axis.

"Are you okay?"

"Just dizzy. That's all. I'm okay now."

Gav gently supported her as they moved through an arched boxwood gateway into a long, narrow hedge-framed garden. Roses, frothy and fragrant, lined a reflecting pool that ran the length of the enclosure; fountains sent up lacy arcs of water at one end, against a facade of alabaster columns, cascading in rippling waves into the reflecting pool.

At the opposite end of the enclosure, stone arches framed a long narrow hallway, all that was left of some ancient palace. Now open to the music of the fountains, the fragrance of the roses, the hint of a breeze, the room stood proud and secure...romantic. The perfect place for a wedding.

K.C. forgot about her earlier sense of foreboding. She forgot about everything except the wedding. And Gav.

She looked up at him, and saw by the expression on his face that he was too moved to speak. They stared at each other, then took in the garden once more.

"Forget the honeymoon in Barcelona," K.C. managed after a moment. "I want to stay here...maybe forever."

"I'll cancel the reservations." He grinned at her and waggled a brow. "Though you know how long it took me to find just the right hotel."

She felt her cheeks turn pink. They'd been stunned to discover that most hotel rooms, whether one-star or five-star, contained two narrow twin beds, spaced at least a foot apart. It had taken Gav a multitude of phone calls, faxes, and translators to find a hotel with what the Spaniards called a *marriage bed.*

He waggled his eyebrow again, and, feeling a bit more clear

headed, she gave him a teasing punch in the ribs. "Keep your mind on the wedding, not the honeymoon, you rogue."

His grin widened. Before he could lift his brow again, she grabbed his hand and, moving carefully, pulled him behind her to the palace ruins.

They had just stepped into the open air room and turned to admire the view of Albaicín when they heard voices from the path alongside the garden.

K.C. looked up at Gav quizzically. "That doesn't sound like the Aznars."

He shook his head. "I didn't think visitors to the Alhambra were allowed in this part of the Generalife."

"Neither did I."

They watched the arched boxwood entrance.

A shrill laugh announced the visitors a moment before they stepped into sight. K.C.'s heart dropped, and she met Gav's frown with one of her own. "I thought this place was private."

He let a huff escape as Arabella and Wyatt stepped into their private garden, looking for all the world like they had been invited.

"There you are!" Arabella waved and hurried toward them. She glanced triumphantly to Wyatt, striding beside her, camera hanging from his neck.

"We promised each other we'd get a picture of the bride and groom in their special place." By now she was standing in front of the palace ruins, beaming at K.C.

Before either K.C. or Gav could protest, the flash popped and the photograph was snapped.

The young couple stared at each other, speechless, then at the Sterns.

But Arabella and Wyatt were already hurrying down the path toward a sweeping tangle of bougainvillea, chatting with each other amiably, just like any other tourists.

"There's something about those two..." K.C. stared after the couple.

When Gav didn't answer, she looked up at him. His jaw was working slightly as he studied the foliage where the Sterns had just disappeared. No longer did he wear the look of the carefree tourist. Now his expression had turned thoughtful, vigilant. Very much the law-enforcement officer.

After a moment he pulled her close, and she leaned into the warmth of his arms. She wondered at the darkness, the shadows, that seemed to fall across the ancient palace ruins—all without a cloud in the sky.

FOUR

WITHIN MINUTES, THE AZNARS ARRIVED, AND WITH THEM WAS THE robust and jovial Duncan MacGowan. He strode to the palace ruins and hurried up the few stairs to greet K.C. and Gav.

"Ah, my friends." He stuck out a hand to pump Gav's hand, then K.C.'s, with equal vigor. "We meet at last!" His brogue was as thick as clotted cream, his eyes no doubt as blue as the highland lochs in his native Scotland.

Formal introductions weren't necessary; K.C. felt an immediate kinship with this man of God.

Marta and Alfredo joined them to chat about the details of the wedding ceremony, diverting K.C. from her uneasiness over the strange visit from the Sterns.

After a few minutes, Duncan invited the four to be seated on the steps, then stood, one foot on the first step, leaning toward them with his elbow on his knee, perfectly relaxed.

"God is in this place," he said without preamble. "We see

evidence of his creation everywhere we look."

K.C. followed his gaze. Shadows were slanted and deep, causing a play of darkness and brilliant light in the late afternoon sun. Even the hue of the roses seemed more intense against the deep shadows beneath them.

"Our Lord is with you—"Duncan looked back to K.C. and Gav—"as you take this step tomorrow. This garden is but a symbol of the riches, the beauty, he has prepared for you...."

There was a rustling behind the hedge. No one else seemed to notice, but K.C. had the strange feeling they were being watched. By the Sterns, no doubt. Though she couldn't fathom a reason for their curiosity.

Duncan continued. "After tomorrow you will carry memories of this place in your hearts for the rest of your lives. I want you to remember that the Lord was here with you as you joined your lives together in him. That no matter what lies ahead, he'll be with you.

"There will be choices to make. As individuals. As one." He looked intently into their eyes. "See that there is no darkness in your relationship. No shadows."

K.C. glanced at Gav and smiled. She couldn't imagine keeping anything from him. Already they were joined in spirit; tomorrow they would be joined as husband and wife. She could see the love in Gav's eyes. No shadows of doubt. No, she was certain, there would never be shadows—deception—between them. Their love was too strong. She reached for Gav's hand, loving the feel of his strong fingers as they closed around hers.

Duncan went on, urging them both to seek God's direction daily, even hourly, as they moved through their life together. "We can't know the future, and sometimes that's difficult when it comes to decision making," he said. "But God tells us to first seek his kingdom, his righteousness…" He smiled. "And the rest will fall into place."

He leaned forward and took hold of K.C.'s hand with his right hand, Gav's with his left. Alfredo and Marta moved closer to where they were seated, as though to encircle K.C. and Gav with love and prayer.

Duncan bowed his head. "Father God—" his rich baritone resonated through the garden—"bless your children K.C. and Gav. May they listen for your voice, may they strive to put your kingdom before all else through the rest of their lives—individually and as partners in the love relationship you have given them."

Following the prayer of blessing, Duncan broke into song. K.C. didn't think she'd ever heard anything quite so beautiful. His thick brogue mixed with the music of fountains, the light brush of leaves fluttering against the breeze. The words were from an old hymn Father Max loved to sing, but she couldn't place the melody. She could almost hear the bagpipes that were surely meant to accompany it.

When the song was done, a silence fell on them, a silence so heavy and precious and fragrant it brought tears to K.C.'s eyes and caused her heart to almost ache with the beauty of the moment.

It had been a Sunday service unlike any K.C. had ever experienced. This godly man had touched her soul, and she knew by Gav's expression, the minister had touched her beloved's soul as well. It was as if an unseen presence had been with them, a presence so alive, so real, she could almost hear him breathe.

"Thank you," she said softly. Duncan helped her stand. "I don't see how the wedding itself can be a more precious memory than our time in the garden today."

Gav moved to stand beside her. The shadows had grown longer now, and the breeze kicked again into a brisk, chilling wind. K.C. shivered.

Marta stepped toward them. "You will be joining us for dinner, yes?" she asked Duncan.

"I can think of nothing I would like better."

"I am so sorry Nuala could not join you this trip."

"Our daughter is expecting a baby any minute, and my wife wouldn't think of leaving Porto."

They were walking slowly toward the opening in the hedge. In the distance, the strange, hollow sound of the gardener's electric cart carried toward them.

"How did you came to live in Porto?" Gav asked.

"Nuala and I were missionaries in Brazil," he explained as they walked. "We were there for a dozen years before we felt called to Portugal. Always wanted to be involved in church planting." He stepped aside to let Alfredo and Marta through the arched hedge. K.C. followed, then Gav. "We began our first church in Porto, in the north of Portugal, just five years ago. Now some of our parishioners have begun churches all over the Iberian Peninsula."

He smiled at Marta and Alfredo, who stood waiting by the electric cart that had returned for K.C. and Gav. "That's how we met. Two of our church members moved here a couple of years ago and started a home church in the heart of Granada."

"We were invited to visit," Marta said. "And now we would not go anywhere else. We are family. Closer than blood relatives."

Alfredo nodded. "We were not there long before Duncan and Nuala visited from Porto."

Duncan chuckled and placed his hand on Alfredo's shoulder. "I count this man among my closest brothers." There was a look of understanding in his expression that told K.C. that Duncan MacGowan knew about the tragic Franco years.

Alfredo nodded. "And you are closer to me than my own brother, my friend."

K.C. glanced at the electric cart with gratitude. She was suddenly too weary to stand another minute. It didn't matter that the vehicle was smaller than the one that had brought her and Gav to the garden, so small that it held only one passenger. Though she would miss Gav on the short ride to the hotel, at least she would be off her feet.

"It appears I'm the lone passenger. Guess I'll meet you at the inn."

Gav frowned. "I'll walk beside you. The driver can move slowly."

The poker-faced Spaniard didn't indicate he would do as requested, or that he had even heard. He was dressed in an impeccable, pressed and creased khaki uniform. His gaze seemed fixed on K.C., and her heart fluttered nervously.

She was being foolish, she decided. It was only a ride through the Generalife to the inn. She laughed. "Don't be silly. You all have a nice visit as you walk. I'll head back to the inn and rest before dinner." She looked down at her foot, then back to Gav. "I could use the rest."

Gav glanced at the driver, seemed to study him a minute, then nodded. "All right. I'll check in on you when we get there."

She laughed nervously. "The Aznars arranged this with the gardeners themselves. Everything will be fine." She flicked an imaginary speck from her sleeve, then grinned up at him. "Really."

He looked at her intently, and she noticed the flicker of concern in his eyes.

She brushed his face with her fingertips. "I'm going to try to get some sleep. Why don't you rest, too, honey?" She could see the fatigue in his face. "We're still battling jet lag. And tomorrow's our wedding day."

He chuckled. "You're telling me not to disturb you?"

"Well, not exactly. But I think we could both use a siesta before dinner."

Marta stepped up. "Yes, please. You need rest. We will not be serving our midday meal until four o'clock. There is plenty of time."

Gav helped K.C. scoot into the back of the vehicle. "Hold that foot up. Don't let it drag…or get close to anything."

She grinned at him, holding her leg straight out.

The little cart started forward, smooth, silent, except for the crunch of gravel under the tires. All four—Marta, Alfredo, Duncan, and Gav—waved. They started to stroll down the same path, then stopped. Duncan pointed to an overlook, which likely afforded a breathtaking view of Albaicín. K.C. wished briefly she'd waited a moment longer so she could have seen it with them.

She craned around to look forward. The cart had nearly reached a hairpin turn where the small gravel road led into a thick woods. She shivered, then looked back again toward Gav.

He seemed to sense her gaze and waved once more.

She blew him a kiss. He caught it, jumping as if she had lobbed it over his head. Then he wound up his arm like a major league pitcher and threw one back to her.

K.C. giggled and reached to catch it.

Just then the cart turned into the curve, silently moving into the woods. It seemed very odd to K.C. when the cart slowed to a snail's pace in the heart of the dense forest.

Odder yet, when the cart came to a complete stop.

When the cart drove out of sight, Gav urged the rest of the group along by lengthening his stride. He didn't know why it bothered him to see K.C. pulling away like that. They would only be apart a few minutes. A half hour at the most. He studied the road where the hairpin turn had taken her from sight. Maybe it was because she looked so small and vulnerable when she blew him that last kiss.

Then he laughed to himself. *Small and vulnerable?* K.C. might be petite, but she was petite like a small stick of dynamite. Dynamite with red-gold hair and eyes the color of the Pacific Ocean at dawn.

At Alfredo's urging, the group moved to yet another overlook.

Alfredo glanced at Duncan. "I have told our friend Gav about the Franco years."

Duncan nodded, his eyes meeting Gav's. "They were terrible times for Alfredo and Marta."

"I know." Gav saw deep sadness in Marta's eyes again. "And it seems they go on." Gav slowed his pace and looked to Alfredo. "You were about to tell K.C. and me about new information?"

Alfredo nodded. "It is probably nothing. But we received a letter recently. It was unsigned but was on university letterhead. That's why I wanted to mention it to you. Because you're going there."

Duncan was watching Alfredo intently. "Was it about the children?"

"Indirectly," Alfredo continued. "It raised some questions about them. That is all." He cast a loving but worried look at Marta.

"What were the questions?" Duncan halted at a clearing near a fountain, and the others stopped with him.

Again Alfredo glanced at Marta, as if asking silently for her permission to open the old wounds. She inclined her head, and he turned again to the others.

"The writer asked if we had a boy and girl removed from us on a certain date. A certain year."

"Were they the proper dates?" Gav asked.

"Yes. They were accurate."

"Was that all?" Duncan laid a hand on his friend's shoulder. "Did the writer ask for money?"

"Not this time. Which is odd. We have given so much through the years only to find nothing at the end of a very long road. Some—how do you say?—detectives promised us the world. But in the end, all we had were empty hands and empty pockets."

"And empty hearts," whispered Marta. "With each failure, it seemed our sadness was more painful than before. This time may be no different."

"It may be someone who has seen records of our search," Alfredo said. "I am certain that the word has been broadcast." He laughed, though there was a bitter, hollow sound to it. "And we are not the only family grieving for lost children."

He walked a few more steps before adding. "There is a list somewhere, I am certain, with all the orphaned children. Though the sad thing is, they do not even know they are orphaned. Many were so young that they probably believe the families who took them in are their real parents and sisters and brothers."

Marta was crying softly, and Alfredo put his arm around her shoulders. "It is so hard," she said. "Even a letter such as this raises my hopes once more."

They passed another fountain and moved closer to a wooded area Gav had noticed on the way to the garden. "Would you like us to take the letter with us to Salamanca? See if we can find out anything?"

"Yes," Alfredo said as he led the group to a shortcut that bypassed the woods. "That is why I brought it up. We know you will be doing research at the university. Perhaps..." his voice fell off. "Perhaps it's nothing. But for our peace of mind, we would be grateful for you to look into it."

"Perhaps the university office might know who has access to the official stationery," Gav said.

"It can be purchased at any souvenir shop," Marta added quietly.

Gav offered her an encouraging smile. "I'll do what I can." But he knew they had little chance of finding the writer.

As they walked, Alfredo explained how the investigators had worked through the years, the cities they had covered, the government agencies they had contacted. The names of José and María Aznar, children of former political prisoners Alfredo and Marta Aznar, were probably well circulated. Especially in this day of Internet communication.

Almost anyone could be out to make a fast buck off the grieving parents. It disgusted him that money was more than likely the motive behind the inquiries. The writer hadn't yet asked for money, but Gav suspected another letter would follow. The bait had been set.

Gav glanced at K.C.'s closed door on his way to his room, up another flight of stairs and down the hallway. The polished wood floors creaked as he stepped across the landing. He slowed his steps, not wanting to disturb K.C. should she be asleep. He smiled to himself as he pictured her beautiful face in slumber. Oh, how he cherished this woman! How thankful he was that God had miraculously brought her back into his life.

Once, long ago, he thought he'd lost her. Forever. He'd broken their engagement. Dropped out of seminary within weeks of graduating. Removed himself from K.C., his childhood friend and longtime sweetheart. He'd been confused, knowing only that he must seek God's direction after a lifetime of planning for the ministry. After he realized it hadn't been God's call he was hearing, but his own. And K.C.'s, he'd thought mistakenly. When he broke their engagement within weeks of the wedding, he didn't think K.C. would…or could…ever forgive him.

But God had restored their relationship. And now that they'd come together again. No longer were they two. They were three, with their heavenly Father a living part of their relationship.

Surprisingly, he had called them to ministry after all, though not inside a church. Besides being sheriff of Sugar Loaf Mountain, Gav's calling was researching cults and working to get kids out of their tangled webs; K.C.'s gift was journalism, especially teaching students who had a burning desire to write and didn't know where to start. Their trip to Salamanca would allow each of them to work in the areas they loved the most. He, researching a cult with roots in medieval Spain; K.C., teaching American journalism students. It was the journey of a lifetime.

He walked up the remaining stairs, musing about the twists and turns their lives had taken. And tomorrow, K.C. would be his bride.

He turned down the hallway toward his room, planning to rest for a few minutes, then dress for dinner. He would wait until the last possible minute to stop by for K.C. She needed rest after the stress of the morning.

He unlocked his door and stepped inside. The light was dim, and at first he thought the mess he saw in front of him was the same he'd left earlier. After all, it had been a morning—make that a day—of confusion and hurry. The run. K.C.'s fall. The hurry to the doctor's office. Then lunch. The time at the Generalife.

But a sense of uneasiness overtook him as he stepped further into the room. He might have left in a hurry, not noticing that his running clothes were scattered across the bed, or that his books and papers and files were strewn on the bedside table.

But this...this...wasn't anything close to what he'd be likely to hurry off and leave.

He stopped. Dead still. Someone had been in his room.

He glanced around, chiding himself for his paranoia. It'd probably been K.C.

Of course. She might have gotten the key from downstairs—it would have been easy to reach across the front desk and retrieve it from its cubbyhole—and come in to grab a book or their camera...something.

He moved to the window and opened the shutters, letting in the dim light of dusk. Then he stepped to a lamp and turned it on.

That's when he noticed the open briefcase, its contents scattered. Then his open backpack. Its contents strewn. His suitcase open, obviously pawed through. The closet doors wide open. His jackets draped haphazardly on their hangers, pockets turned inside out.

Stunned, he didn't move. Then he remembered the laptop. His files. His months of research. His notes. His Internet list to Web sites connected to the cult.

He hurried to the dresser in the corner near the window. After accessing his e-mail account early that morning, he'd tucked the laptop in the bottom drawer. Figured it would be safer to be out of sight when the maid came in.

He knelt and yanked out the drawer.

It was empty.

Maybe he'd been mistaken. Perhaps he'd left it in a different drawer. The next one up. He yanked it out, then the others, one at a time. Each was as barren as the one before.

He settled back on his haunches, his mind racing. The room had been ransacked. But for what?

He didn't have any valuables. His passport was in a pouch, hanging on a string around his neck under his clothes. His camera was an older point-and-shoot model. The laptop, though powerful and fast, was beat up, already out of date by today's standards. No good to anyone but himself.

He sighed heavily and turned to leave the room. He'd have to tell Alfredo and Marta. And of course the police would need to be involved. He hated even to do that, wanting to avoid anything that might complicate—or lessen the joy of—their wedding day. He dreaded telling K.C.

Then it occurred to him that her room might have been hit as well. A niggling worry crept into his mind, filling him with a desire to see her immediately. To see that she was safe.

What if she'd burst in on the thieves?

His heart pounded, and he raced from his room, taking the stairs two at a time. Seconds later, he rapped at her door, lightly at first, not wanting to alarm her if she slept. But when there was no answering call, he knocked again. Harder. Still no response.

"K.C.?"

Silence.

"K.C.? Kace? Are you awake?"

No answer.

He tried the door. Surprisingly, it was unlocked. He pushed it open and stepped inside. "Kace?" It took a few seconds for his eyes to adjust to the dim light.

Her room looked just like his. Clothes, books, papers, strewn and scattered about. Cosmetic case overturned. Suitcase wide open. Jewelry case emptied.

But there was no sign of K.C.

FIVE

GAV RACED DOWN THE STAIRS TO THE FRONT DESK. NO ONE WAS there, which wasn't surprising. In a short time the Aznars would serve the midday meal to their guests. They were probably in the kitchen or dining room.

As he followed wafting scents of roasting lamb, he prayed that when he opened the door K.C. would look up at him. He could see her now—apron on, helping Marta, laughing at his worried expression.

But when he burst through the door, only Marta looked up at him in surprise, then set down a large roasting pan. She stepped toward him.

"Have you seen K.C. since we got back?"

Marta frowned. "No, but I have been here in the kitchen.... I have not seen any of the guests. Is something wrong?"

He took a deep breath. "My room's been...gone through. My computer's been taken." He shook his head, trying to comprehend it himself. "And I checked with K.C. Or at least I tried to. She wasn't in her room."

Marta reached back to untie her apron, the worry on her face adding to his fear.

He hesitated, refusing to think the unthinkable. "I figured she'd come down to help you prepare the meal."

Marta shook her head. "No. I haven't seen her. But let's check with Alfredo. He is setting up the dining room. Perhaps she is there."

They hurried back into the hall and through the double French doors. Alfredo was setting out the plates and flatware. He looked up with a warm smile of greeting as they stepped into the dining room. His smile faded when he saw their faces.

Gav quickly told him what had happened, hoping against hope Alfredo would smile at him and tell him not to worry, that he was overreacting. Instead, Alfredo listened, growing visibly alarmed. Gav finished his explanation, waiting, heart pounding—and felt his dread double when Alfredo, his face somber, stepped to the phone and called the police.

Gav couldn't deny it any longer.

K.C. was missing.

While they waited for the officers to arrive, Gav, the Aznars, and Duncan MacGowan searched the inn and the grounds. There was no sign of K.C. Even a worried-looking Arabella and Wyatt Stern, who had just returned from touring the cathedral, joined them in the search.

"Maybe she decided to walk out to the citadel to look at the sunset," Arabella suggested with a shrug. "She was so taken with the sunrise this morning."

"I already checked," Gav said. "I really don't think she

would try to walk anywhere. That's what is so disturbing about this. She was in too much pain…too tired. She would have come straight back here. Gone directly to her room…."

Duncan rested his arm around Gav's shoulders. "We'll find her."

"This is impossible to comprehend," Gav admitted to the pastor. "I think about her bursting in on the burglars. That she might be in danger right now—" He was unable to continue around the choking sensation in his throat. Swallowing, he forced the words out. "And I can't get to her."

Duncan nodded. "I'm not going to give you any trite platitudes. But I will tell you that God is with us. And with K.C., wherever she is. Rest in that, son."

Gav drew in a deep breath. "I know it's true. But right now my concern for K.C. is blocking out all thoughts of comfort. I just want to find her. To know she's okay."

"I understand. God does too."

The others had moved closer and were discussing in low tones where K.C. might have gone, everyone offering an opinion.

But nothing anyone said could make an ounce of sense out of the nightmare Gav couldn't seem to escape.

A blue-and-white car pulled up in front of the inn within minutes, and two uniformed men got out. They were introduced as Hector, a distinguished graying man, and Juan, a cocky and smooth younger man. They assumed Gav knew Spanish and fired their questions at him.

He held up a hand in defense, shaking his head. He was irritated with himself for not picking up more Spanish before coming to Spain. He'd now have to rely on translators—and all jumped in to his rescue, Marta, Alfredo, the Sterns, even Duncan.

Hector, the older officer, asked how long it had been since they'd last seen K.C. Marta told him, and he nodded, making notes on a form attached to a clipboard. Gav could tell from Marta's gestures that she was telling the men about K.C.'s twisted foot and the ride to the Generalife in the gardener's cart.

"They would like to see your room, and K.C.'s," Marta said to Gav after a few minutes.

"Of course. Let's go."

They all trooped into the inn and headed noisily up the stairs. Alfredo, who led the way, craned around pointedly at the first landing and suggested that Wyatt and Arabella return to their room or to the lobby. The others continued on to K.C.'s room.

"Is anything missing?" the younger officer asked.

Gav looked around, feeling helpless. "No," he finally said. "Or rather, I don't know. I don't think so."

"Jewelry?" Hector asked through Marta.

Gav looked at the spilled contents of K.C.'s drawstring travel bag. "No, I don't think so."

"Did she have anything valuable?" Juan asked.

"Just the ring on her finger. Her engagement ring."

The officers nosed around, and Gav grew more agitated by the minute. It was growing dark, and if K.C. was out there somewhere, if she had fallen, or...he didn't want to complete the thought. But if she needed help, it seemed they were wasting valuable time. The officers were strolling about the room, picking up this item or that, asking endless questions of Gav. He began to suspect they might be blaming him.

Alfredo looked disturbed as he translated the next question.

"Juan wants to know if you'd had a quarrel. You and K.C."

"No, of course not!" Gav looked to Alfredo. "You were with us. You saw her the last time I did—"

Duncan stepped up and swung his arm around Gav's shoulders. "They must ask hard questions, Gav. They mean nothing by them. Nothing personal. They are only doing their job."

Gav swallowed hard. "Yes, I know. It's just that time's wasting. I think we should be searching for K.C. Not talking. Not taking inventory of our rooms."

Duncan translated, and the two officers exchanged a glance and shrugged. Finally, one suggested they go on up to Gav's room to have a look around. He led them through the doorway and up another flight of stairs. When they reached his room, the scene was repeated, the same questions asked.

By now it was dark outside, and Gav was frantic about getting the search under way. He asked through a translator if more manpower was available. And search dogs. The men nodded and made notes. Gav added that the rooms might be dusted for fingerprints. More notes were taken. More nodding.

Hector scratched his head, then looked apologetically at Gav. He spoke in a calm, professional manner to Alfredo, who translated. "He says that it is not unusual for brides to have second thoughts on the eve of their marriage," Alfredo said. "He thinks that we should give K.C. until daylight to come back on her own—"

"No!" Gav couldn't believe what he was hearing. "Tell him no! We can't wait until morning. K.C. wouldn't *do* this…she wouldn't just disappear without warning."

But in the back of Gav's mind was his own disappearance from her life before their planned wedding day a few years before. No. He wouldn't even consider it. She hadn't had second thoughts. She certainly wouldn't have flown all the way to

Spain only to back out at the last minute. He couldn't believe she would do such a thing. Wouldn't believe it. "We must look tonight."

The officers spoke to each other in Spanish, Juan shrugging, Hector more intent.

Gav turned to Alfredo. "Perhaps we should call the American embassy."

"There's not an embassy here."

Of course. How could he have forgotten? Granada was too small for an embassy. "The consulate, then. Maybe they can intervene."

Alfredo agreed, and the group headed down the stairs to Alfredo's small office. Within seconds he had the U.S. consulate on the phone and handed the receiver to Gav.

A pleasant Spanish woman spoke to him in broken English. Gav explained what had happened. It was Sunday, she explained, and normally they were closed, but she had just stopped by her office to get caught up with her work. She was sympathetic and suggested he come in the following day to fill out the necessary paperwork.

"Paperwork?" He pictured mounds of red tape and felt his anxiety reaching a boiling point. He fought to keep his cool. "Maybe you don't understand." His words were measured, slow. "My fiancée is *missing*. She has been gone for a couple of hours now. We think there was foul play. Her room is a mess..." He realized how foolish this must sound. "It's been gone through."

"Is anything missing?"

"No. We don't believe so, but—"

The woman broke in, though her tone wasn't rude. "Actually, Mr. Gavin, a person missing for just a few hours does not warrant filing a report." She sounded sorry.

"I'm in law enforcement in the States. I understand how and why you work as you must. But I also know K.C. Keegan. Something has happened—"

"I am sorry, Mr. Gavin." She sounded ready to close the conversation.

Gav tried again to explain the circumstances, why it was imperative to begin the search immediately. But the woman held her ground—though before hanging up, she did encourage Gav to come into the consulate and fill out the forms so that when the necessary time had passed, that much would already be accomplished.

The officers, who now stood near the lobby, gave him a questioning look. Gav shrugged and walked toward them. Alfredo strode alongside to translate.

"They have called for a fingerprint specialist," Alfredo explained a moment later. "Perhaps something will turn up."

"I see," Gav said. "And the search team?"

"They will send a team up here at dawn. No sooner."

He caught his breath, again feeling the mix of frazzled emotions and physical fatigue ignite into what was sure to be a major explosion. But he also knew that his reaction would serve no purpose, wouldn't change the mind-set of the officers.

He closed his eyes for a moment, gulped in a calming breath, then said, "Is there anything against your department's policy for providing supplies—some powerful lights, perhaps some search dogs—so that my friends and I can search the premises?" He paused, letting Alfredo translate, before going on. "I am in law enforcement myself. Can't we bend the rules? If the circumstances were reversed, I would do the same for you."

His mention of law enforcement made a difference. Hector had new respect in his eyes. "Sí. Yes, we will comply with your wishes."

At least Gav could breathe again. He nodded. "Thank you.

Gracias, Señor." He shook both their hands. "Gracias. I'm grateful. Very grateful."

The officers called in the request, then in a surprising turnabout stayed to help. Gav suspected that Hector, whose demeanor was more sympathetic, had talked the younger officer into offering assistance. Within minutes, another patrolman pulled up with the high-powered searchlights.

Some of the other guests, hearing what had happened, joined the search. Gav was even grateful for Arabella and Wyatt, who put aside their petty bickering and artistic affectations and seemed genuinely helpful.

By eight in the evening seven men and four women were ready to head out from the inn. Hector and Juan, now off duty, took charge. Hector's teenaged son, Rico, drove up in a battered van, swung open the back door, and clipped leashes on a pair of German shepherds.

The big dogs bounded to the ground, straining against their leashes, panting and wagging their tails. Gav pulled K.C.'s scarf from his pocket and, after a nod from the officers, held it to the dogs' noses, patting them and speaking softly about K.C. There were some answering whines and a few more tail wags, and it occurred to him that the dogs seemed to understand perfectly.

The plan was to spread out, half the team heading toward the citadel, the other half toward the Generalife. Flashlight in hand, Gav headed toward the Generalife with Hector, his son Rico with one of the dogs, and Duncan.

After two hours of scouring the hillsides, gardens, and palace ruins, Gav was becoming more heartsick by the moment. They wound along tourist paths and gardeners' routes, but the dog remained calm. No sniffing the ground. No barking.

In the distance, the other searchers' lights could be seen bobbing through the foliage near the citadel, but there was no telling bark or bay from the dog.

Gav was heading back to meet the others when it hit him. He halted, and Duncan stopped beside him, looking at him in surprise. Hector, slightly in front of them, turned, his expression curious.

Gav directed his words to Duncan, asking him to translate. "We haven't been thinking this through…any of us." He couldn't help casting an accusing look at Hector. "We are assuming that K.C. arrived back at the inn. What if the gardener didn't take her there?" He nodded to Duncan. "Remember? It took us nearly an hour to get back to the inn. What if K.C. never made it?"

Hector stepped closer. "The gardener brought her back?" He asked through Duncan.

"Yes. We assumed he did…."

"Where were you when he picked her up?" Duncan translated, then answered the same question in Spanish, pointing toward the palace ruins farther up the hillside.

A short discussion ensued, and finally, Duncan turned to Gav. "Hector would like to see the place where we last saw K.C. He is sending his son back to the inn to look for the Aznars, to see if they can tell us anything about the gardener. Where he can be located…."

Gav nodded, still chiding himself for not thinking this through earlier. "All right. Let's go. Maybe we can get K.C.'s trail from there."

Rico headed back down the footpath leading to the inn, and the others hurried up the hillside, Gav leading the way this time. He tried not to think of K.C., where she might be…what she might be going through. But she was so deeply entrenched in his heart, it was impossible to keep her from his mind.

He kept coming back to the singular thought: *How can this be?* The words beat a cadence in his mind, right along with his thudding heart and pounding stride. *How can this be?*

They reached the hairpin turn where K.C. had blown Gav a kiss. "It was right here. The last time we saw her, the cart was about to head around this bend." He looked around while the others caught up. "Right here." He again pulled K.C.'s scarf from his pocket and knelt to let the dog sniff it. He fingered its silken folds, remembering the last time K.C. wore it—on the flight to Madrid. Remembering how it framed her face, her gray-green eyes reflecting its hue. Her chin-length red hair brushing the scarf each time she turned her head to look at him.

He swallowed hard and pressed the now-wadded folds into the dog's nose.

This time the dog put his muzzle to the ground and circled a few times, wagging his tail, then trotted back to where Gav still squatted, holding the scarf. With a nod, Hector encouraged the dog to circle farther from the hairpin turn.

The dog panted and trotted, tail still sweeping horizontally, once in a while nosing the ground. But his ears were flopping, his tale wagging. He looked anything but serious about his attempt to follow the scent.

Gav was ready to give up. He stood and stretched his legs, meeting Duncan's sympathetic look. Shaking his head, he stuck his hands in his back pockets. "It was a long shot," he said. "K.C. was in the cart. It's no wonder he's not picking up anything."

Hector led the dog to the edge of a nearby stand of cypress trees. The path wound close to the woods, then veered around it again. On what Gav supposed was a hunch, the officer urged the dog into the trees, his high-powered flashlight picking out a faint trace of wheel tracks along a seldom-used path.

Gav and Duncan exchanged another look and followed. Though he wasn't visible, the dog was now yipping and sniffing, the sound carrying back to the two men.

Gav's heart dropped. Without a word, he sprinted toward the thick copse of trees. Duncan followed, the dog now barking wildly somewhere in the darkness.

"*¡Aquí!*" Hector called. "*¡Aquí!* I have found something! Hurry!"

SIX

K.C. WAS TRAPPED IN A BRILLIANT WHITE LIGHT. EVERYTHING WAS white: her wedding gown; the creamy gardenias, fresh-picked from the bush at her aunt Theodora's Sugar Loaf cabin; the tulle that covered her face, floated over her hair, and draped onto the aisle behind her.

Frantically, she glanced around for Gav, studied her watch, then scanned the whiteness again. The day was wasting—it wouldn't stay light forever—and the time for the wedding was about to pass.

Where was he?

She tried to move, knowing she needed to search for him, but her legs had no strength at all.

Nausea surged over her like ocean waves. She was being pulled from shore...from the safety of consciousness...in a riptide.

She heard a sigh, long and raspy. Someone must be with her. Someone else fighting the pull of the current. Then, she realized, it was her own voice. Her own troubled sigh.

It frightened her to know she was alone after all. Gav wasn't near. No one was. She fought to open her eyes.

But her lids were too heavy. And she was too weary.

For a moment she thought she heard the drone of airplane engines. A plane? It couldn't be. Not this far out in the brilliant white ocean. Then she let the current pull her under once more.

Gav stepped closer to the electric cart, its metal surface gleaming in the shaft of the flashlight. There were no signs of K.C. or the driver. No footprints. No indication of struggle. Only the dog still nosing and sniffing and whining around the vehicle.

And Hector, standing to one side, shining the flashlight at what appeared to be an envelope, frowning at something scrawled across the front. He looked up at Gav and Duncan absently, then continued turning the letter this way and that, as if deciding what to do with it.

Hector met Gav's puzzled gaze. Finally he nodded and handed him the missive.

Gav's name was scrawled across the front. And in a chilling heartbeat, he recognized the handwriting. It was K.C.'s.

He moistened his dry lips and swallowed hard. Then he slid his finger beneath the seal, pulled out a folded note, and began to read in utter silence.

Dear Gav,

I am sorry to leave you so abruptly, but I couldn't do it any other way. I couldn't face you with the news that our wedding must be called off.

I am sorry for attempting to lead you to a wrong conclusion by adding a bit of mystery to my leaving—the state of our rooms, this note left on the cart hidden in the woods. But I needed to give myself time to get away from Granada. I knew you would try to stop me, and I couldn't let that happen.

As you have guessed, I'm having second thoughts about the wedding. I need time alone to think things through. Please do not attempt to find me, or to contact me. I will be in Salamanca next week as planned, but I beg you not to join me there.

Before you condemn me for my actions, please remember that you once left me at the altar—wondering where you'd disappeared. I'm not doing this in retaliation. Merely for the same reasons you did. I did it to give myself time to think.

My best to you, Gav, as you attempt to understand what led me to do this.

Love,

K.C.

P.S. I took the laptop because it contains the files I need for my work at the university. I will return it once I'm back in California.

Gav stared at the letter. His hands shook. He felt cold, bitterly cold. He read through the words once again. None of it made sense, not considering the K.C. who'd blown a kiss to him just as she rounded the corner.

"I don't believe it." He smacked the letter against his palm. "I don't believe one word of it." The other men exchanged looks but remained silent.

Gav studied the writing again. It was hers. There was no doubt. "I don't believe it," he said again. This time his voice didn't sound as certain. Not even to himself.

He believed in K.C.'s love. They had come through so much. Now this? He let out a shuddering breath. How could this be?

"What is it?" Duncan stepped closer. "The letter is from K.C.?"

"Yes. But none of it's true. It can't be."

"May I see it?"

Sickened, Gav handed him the letter. "It might be K.C.'s handwriting. But those aren't her words."

Duncan scanned the missive, then looked up at Gav. "Is there any way someone else could have known about this? About you leaving her at the altar, I mean?"

Gav shook his head. "Only our family and friends." He tried not to think how he had agonized when he'd made a similar move during their first engagement. For weeks he'd known he needed to walk away from K.C., yet had never said a word to her about it—not until he'd actually left. That was the only reason he could entertain the slightest belief in the words in the letter. He, of all people, understood fully.

Hector said something in Spanish, and, sick at heart, Gav asked Duncan to translate the contents of the letter to the officer.

When Duncan had finished the older man nodded slowly, then turned to leave, the dog at his side. Duncan draped his arm around Gav's shoulders, and they headed back to the inn to tell the others to call off the search.

"It can't be true," Gav said. But his heart was sinking. "She wouldn't do this. Not now. Not after all we've been through. We've changed. Both of us have...." His voice choked.

Desperation threatened to overwhelm him, despite his most determined denials. Because as much as he resisted it, he couldn't silence the fear that perhaps...just perhaps, K.C. had indeed changed her mind—just as he had done before.

And if that was true, Gav wondered how he could recover from the heartbreak.

K.C. again felt, rather than saw, the white light around her. This time—as she struggled to regain consciousness, to reach the safety of that shore—she felt herself nearing it. The nausea wasn't as pronounced, the headache not as overpowering as before.

She moaned and immediately sensed that someone in the room heard her. Was moving toward her.

"Where am I?" Even the muffled sound of her voice caused her head to pound.

The voice than answered was female. Low, pleasant. Ageless. Soothing. Spanish. She had no idea what the woman said. A moment later, though, a hand touched her forehead. The touch was gentle and cool.

K.C. attempted to open her eyes, prepared for waves of painfully brilliant, blinding light to overtake her. Then just as quickly, she decided to take the route of less pain. Keep her eyes closed. At least for now. Let the touch of the hand soothe her.

How did she get here? Her last memories were of the inn…the gardens…waving good-bye to Gav.

Gav!

"Where am I?" Her voice was hoarse. "Where's Gav?"

The woman had moved away from her now and answered from across the room. This time, however, she answered in English. Her accent was thick, and K.C.'s head hurt almost too much to try to concentrate. She caught only a spattering of words. *"Valle de los Caídos…"*

K.C. thought she'd heard wrong. "What?"

"Valley of the Dead," the voice translated in a heavy Spanish accent, then went on. "A time to rest…not to worry…you are safe."

K.C.'s mind was stuck on Valley of the Dead. For the briefest instant she wondered if she was dying—or was already dead. The pain was too great, she thought rationally. She was surely alive. "Why am I here?" Again she tried to squeeze open her eyes. "Is this a hospital?"

A low chuckle was her answer. "No, K.C." She spoke in the purest Castilian form of Spanish, making K.C.'s name sound more like *Kathy* than *Casey*. "No hospital...but sick...very sick."

K.C. swallowed hard and murmured that she was thirsty. A straw was held to her lips and she drank. A few moments later, she drifted to sleep once more. This time her dreams were empty and dark.

Blessed darkness had fallen when K.C. woke again. The pain in her head had lessened, and she opened her eyes. For a moment she was disoriented, forgetting briefly that she'd somehow left her room at the Granada country inn. Then she remembered the blinding light, the soft Spanish voice, the nauseating pain....

She was in bed, though still dressed in her clothes. The room temperature was comfortable; she was covered with only the bedspread. She frowned and ventured moving her head, glad to find that the pain had subsided enough to allow movement without the howling misery from before. She didn't seem to be in a hospital, but she searched her mind for a memory of an accident. A car wreck. A fall. She tried to remember. But nothing came to her.

A night-light glowed from the direction of what must be a bathroom, casting just enough light for her to make out a shadowy figure sleeping upright in an easy chair across the room. She supposed it was the same woman who'd spoken to her before.

The woman stirred as if sensing K.C. no longer slept. She turned her gaze toward the bed. K.C. didn't know whether to feign sleep or let the woman know her charge was awake.

Curiosity won out. "Where am I?" She vaguely remembered asking the same question earlier, but couldn't remember whether the woman had answered.

"Santa Cruz del Valle de los Caídos." The woman reached over to a table and turned on a lamp, keeping it soft and low, for which K.C. was grateful.

The woman stood and stretched, a feline, long-limbed stretch, then moved over to the bed. K.C. was struck by her ageless look. She might have been twenty or forty. Her complexion was flawless and her dark shoulder-length hair gleamed even in the soft lamplight, framing a pleasant, heart-shaped face.

"Who are you?" K.C., still afraid to move her head, stared up at the woman.

The woman smiled. "I am Danita."

K.C. returned the smile. "That's a pretty name."

Danita nodded. "Gracias." It sounded like *grathias*.

"My name is K.C. Keegan."

"I know, K.C."

"How do you know that…?" K.C. frowned, again searching her mind for a hint as to what had happened to her. "Why am I here?"

Danita picked up a ceramic pitcher and poured water into a glass on a bedside table and handed it to K.C.

Gratefully, K.C. took a sip.

Danita drew in a deep breath, and there was a hesitancy to her tone when she continued. "You came with us willingly, once we explained."

"Explained what?" She tried to sit up, and Danita reached to help, fluffing her pillows and easing K.C. back against them.

"That you needed time to think through your...decision to...ah, marry. You remember, yes?"

"That's ridiculous!" K.C. tried to swing her legs off the bed, but they seemed made of lead. She groaned and leaned against the pillows again.

Danita laughed, an incongruously pleasant sound, at K.C.'s bewilderment. "Do not worry, *mi amiga*. This will pass. You will be well again soon."

"You've given me something...?" She thought about the white light, the spinning, the pain in her head. Her extreme thirst. "I haven't been sick." She frowned again. "I've been drugged. You...you drugged me."

Danita shrugged and laughed again. "You will soon understand."

K.C. closed her eyes and rested against the pillow. "When—?" She opened her eyes and stared into Danita's dark ones. "I want to know. Right now. I must know what happened."

Danita looked at her watch. "You must rest until morning."

"You can't hold me here against my will." She sat forward, again trying to move her leaden legs. "I want to leave. To go back to the inn. To Gav..." The effort was too great, and her head was beginning to pound again. "Please," she breathed, "please, take me to him."

Danita held the glass to her lips. "Drink."

"I must go. Now..." Her eyes were heavy again, and flashes of light, an aura, flickered somewhere behind her lids. Her breathing slowed and she fought to keep from drifting away from the safe shore of consciousness.

Somewhere in the velvet darkness, a nagging thought wouldn't leave her. Something important she had to do. But she couldn't remember what it was. Only that she needed to rest.

Gav was awake all night. He paced his room, going over the moments he and K.C. were together before she left. Once in a while he walked to the window, pulled back the curtain, and stood utterly still, looking out into the night. But most of the time he paced. He needed to keep moving. Mind, body, heart.

He hurt for K.C., for the hard decisions she must be working through. But he was sure his heart ached just as badly as hers.

Toward dawn, he put on his running shoes and headed out of the room, down the stairs, and toward the citadel, the same place where he and K.C. had watched the sunrise the morning before.

How happy she had seemed. Had he done something wrong? Or was leaving him something she had been considering even then? He wondered, not for the first time, why she hadn't just told him she'd changed her mind before they left home? Of course she'd been hired to teach in Salamanca; that's why they'd decided to marry in Spain.

He pressed his shoe against the stone wall and stretched his calf, leaning into it, thinking. He repeated the motion with his other foot. And as the sun slipped over the horizon, he began to run. And pray. Just as he did every morning.

Only usually, he and K.C. ran together. Prayed together.

How could he have been so wrong about her? How could he have missed picking up on her misgivings?

"Lord, help me through this," he prayed as he ran. "I miss her. I don't know how I can go on without her…" His feet thudded along the dirt pathway. "I want to be angry…dismayed…

but I can't find it in my heart to feel anything except loss. The pain of loss.

"Father, she was part of me. Heart and soul. My best friend...."

Tears stung his eyes. "I can get along without her!" But he knew it wasn't true.

He picked up speed. "I don't understand her, Lord. Why didn't she tell me? Why did she wait so long!" He thudded on, the image of her face before him. He saw again the things he loved about her... her flaming red hair, the way she pushed up her glasses absently, her habit of twisting a strand of hair when lost in thought.

"But, Lord, how I love her! How I miss her."

The sun was higher now, and he tried not to see the glory of it. The beauty that he and K.C. should be seeing together. This was to be their wedding day!

He pressed his lips together and kept running.

Wedding. Ha! Some glorious day this would be. After his shower, he planned to catch a cab to the airport. Make his way back to Madrid. Change his British Airways ticket to London and San Francisco. He hoped to be home within twenty-four hours.

K.C., according to her note, planned to go on to Salamanca. That would give them a week of separation to think things through.

But she must have already made up her mind. Otherwise, she wouldn't have taken such drastic steps. He needed to face reality and get on with his life as quickly as possible. That was obviously K.C.'s intent as well.

He headed around the citadel wall, along some gardens, past a row of still-closed gift shops, and back to the inn.

Just as he arrived there, the Sterns were loading their luggage into the back of a car. Wyatt turned and saw him, then said something to Arabella, who turned toward him with a sympathetic expression.

"We heard about the letter," she said, slowly shaking her head. "I never would have guessed K.C. would take off like that." She pursed her lips. "We are so sorry."

Gav attempted to hurry past them, but they stepped between him and the front door, so there was no way to avoid them.

Wyatt put out his hand to shake Gav's. "You look us up when you get back to the States, now, son. We'd love to have you pay us a visit." Gav nodded while Wyatt continued pumping his hand. *"Mi casa, su casa."*

Arabella rolled her eyes.

"Thank you for helping last night," Gav finally managed. He chided himself for being ungrateful, for letting the two irritate him so.

"It was nothing," Wyatt said smoothly. "We were happy to help out a fellow traveler."

"Happy isn't the appropriate word, Wy," Arabella said. She shook her head, her expression saying louder than words that her husband couldn't ever get the finer nuances of social behavior right.

"You folks heading back to New Mexico soon?"

They exchanged a glance. "We plan to travel into western Spain, overnight at some paradors, take in the sights."

Salamanca was in western Spain, but Gav didn't comment. He wondered if they would try to see K.C. She had mentioned her teaching plans to them the first night they met, and he was sure that the contents of K.C.'s letter had spread like wildfire among the guests.

Arabella reached for him and kissed the air on both sides of his face. "Now you take care of yourself, Gav. You've been through quite an ordeal...." Her voice fell off as she looked at her watch. "We really must be off, Wy."

Her husband nodded and shut the trunk. He opened the passenger door, and Arabella slid onto the seat.

They drove out of sight. Gav stood staring after them, wondering what troubled him about the two. There was something he was missing. About them. About the way they'd hovered over K.C. yesterday morning when she hurt her foot. The way they'd followed them to the garden.

But he couldn't place what it was exactly, and after a moment, decided it was just his overworked sense of anxiety.

He headed back into the inn to pack.

The sun was high when K.C. woke. Danita was nowhere in sight.

K.C. tried to swing her legs from the bed to the floor. They weren't as heavy as they'd been the night before, but as she attempted to move them, she looked down at her swollen ankle, and knew it wouldn't bear her weight—even under the best circumstances. So she leaned back against her pillows, trying to make sense of her predicament.

She hadn't had long to consider where she was or why when a knock sounded at her door. It opened, and Doc Rafael strolled into the room.

Suddenly K.C. felt like Alice at the Mad Hatter's tea party. Nothing made sense. Why would Dr. Rafael come to see her?

She'd been sick, at least that's what Danita had told her. Was he here to check on her ankle?

Doc crossed the room to stand by the bed. "How are you feeling this morning, K.C.?" He glanced down at her ankle, but made no attempt to examine it.

She studied him as he crossed the room and brought back a chair to sit by her bed. He tugged at his mustache. "You are probably wondering why I have brought you here."

"You brought me here?"

"Yes, here to the Valley of the Dead." He nodded. "You do not remember?"

"No."

"Ah." His cold eyes assessed her, and she shivered.

"Was there...an accident?" She searched her mind for the hundredth time but came up with nothing.

He laughed softly. "No, there was no accident. And really, Señorita Keegan, there is no need for you to know the details. Only that you are several days' journey from Granada."

"Several days have passed?" She was incredulous.

He laughed heartily. "No, no. We came by plane. You are near a monument in the Valley of the Dead. A war memorial built by Franco. His tomb is not far from here."

Alfredo's words came back to her: "The place was built by the sweat, blood, and tears of prisoners from the opposition...Franco's Folly."

"And I hope you appreciate your accommodations." He glanced around the room appreciatively. "There are those who wanted you placed in one of the prison cells." He laughed.

No wonder the room was so dark. She remembered reading in the tour books that the basilica was carved deep into a solid granite mountain. "What am I doing here, Dr. Rafael?"

"You can call me Doc. Actually, I prefer it." He laughed again, apparently enjoying his role.

"Please, tell me why I am here. And what have you done with Gav? Where is he—?"

Rafael put up his hand to stop the tirade of questions. "First of all, you are not to worry about Señor Gavin." He chuckled again. "You have broken your engagement to him."

"What?"

Rafael repeated his words, watching her as if he took special pleasure in her dismay.

"That can't be!"

He leaned across the distance between them and grabbed her arm, roughly pushing up the sleeve of her shirt. A red lump was visible jut below her shoulder. "You received an injection Señorita Keegan. You don't need to know the Latin term for the, ah, shall we call it medication. You only need to know it made you cooperate with us." He laughed, letting her arm drop. "At least long enough to write your beloved a good-bye letter."

K.C. sat forward. "No!" She couldn't believe what she was hearing. It was all a bad dream. "No!"

"Sí, Señorita Keegan. We know you are a writer. We saw how you have a way with words." He leaned forward. "You even embellished what we dictated to you. We were surprised how easily you gave in to our request that you tell your beloved to—how do you say?—take a hike."

"Why?" Her voice was low. "Why me? Why Gav? What reason do you have to do this?"

His full lips widened into a smile, and he patted the hair laid across his baldness. "It will be a pleasure to tell you what we have planned for you…for your Señor Gavin."

"He won't believe the letter." Gav would see through the sham of the thing. She was sure of it.

"He has already accepted his fate, my dear. The last I heard he was changing his British Airways ticket to return home immediately." He stared at her.

"Then why am I here?"

Rafael studied her for a long moment, the fingers of one

hand drumming his knee. "Your fiancé is studying an organization located here in Spain, yes?"

Medieval Spain. But she wasn't going to tell him that. "He studies cults—organizations—that are based all over the world. There's nothing unusual about that."

Again, he watched her with those piercing eyes. After a moment he went on. "You see, we could not have him studying that particular—how do you say it?—cult."

She almost laughed. "You kidnapped me to get Gav to stay away from—" She stopped herself before divulging the name of the medieval society that had captured Gav's attention. "I demand that you return me this instant to Granada."

"You can demand nothing." His voice was low. Without emotion. "You are nothing to us. Your fiancé is nothing to us. There are things about to happen more important than you can imagine. No one can be allowed to get in the way…." His voice dropped menacingly.

"I am an American citizen."

"Prove it." His eyes glinted. His tone said he'd won. "Show me your passport."

She saw her suitcase on a table across the room. Her purse with the contents spilling out. "Where is it?"

He laughed. "It will be returned to you soon enough."

"I'll go to the authorities."

He raised a brow, amused. "Yes, yes. Of course you will."

"What's to stop me?"

He stood and walked to the window, then turned to look at her. A cat looking at a bug. A lizard eyeing a mosquito. "You will teach your class in Salamanca as planned."

She nodded. "And what do you have to do with that?"

"Nothing." He stepped closer. "If your Señor Gavin returns home as he now plans, then there will be nothing for either of you to fear. You can kiss and make up at the end of your time in Salamanca. All will be forgiven. Forgotten."

"And if he doesn't return home?" She had held that hope in her heart since hearing what had been forced upon them.

"He is not to look into the secret society on which he is conducting research."

"And if I can't stop him?" She thought of Gav. Her stubborn Gav. Once his sights were set, nothing, no one could get in his way.

Rafael paused and stepped closer, leaning over the bed. "Snatching you right from under his nose was child's play. Surely you see that."

She stared at him, pushing her chin forward, trying to look unafraid. But he was right.

"If he doesn't head back to the United States, if he does in fact come after you, you will both be sorry. Very sorry indeed."

She continued glaring at him with narrowed eyes. "Gav doesn't cower before empty threats."

"That is what you believe this to be? An empty threat?" He laughed again. A soft, evil sound. "Think about it, my dear. Look at you. Look what we have done with the greatest of ease. Nabbed you right from under your beloved's nose. Whisked you away by plane. You are under our power. We can keep you here. Or imprisoned elsewhere." He smiled. "You and your Señor Gavin do not stand a chance against us." He paused, studying her. "And if you do not fear for your own life, Señorita, I am guessing you will fear for your beloved's."

K.C. refused to shiver.

He laughed as if understanding the fear beneath her bluster.

"It is only because we choose to have you reappear in Salamanca that you will indeed reappear." He leaned closer. "Believe me, if we did not want you there, Señorita Keegan, you would not go. And anytime we feel you have broken your agreement with us, your beloved will suffer the consequences—that is, if he does not return to the States."

"You don't scare me," she repeated, but her pounding heart told her what a liar she was.

"If your actions bring harm to your fiancé, I think you might regret it."

She stared at him, unblinking.

"Am I right?"

Still she didn't answer.

He gave her a knowing smile and stepped even closer. "You see, my dear, I know all about you. I know what you will do to save the one you love, and I admire your brave disposition. But in your heart, I believe you know we will do as we wish. This mission cannot fail. Your fiancé is a threat to us. If he shows up uninvited, you must convince him to leave you. To leave Salamanca."

K.C. turned her head to the wall. "Actually, I don't think you need to worry. I doubt that he'll come back."

"We know about what happened between you a few years ago. That's why we planned this little—how do you say?—escapade." His smile, his tone, everything about him dripped arrogance.

She turned to glare at him. "How could you possibly know about that?"

His full lips split into a grin. "You would be surprised what we know about you, Señorita Keegan."

SEVEN

GAV TOOK A SEAT NEAR HIS GATE IN THE INTERNATIONAL TERMINAL of the Madrid airport. He held a cup of café con leche in one hand and with the other tapped his ticket against his knee.

He checked his watch. An hour until boarding time. He faced the center of the terminal where dozens of brightly lit duty-free shops circled the area. Restless, he checked his watch again, then stood and tossed his coffee cup into the trash receptacle. He had several large denominations of Spanish pesetas in his pocket. Might as well get rid of them.

Wheeling the TravelPro along behind, he headed toward the first of the shops. Ties and scarves. He quickly moved on. Past a *tapas* bar, past the perfumes and the gourmet sausages and cheeses. A bookstore beckoned in the distance, and he headed that way, the wheels of the carry-on clacking on the polished vinyl floor as he went.

Once inside, he paused. Most of the offerings were in

Spanish. A few shelves held German books, several others French. He finally spotted a small replica of the British flag across the store and moved toward it.

Setting his suitcase upright beside him, he started flipping though some of travel books displayed on a nearby table, thinking he would grab a few to show the folks back home. Slick photos. Gripping descriptions. The stuff of tourists and travel. A book on Salamanca caught his eye. A photograph of the cathedral was on the cover, its golden towers etched against a midnight sky.

He and K.C. had spoken of what it would be like to stand inside, looking up at the high arched ceiling, as tall as a football field standing on end. They'd promised each other to repeat their vows at the altar of that ancient place. K.C. said she planned to walk down the aisle in the footsteps of the ancient monks. She had wanted him to record the moment on videotape. No, he didn't want to purchase the book on Salamanca. It hurt too much to consider the memories it evoked.

He reached for another. Ávila, a small, completely walled city on the road from Madrid to Salamanca. Its picture made it look like the stuff of fairytales. There were two pages devoted to Teresa of Ávila, a spiritual teacher and prayer warrior from the sixteenth century. She had founded monasteries in Ávila and Salamanca. He remembered that K.C. had read everything she could find on Teresa, who'd become something of a hero to her

Teresa of Ávila. On the plane over, K.C. had read a collection of her writings.

"Listen to this, Gav," she'd said as the sun was fading. She'd read it to him in the form of poetry. He couldn't remember the exact words, but certain phrases returned to him now.

Let nothing, O Lord, disturb the silence…
Let nothing make me afraid.
Let me now, in the dying moments of this day,
Cast aside my concerns,
And commend myself wholly to your care.
For if I have you, God,
I will want for nothing.

K.C. had then taken his hand, put it against her cheek, and looked up at him with glistening eyes. God's love glowed in her face; his peace shone in her eyes.

She hadn't been hiding anything from him. He was sure of it. There had been no shadow in her soul, no thoughts of turning from him. Not then.

So when had she gotten cold feet?

He frowned, set aside the Ávila book, and reached for the book on Salamanca. This time he didn't hesitate. He opened it to the cathedral, studying the glorious photographs of the interior, the ornate altar, the towering gothic ceilings, the carved choir…the aisle where K.C. said she wanted to walk into his arms.

Something didn't make sense.

Could she have been coerced into writing the letter? But who could have done it? Outside of family and close friends, no one knew their history. Few besides K.C. knew about the earlier broken engagement.

He thought through the morning before she disappeared. Again, there was no sign that she was lost in an internal struggle, that she was thinking of fleeing from him, from the ceremony.

But that was the one sentence in the letter that convinced him it was from her heart.

He placed the book back on the table and turned to look

for a couple of paperbacks for the long flight home. He found an older New York Times bestseller by Jim Brown and a new release by the same author that was skyrocketing to the top of the charts. Gritty and compelling detective stories, both. Page-turners by an author sure to deliver.

Just what he needed to keep heart and mind from dwelling on K.C.

He headed to the register, grabbed a couple of packs of gum, then paid for his purchases. He hadn't made much of a dent in his leftover pesetas but figured he'd give the rest to the flight attendants when they collected for international charities.

A moment later he was rolling his suitcase back to the gate. More people were milling now, readying to line up and board. He checked the monitor and saw that his flight had been delayed.

With a heavy sigh, he sat down again. Around him babies fussed. A few people, obviously traveling together, were bent toward each other in earnest conversation. A woman guffawed, a loud and boozy laugh, and Gav hoped she wouldn't be seated near him on the flight.

He pulled out one of the Brown books—the newest release, *Millennium Force*—and flipped it over to read the back cover. It was an intriguing story…an international organization hoped to put a one-world government into place through a crash of the world economy brought about through computer hacking. Bad guys were nerds, planning to use both their hostilities and expertise to pull this off. Their existence was known only by e-mail addresses and Web sites. No one could get beyond the web of DNS servers that hid them.

At the bottom of the back cover text, a line jumped out at Gav: *In a chilling chesslike game,* Millennium Force *hackers found out everything they needed to know, from world banking practices to the cereal their opponents had for breakfast. There wasn't information anywhere in the world they couldn't find.*

Gav frowned, then flipped over the book, opened the cover, and tried to read the first line. But he couldn't concentrate. *There wasn't information anywhere in the world they couldn't find.... There wasn't information anywhere in the world they couldn't find....* The words played like a broken tape in his mind.

He put the book away, and headed over to the monitor to check his flight. Just as he spotted it, his flight was announced, first in Spanish, then in German, French, and finally English. Gav wandered back to the line that was forming at the gate. A child wailed nearby, and the woman with the raucous laugh got into line behind him. Gav took a deep breath and checked his watch again.

There wasn't information anywhere in the world they couldn't find....

What if someone had been able to document his and K.C.'s engagement years before? He had exchanged e-mail letters with Father Max, his pastor friend and confidant, when struggling with his decision to break the engagement.

He frowned, remembering a recent TV news magazine segment about how e-mail posts were not actually deleted anywhere, but remained on the user's computer. Copies of all e-mails remained on servers somewhere in the maze of DNS systems.

Could a hacker have pulled up the deleted posts he'd exchanged with Father Max?

It couldn't be. Why would anyone bother?

He sighed again, impatiently, and reached in his jacket pocket for his passport, which would be checked along with his ticket.

There wasn't information anywhere in the world they couldn't find.

But her handwriting, he argued with himself. *What about her handwriting?*

They easily could have coerced her into writing the letter. Or could they? It looked as calmly executed as if she'd been jotting down a recipe.

But a nagging thought wouldn't leave him alone. What if he was leaving K.C. in the clutches of someone who had plotted against them? Cult practices ranged from the bizarre to over-the-top paranoia.

He laughed to himself. Talk about an overactive imagination.

Maybe he just couldn't let himself believe that K.C. had broken the engagement. That was it. His pride couldn't accept it. That's why he was entertaining the thought of staying.

Staying?

The line was inching forward now. People were showing tickets and passports. He tapped his impatiently against his thigh. Staying? How could he even consider it? He looked at his watch, trying to decide.

The British Airways 747 loomed beyond the window. Hundreds of people were lined up, moving forward a few feet at a time.

But what if K.C. needed him?

He clamped his jaw. What if she didn't? What if she would simply be irritated if he walked back into her life again, joined her in Salamanca, where she'd specifically told him not to go?

He glanced down at his ticket. Could he get a refund, or at least an extension on the departure date?

His first inclination, he'd found through the years, was usually the correct one. From taking a multiple-choice test to deciding what SUV to buy. Gut reaction. He counted on it. Always. Never let him down.

He inched forward, now drumming his passport on his

thigh in a nervous rhythm. The woman in front of him craned and glared.

He smiled at her. Moments later he reached the agent and handed over the ticket and the passport.

K.C. seated herself across the table from Doc Rafael and Danita in the dark dining room near the basilica. It was the first evening she'd been allowed to leave her room. She glanced around for an exit, though she was fairly sure she wouldn't be given an opportunity to make a run for it. Gray stone walls, no windows. Charming place.

She laughed at the irony. Even if she did get away, where would she go? She was in the remote woodlands known as Santa Cruz del Valle de los Caídos. Valley of the Dead. How fitting.

The dining room was empty except for the three of them. Rafael seemed to sense her mood and leaned forward with a wry smile. "I wonder if you can enjoy the extraordinary beauty of this place, my dear, the thought that went into the building of it. We will give you a tour of the basilica later."

"I can't imagine there's any beauty in something where prisoners were killed as they built it."

Doc Rafael gave her a patronizing look. "Ah, my dear, most people don't understand the reason this magnificent place was built."

"They don't understand that it's a monument to Franco, to the worst of a man's folly," she said.

Danita leaned forward. "You are mistaken about lives lost while it was being built—"

"You are saying prisoners didn't build it?"

"Well, yes, they did—"

"That they were forced to build it?"

"Sí."

She raised a brow. Her point was made.

But Danita wouldn't give up. Fervor was hot in her dark eyes. "You do not understand. You *cannot* understand our people."

"I understand what a brutal dictator can do to his country, to his people. Especially to those who oppose him."

Rafael held up a hand. "We will not solve the ills of the past by discussing our recent dictator."

The women fell silent, and K.C. studied Danita as a server poured them coffee. The woman was younger than she had first thought. And pretty. Her features were dainty, her wrists small, her fingers slender. The corners of Danita's mouth turned upward more than they turned down, disconcerting at the very least, since the woman was part of some strange plot against K.C. Danita's command of both languages and her demeanor told K.C. that she was well educated. Under different circumstances, K.C. might have liked her.

She wondered what was behind the actions of this woman and Doc Rafael. What were they afraid Gav might find out? What did it have to do with the cult he was researching?

She frowned as she studied the two; this was the first time she had observed them together. The obvious difference between their ages made K.C. think they might be father and daughter, but she saw no sign of affection between them.

"How much longer will I be here?" K.C. waited while a plate of eggs and ham was set before her. She hadn't been asked what she wanted, but the choice was right for her growling stomach. Next, a basket of warm rolls was served, and a small dish of fresh strawberries.

Danita handed K.C. the basket, her dark eyes meeting K.C.'s for a brief instant. "You will leave tomorrow morning."

"For Salamanca?"

Rafael laughed. "No."

"Where, then?"

"We have quite a tour planned for you." Doc gave her a benign smile, then reached for a piece of dark bread, broke it, and placed in on his plate. "You see, my dear, once you reach Salamanca, you will be asked where you've been. What you've been up to. We must make sure you do not give away any information about what has happened to you. We have determined the best way to do this is to provide you with tour guides to show you some of the finest sights in Western Spain. You will see castles and palaces and museums, vistas beyond imagining. Your mind will be filled with the beauty of—" he chuckled—"of your experience here." He took a bite of his eggs, his mustache wagging as he chewed.

"Rather than the horror of being kidnapped, you mean?" She looked at him evenly.

"We prefer to call it house arrest." He laughed as he spread a piece of bread generously, in one precise motion, with sweet butter. "It can be pleasant if you cooperate. Unpleasant if you do not." He popped the roll into his mouth.

"We did not mean to frighten you," Danita said gently. "What we have done is very necessary. Someday you will understand. Someday the world will understand."

"The world?" As K.C. spoke, Doc gave Danita a warning look.

"In a manner of speaking," Danita said, and went back to her supper.

As soon as the meal was over, Doc helped Danita from her chair, then the two of them helped K.C. to standing. He'd brought her a small cane to help ease the difficulty she still had walking, and she took it from him.

"We will tour the basilica now." He met K.C.'s challenging stare with an unblinking one of his own.

K.C. drew in a deep breath and gave him a slight nod. "All right, lead the way."

They wound through a long, wide stone hallway, leading, K.C. assumed, from the bowels of the granite mountain. Strange. It was luxuriously appointed, from the Persian carpets to the crystal chandeliers, with centuries-old sideboards spaced along the way. But still no windows. Incongruous, to say the least. She hobbled along with Danita and Rafael, anxious to be free of the place. But as they walked she wondered about the maze of secret passages Alfredo had worked in....

Could they still be found? Or, more important, accessed?

It was worth pondering.

Minutes later they stepped down some wide stone stairs and onto an expansive courtyard. The sky was clouded and the air brisk. K.C. blinked in the dull gray light. She hadn't seen real daylight since her arrival.

Danita was smiling and looking behind K.C., straight up the mountainside.

K.C. turned and squinted against the sky. A massive concrete tower in the form of a cross rose skyward some five hundred feet.

She swallowed an emotion she couldn't fathom, an abhorrence that made her ill. The gleam of elevator cables caught her attention. She moved her gaze slowly up the vertical rise of the cross and saw the elevator port at the top, where tourists could tramp along the horizontal crossbar to gaze out at the valley from the observation deck. A Disneyland ride in the worst of taste.

She shivered. It reminded her again of the folly of humanity, a cold and sterile monument in the form of what was properly a symbol of the greatest sacrifice from time's beginning: the death of God's beloved Son, sent to die an agonizing death for the sins of all the world.

Chilled, K.C. turned away from the stone edifice. Doc gave her a pleased nod. Apparently he thought the tears in her eyes meant she'd been moved by the monument. He turned to lead them into the basilica itself.

K.C.'s spirits dropped even further when she saw the vast, cold emptiness of the courtyard, the entry to the cathedral. She had hoped that the place would be teeming with tourists, even one person she could ask for help. But it was obviously after hours or a day the monument was closed.

She hobbled through the ornate narthex into the vast barn of the basilica, each step more reluctant than the one before.

Her shoulders proud, Danita swung open one of the ornately carved wooden doors and K.C. stepped inside.

Danita kept her gaze on the front of the basilica as she moved to stand beside K.C. "Franco's tomb," she whispered.

K.C. followed her gaze, and her spirits lifted. A woman draped in dark colors and wearing a wide-brimmed hat knelt by the tomb.

Doc leaned toward her. "Do you know, my dear, that this was to be the largest cathedral in the world?"

She shook her head mutely, still watching the figure at the tomb.

He laughed again as they moved slowly down the center aisle. "But the pope would not allow Franco to build it larger than that at the Vatican. Franco gave in of course, not wanting to upset the pope. He finally scaled it down so that it is a mere few meters smaller."

They had almost reached the front of the massive barn of a church. The walls were stark, granite-hued gray. There were no windows, because the entire basilica had been carved deep into the hillside. K.C. felt as though she was in a cave. Then she shivered again. She *was* in a cave.

Danita stopped to explain one of the paintings that lined both sides of the basilica. Her eyes were shining with delight at the magnificence of the art, the talent of the artist. She was obviously well read, and knew art and art history well, for she explained succinctly what K.C. was looking at.

They turned again to head down the aisle. The woman had disappeared, and K.C. let her gaze travel along the massive expanse of the place, across the choir, the retrochoir, the chancel. It was too full of shadows to see clearly, but still she searched. If she could only get to the woman, tell her she needed help. Make her understand, whether she spoke English or not. She *had* to understand. She searched her mind for the tidbits of Spanish she could remember.

Help. *Socorro!* That would be a start. What was the word for trouble? *Problema!* Yes. *Problema*. Another she could use. And she would point to Danita and Rafael. She was pretty good at charades. She would make the woman understand.

As Danita led the way up the stairs to the tomb, Rafael hovered at K.C.'s elbow. She craned around to look for the woman. It appeared she was strolling into one of the side chapels. She prayed there wasn't a separate exit and willed the woman to turn around and head back toward her.

Danita stopped at the tomb of Franco. Her eyes misted, and for a moment she didn't speak. "This is the place," she said simply, "where Franco is buried."

K.C. nodded, and from the corner of her eye saw the woman turn to head back to the chancel. From the shadows of an alcove, a man stepped out to join her. They strode forward, the man's hand beneath his companion's elbow. Then the woman removed her black felt *vaquero's* hat, letting her abundance of hair fall free. Au naturel.

They were both dressed in black, dripping in silver and turquoise.

A burst of hope filled K.C.'s heart. It was the Sterns. They would understand...and help.

"Good afternoon, K.C." Arabella said. "Imagine meeting you in such a place."

And she laughed.

Eight

One week later, K.C. leaned against her seat on the train from Madrid to Salamanca. Arabella sat beside her on the aisle side, seemingly lost in her thoughts. Wyatt was two rows back, also on the aisle. The rail car was filled with passengers, mostly Spanish, many probably on a pilgrimage to spend Holy Week in Salamanca.

K.C. stared through the window, watching the bleak landscape slide by. For the hundredth time since she boarded an hour before, her thoughts turned to Gav. Oh, how she missed him! His crooked smile. The light in his eyes when he looked into hers. His low, rumbling laugh. She sighed and closed her eyes, picturing him. Was he home by now? What was he thinking? Did he believe the letter? Or did he have faith in her love?

Oh, Gav...how I wish you were here, touching my hand, telling me this will all turn out okay....

What if he did have faith in her love? What if he showed up at the university to rescue her? His life would be in danger. No matter how nonthreatening her captors seemed, she had seen things during the week of so-called *tourist travel* that convinced her they were serious.

Dead serious.

Her stay at the Valle de los Caídos had been only the beginning. She had toured art museums and cathedrals, theaters and paradors. Always accompanied by the Sterns. They seemed to be determined that she experience firsthand museums that showed the horrors of Spain's Civil War, especially those featuring the atrocities carried out by the Republicans, Franco's opposition. It hadn't taken her long to understand that the entire trip was meant to sway her political theories. It angered her that they thought her so naive.

Since the train left Madrid, the landscape had changed drastically. From the expanse of city buildings, they'd moved into the country of rolling, forested hills and lush undergrowth. But now the land had spread into one great plain, barren except for a few groves of olive trees along the way.

The spring weather hadn't warmed since K.C. had left the Valley of the Dead. If anything, the wind and cold seemed to cut right through her.

Arabella looked across the double seat they were sharing. "How do you like Western Spain?"

K.C. lifted a brow. "I'd prefer to experience it on my own. But it does have a wild, windswept kind of beauty."

Arabella followed her gaze across the barren land. "I agree."

The sound of metal wheels on metal track, the blur of sunlit scenery…it all made her drowsy, leaving her almost mesmerized by the sound.

She leaned her head back against the high upholstered seat.

She'd made it through one week. She would make it through another in Salamanca. She would keep her mouth shut, as directed. Then she would go home, find Gav, and explain. She closed her eyes. One week. One day at a time. She could handle it. Of course she could.

The rhythm of the wheels continued, and she drew in a deep breath. *Lord, help me. Help me keep my focus on you. On getting through this week. You are with me. Help me, Lord. Help me.*

She opened her eyes to find Arabella studying her. The woman's eyes were piercing, cold. K.C. turned away to look through the window.

"You were praying just now."

"Yes." K.C. kept her gaze on the passing fields.

"I no longer believe in prayer."

"I don't believe in prayer, either," K.C. turned to her. "I believe in the Lord who answers my prayers. There is power in the One who's listening, not in the words themselves."

Arabella laughed, quirking a brow. "What about all the prayers that go unanswered? What kind of a God refuses to answer the most desperate prayer?"

K.C. studied the woman for a moment. "Sometimes his answer is no. It's not that he doesn't hear. He just knows better than we do what we need."

"Even the death of a child?" Arabella's mouth twisted, and a dark look shadowed her eyes.

K.C. sat up, studying the woman. "You had a child who died?"

Arabella stared at her without answering, and K.C., with a slight nod, moved her gaze. She knew the answer without a word from Arabella. She could see it in her eyes.

But the older woman persisted. "You think God can rescue you from this? That he can save you?"

K.C. turned toward her again. "He is with me. There may be reasons I'm here that I don't know about." She leaned forward. "I'm not praying for rescue."

"Ha!" Arabella's laugh was brittle. "I just bet you aren't." Her silver bracelets jangled as she swept back her dark hair.

K.C. didn't debate the point, but kept her gaze on the woman beside her. "When a child is lost, we can't know why. We may never know why tragic things happen to us. But the solace is that our heavenly Father knows. And he's with us."

Arabella dismissed K.C.'s words with a wave of her hand. "You've obviously not ever felt the kind of pain I have."

K.C. agreed in her heart, but it didn't mean that the sorrow and terror she had felt—after waking to find she'd been kidnapped, after finding Gav had been sent away from her and her wedding had been canceled—was any less significant. "Losing a child must be the most painful experience a woman could have."

Arabella turned away from K.C. to stare at the passing landscape. Both remained silent as the train continued on to Salamanca.

"Ladies..." Wyatt stepped toward them. "We have only a few more minutes until we arrive at the station."

K.C. nodded and drew in a deep breath, wondering what else was in store for her.

"We will be staying at the same hotel as you," Arabella told her. "You can tell anyone who asks that we're your personal tour guides and friends. You will refuse to go anywhere without us. Especially after the loss of your fiancé. I'm sure your colleagues will understand."

K.C. nodded absently, her eyes now on the horizon. From

out of nowhere, it seemed, a crop of bell towers sprang heavenward from the flat dismal plains. The structures caught the slant of the late-afternoon sun, superimposed on the pearl twilight sky behind them. There was something about the ancient, glorious buildings that spoke of God's ageless presence, and K.C.'s eyes filled with tears.

Wyatt leaned over the two women to peer out the train window. "Salamanca's two cathedrals." He nodded toward the bell towers. "The older was begun in 1150, the newer in 1491, the year before Columbus sailed for America." He delivered the information blithely, with an air of condescension, like a master imparting pearls of brilliance to his acolytes. "As I'm sure you are aware, the university was founded in 1218."

K.C. wanted to scream at him that she didn't care. To tell him to just shut up, that the only information she wanted from him was when they'd let her go. But she just bit her lip and looked away.

He eyed her. "That is where you'll be teaching, is it not?"

K.C. figured he knew full well and didn't bother to answer.

Arabella leaned forward. "Lest you think we won't be diligent in our continuing charge over you—" she smiled—"I've enrolled in your classes for the week. There won't be a moment you'll be out of our sight. Not even in your classroom. Even your hotel room will adjoin ours."

With those words, K.C.'s one hope vanished. The academic sanctuary—the plan to get help from her American colleagues, a plan she'd worked out in her mind over the past several days—was out of reach. Another disappointment in a week filled with too many to list. "How could you arrange that?" she finally managed. "These students are from a local community college in California. They're enrolled for the entire semester, not just for the one week I'm here as the visiting scholar."

Arabella and Wyatt exchanged a look. "We have our ways, dear," Arabella said. "As I'm sure you're now aware. We have our ways."

K.C. suddenly bolted for the aisle, surprising both Arabella and Wyatt. The older woman grabbed K.C.'s arm, but K.C. shook it off and mumbled that she needed to visit the loo. Then she fled to the back of the car, pushed her entire weight against the sliding door until it gave way, and stumbled into the space between the cars.

The window was open, and she headed toward it, gulping the fresh air. After a moment she leaned against the cold steel of the doorframe and closed her eyes. She was suffocating.

A porter stepped toward her, seeming to appear from nowhere. "Señorita…?"

Just then Wyatt pushed through the sliding door and shoved the man aside. "We're nearly to the station." His eyes assessed K.C.'s position by the door. "I suppose you were planning to run as soon as the train stops—"

K.C. cast a desperate look at the porter. She could see by his blank look that he probably understood little, if any, English. She drew in another deep breath, praying for strength. "Actually, I hadn't thought of it." Then she managed a cocky tilt to her chin as she brushed past him. "But you're right—" she tossed the words over her shoulder—"it would have been a good plan." She felt surprisingly calm as she headed back down the aisle to her seat.

Arabella patted the seat next to her as K.C. stepped toward it. "There, there, now, dear. Do you feel better?"

"I won't feel better until this is behind me," she muttered, then stared through the window as the Salamanca train station came into sight and the train slowed.

That night, after the three had checked into a hotel just off the *Plaza Mayor,* K.C. hoped for some time alone. She needed time to plan her next move. If there was to be a next move.

She got what she wished for. She had been placed in an adjoining room next to Wyatt and Arabella. She stretched out on her small bed and hooked her arm across her eyes. She was weary, too weary for words. She wondered how she could possibly get through the week, expending the energy needed to teach students the elements of good journalism. Ha! Good journalism. The truth at the heart of every story. The irony almost made her laugh.

She lifted her arm and stared at the door. She thought for a minute about hobbling down the stairs, looking for a pay phone. If she called for help—even home to the United States— assistance would come, all right. But if Gav happened to be here in Salamanca—as she half-expected him to be—his life would be taken in exchange for her moment of folly.

Or was it folly?

What did these people want? What could be so important to this group that they were willing to go to such extreme lengths to keep Gav off their trail? What had he looked into while researching his latest cult that endangered his life? What if she did try to call him in the States? Would he even speak to her?

She sighed, her arm again snug across her eyes. Weariness settled over her like a blanket, and she drifted into that dark place between semiconsciousness and sleep. Her breathing slowed; she turned onto her side, facing away from the adjoining door.

Then the door creaked open, pulling K.C. from her waking dreams. Eyes still closed, she feigned long, deep-sleep breaths.

"She's exhausted, poor dear," Arabella whispered. Then the door creaked as it was pulled closed, though not completely shut. Arabella's and Wyatt's voices drifted into the room.

K.C., still not moving, caught her breath. The voices were muffled, and she could make out only snatches of words, from time to time, a phrase.

"Darling, you must consider the consequences...." Arabella's voice was low.

Wyatt's answer was muffled. K.C. barely made out something that sounded like "the only way."

Then another machine-gun spurt of words, and finally sobs. After a moment of silence, Arabella spoke again, apparently moving toward the door between the rooms. "You don't understand...you never understand. I don't know why I expect it to be any different. You have no passion for the cause."

After a few minutes, the voices rose again. K.C. couldn't help smiling to herself. *Argue. Go ahead, go for it! All the better for me to hear.*

Then the door clicked shut.

Arabella sat back, her heart aching, as Wyatt delved deeper into the subject that divided them.

"Danita is not your granddaughter. You might as well forget it."

Arabella took a deep breath. "She's the right age. Even her coloring..."

"You don't even know if the baby you gave up lived, married, had offspring—"

"On the other hand, we don't know that the child did not." Her laugh was short. Bitter. "Though I can see you don't care one way or the other."

"We have deeper, more important issues to consider than whether the young woman is or isn't your granddaughter."

Arabella leaned forward, her heart catching in her throat. "You'll never let me forget what happened, will you? You can't forgive me for loving someone else—even though it was years before I met you."

His eyes glinted. "That was before we married. I care nothing about it." He paused. "But my dear, it is not I who cannot forget. It is you."

"My child's father was a Spaniard."

Wyatt's gaze flickered over her face, though his expression remained bored. "And you two worked as spies for Franco. Yes, I know. You don't need to remind me how Miguel Vargas was bigger than life." His fingertips tapped a staccato beat on the chair arm. "Martyrs usually are."

She turned away from him. "We were to marry. After our last mission."

"He was killed, and you were left alone. Pregnant. In a foreign land." He gave her a shrug of indifference.

"I was only sixteen."

He let his gaze drift from her face to the window. "We've talked about this before. Ad nauseam."

Arabella bit her lip as tears filled her eyes. She didn't want to show her husband her vulnerability. "I gave her up. I didn't see how I could care for her. I was little more than a child myself. But the first time I saw Danita...I saw something in her eyes. Something of Miguel."

Now Wyatt was staring at her again. "You didn't feel guilty until we lost our child...." There was pain in his eyes. "You also didn't think of your first child as female until then."

"God punished me for giving up my firstborn."

"I didn't think you believed in God." His look was mocking.

She ignored him. "Danita knows nothing of her background. She says there are mysterious circumstances that no one will explain."

Wyatt's eyes glinted dangerously again. "You didn't tell me that you'd spoken to her about this."

"I—I didn't tell her what I suspect. I merely asked her about her family." Arabella didn't say that when she'd tried to probe deeper, Danita immediately put a wall between them. An emotional distance. Quite suddenly and quite firmly. After a moment Arabella went on. "Don't you see, Wyatt? Franco arranged for the adoption. He would have seen to it that Danita was placed with a family with known loyalties. She grew up knowing what was expected of her. That she should continue the fight for fascism."

"So could thousands of other orphans, Arabella. Think about it. You're a rational woman, but you're dealing with this in a completely irrational way."

"But it all fits." She stared at him, setting her lips in a straight line. "I refuse to give up believing that Danita is my grandchild."

Suddenly, Wyatt moved toward her chair and knelt before it. He took her hand in his, held it against his bearded cheek. "I'm sorry, darling, if I seem cold. We both believe in Tres Equis and what they're trying to accomplish or we wouldn't be here. We wouldn't have contributed to their cause—or taken part in this kidnapping." He glanced toward the door separating their room from K.C. Keegan's.

"Danita is a leader in a cause we believe in. She's captured your heart because you see in her something of yourself, a fervency similar to yours when you and Miguel Vargas worked for Franco."

He paused. "She also has captured Julian's attention...

which makes her—or perhaps I should say her future position in government—that much more attractive to you."

Her husband's gaze now held hers captive. In spite of his earlier hostility, he was looking at her with eyes of love and understanding. She melted. Neither one of them had ever gotten over their little Carlotta's death. And the fact that Arabella had once loved another man and borne his child—a child who likely lived—hurt and angered Wyatt.

She understood and squeezed his fingertips. From now on she would keep her suspicions about Danita to herself. Because no matter what her husband said, there was more to the connection between herself and Danita than just political ideology.

Wyatt touched her face, letting his fingertips trail lovingly down her cheek, then kissed her palm. "You must remember you were but a student, an idealistic exchange student, when you fell in love with Miguel." He chuckled, cutting his eyes to the door once again. "Fighting for a cause is romantic—"

"Is that why you're going along with this now, my love?" Her voice held a measured innocence, but deep down she thought Wyatt probably didn't have a political bone in his handsome body. A memory of Miguel's impassioned face tugged at some corner of her mind, and she sighed. "Because the cause is romantic? You fancy yourself some sort of Hemingway. Wealthy American, artistic and adventurous, here for the sport of it?"

Wyatt's cheeks flushed, and he stood abruptly. "Why must you always compare me to Miguel?" He turned away from her. "It seems you will never be satisfied."

"I just don't believe your heart is in our cause," she said to his back. "You have no passion. Even Julian says—"

He whirled.

"Hit a nerve did I, my love?" She quirked a brow and stood, now staring at him eye to eye.

For a moment the only sound in the room was the creaking and groaning of an ancient radiator in the corner near the window. Finally Wyatt spoke, his words mixed with a tired sigh. "It's nearly time for supper."

"I'll see to K.C."

Turning the brass handle, she pushed the door open, hurried inside K.C.'s room, and looked around, puzzled. The bathroom door was ajar, and one glance at the small, empty room confirmed her fears.

She whirled and nearly ran into Wyatt who was following only a few steps behind.

His face blanched. "She's gone?"

Arabella nodded. "Yes. She's gone."

NINE

LATE THE FOLLOWING MORNING, BACKPACK SLUNG ACROSS HIS back, Gav bounded down the steps leading from the *autobús*. No Greyhound, this. No, he'd been pleasantly surprised at the luxurious upholstered seats and the strains of Mozart drifting from the stereo system during the two-hour drive from Madrid.

He looked around, getting his bearings. The Salamanca station was smaller and emptier than he'd expected. He reached for his pocket dictionary, flipping through until he found the words he needed, then headed through the double glass doors to the information booth.

He smiled at the woman seated behind the counter. "Can you tell me how to get to the university?"

She frowned.

"*Universidad*," he repeated.

"Ahh, sí." She finally returned his smile, then fired off a rapid answer in Spanish.

He grinned sheepishly and shook his head. "No. Please. Too fast. I'm sorry."

Now there were three people in line behind him, one woman jostling a crying baby. An older woman shuffled up to the counter and complained loudly. Though she spoke only Spanish, her irritation was clear as she glared at Gav.

The woman in the booth shrugged at Gav, then pointed toward the street where taxis were queued. Her look said he might as well be from Mars, asking directions to another planet in the solar system.

"Gracias." He smiled at the line of sullen-looking people. No one said *de nada* in return.

He sighed as he hefted the backpack into place and headed through the doors to the taxi stand. Probably better not to walk anyway. He wanted to avoid being seen. He did know—from some vague and roughly drawn tourist maps—that the heart of Salamanca's historical district was not large. Besides the university, it contained the cathedral, several monasteries and churches, colleges and convents. The town's narrow cobbled streets all led to the Plaza Mayor.

In the medieval sector everyone walked; the only vehicles were taxis and delivery vans. He didn't want to risk being recognized by K.C. or anyone else until he sorted out some answers to his questions.

A cab pulled into place at the head of the line. Gav looked through the window at the cabby. *"Universidad?"*

The man nodded to the back door, and Gav crawled in, barely closing the door before the cabby pressed the accelerator and the car leapt forward. Within a few minutes, they'd left the modern architecture of the outer city and were winding through dark and narrow streets. The ancient setting clashed with a soccer game blaring from the cabby's radio.

Soon the cab pulled to a halt near the cathedral. The driver fired off something in Spanish. Even if Gav could have understood the stream of Spanish, he wouldn't have heard him over the shouting radio announcer. He glanced at the digital readout of the fare and figured how many pesetas he owed, counted out the bills, and handed them to the cabbie, who shrugged and drove off.

He'd been let out of the cab about a block from the cathedral, and hefting his backpack onto one shoulder, he strode toward it. As the bells in a nearby tower tolled eleven o'clock, young people carrying books and backpacks surged from buildings across the square from the ancient golden-stoned edifice.

Gav remembered that the University of Salamanca was across from the cathedral and headed toward a square that looked promising. He encountered more students along the way and heard snatches of Spanish, French, and something guttural that sounded German. But no English.

He'd read that at any given time, as many as forty thousand students were in Salamanca studying at various colleges, language schools, and of course the university itself, once considered the best in the world. Though he was in the heart of the city, he could have sworn he'd landed on a major university campus.

He stopped to check his tourist map, turned it around, and checked it again. It showed that the university was just around the corner from where he stood. Frowning, he followed a fresh stream of students heading out of modern glass doors—automatic doors—smack dab in the façade of a building that had to be a thousand years old.

Stepping inside a modern office building, he had to blink twice. The building had obviously been gutted of all that was original. Inside, behind gleaming glass and chrome counters, computers hummed, fax machines spilled out their incoming faxes, and beautiful young Spanish women hurried about.

He stood at the counter until one of the young women spotted him and stepped forward.

"Do you speak English?"

She nodded. "Sí, yes. How may I help you?"

"My…fian…ah…my friend, Katherine Keegan, is scheduled to teach classes this week, beginning today, I believe. As a visiting scholar. I need to see her, get in touch with her. Can you tell me where her class will be meeting?"

The woman nodded crisply. "I do not recognize the name. Which college is she affiliated with?"

"It's a semester abroad program from California. I only know that it's somehow connected to the University of Salamanca."

She smiled. "There are many colleges here. Some are connected with us. Some are not."

"Can you check under Pelican Bay Community College?"

"Certainly." She stepped to her computer terminal. After a moment she turned back. "Yes, it is here. Can you tell me your friend's name again? And you say she is faculty?"

"Her name is Katherine C. Keegan. Or she might be listed as K.C. Keegan. She's the visiting scholar. She's here only for the week, so she may not be listed with the regular faculty."

The woman frowned, now scrolling with her mouse. "Oh, yes. Here it is. I found Pelican Bay. And Katherine Keegan. She is on the list." She glanced at Gav. "But she is also reported as absent today." She frowned. "Perhaps she is ill after the long flight."

Gav didn't bother to explain. "So that means she is not here today."

"Sí, that is correct."

"Do you have her hotel, the address and name—where she's staying?"

"I cannot give you that information. You will have to see those in charge of that program."

"And who might that be?" He was getting impatient.

The woman scribbled something on a notepad, tore off the top sheet, and handed it to him. "Perhaps you can leave a note for your friend to call you. This is the address of the faculty office."

Gav nodded and placed the paper in his shirt pocket.

"But you will not find anyone there right now." She glanced at a wall clock. "It is nearly time for siesta. This office will be locked."

He let out an exasperated sigh. "Until what time?"

She gave him a surprised look as though he should know the answer. "Until four o'clock. All businesses close for siesta. Three hours."

He tried to swallow his annoyance. "Thank you."

She looked sympathetic. "There is a coffeehouse across the street from the *colegio* office. Perhaps you can eat lunch while you wait."

Eating was the last thing he felt like doing. With K.C. reported as absent, he was more worried than ever—also convinced that she had indeed met with something other than a case of cold feet.

He thanked the young woman and headed out the doors to the cobbled street beyond the university office. He rounded the corner of the ancient façade and hurried down another street. Suddenly, in front of him loomed the towers of the cathedral. He halted, looking up, and took a deep breath. They held a golden sheen in the early afternoon sun, almost too bright to keep his gaze on for longer than a half second. A purple blue provided a backdrop for a few drifting clouds.

A clicking sound drew his gaze further up the bell tower. A stork in a three-foot nest gazed down at him from the top of the tower, looking as perplexed as Gav felt. The clicking sound came from the giant bird's bill. Gav grinned, then, turning in a circle, noticed the big birds were roosting on nearly every high point on the ancient buildings.

He stepped closer to get a better look at the bird right above him. Gav chuckled. How K.C. would love to see this! He could almost hear her laugh. She'd probably imitate the clicking sounds, try to figure out a way to reach the nest for a closer look.

The thought of K.C., the pain of missing her so, brought a sting to his throat, and he swallowed hard.

Where are you, my love?

He'd hoped and prayed that he would find her here in Salamanca, safe. That she would assure him she'd merely had a case of cold feet. That she would beg his forgiveness....

He walked closer to the cathedral. The streets were emptying now, siesta about to begin. The place seemed to beckon him, as if God might meet him there to give him rest for his weary, worried soul. He quickened his steps, bounded up the wide stairs leading to the twenty-foot, carved wooden doors, and tried the iron handle. It held fast.

Taking the steps three at a time, he headed back to the wide plaza around the cathedral. He sprinted across the grounds, around the building, and down the narrow street, looking for other entrances that might not have closed for siesta.

He tried some large double side-doors. They were locked too. Then he noticed a small alcove. No door was in sight. He turned, intending to continue his search, but something held him fast. With a frown, he studied the alcove again. Then, following an urging he didn't understand, he walked toward it.

A small open door greeted him as he rounded the corner. Smiling to himself, he stepped from the sunlight into a small, dimly lit hall. He stopped, blinking to let his eyes adjust before continuing down the hallway.

Stepping toward the alcove, he put his shoulder against one of the heavy wooden doors to push it open. It gave way, creaking as it swung inward. Suddenly he was inside the cavernous room. He halted dead in his tracks, his mouth falling open.

His gaze was drawn upward—rather, it *soared* upward. Glorious gothic arches towered above him. Slender pillars led away to vaults and domes too magnificent to take in…stained glass windows with their rainbow light…the cold hush of ancient stone.

Splendor and power were everywhere…and yes, the awesome sense of holiness.

It was still, so still that Gav could hear his heart beat. And so large, he must surely have shrunk to nothing. He turned a complete circle, awestruck, still looking upward.

K.C. stepped into one of several small, open chapels to the side of the cavernous cathedral and closed the iron gate behind her. Its click was magnified in the silence. She dropped the iron key into the pocket of her novice's robe and took her seat in a wooden pew, facing an ornately carved marble crypt, her back to the transept.

She pulled the nubby cloth closer, letting the folds fall over her running shoes. She had to smile at her costume; it had been Sister Calandria's idea. Dressed thus, K.C. could slip around town as one of dozens of novices visiting Salamanca during Holy Week. Sister Calandria, who spoke perfect English, had commanded her not to speak. Many novices take vows of silence, she had explained.

It was still a wonder that Sister Calandria had believed K.C.'s story. Not only believed, but had granted her sanctuary in the small Convent of Saint Teresa until K.C.—and, she suspected, Sister Calandria—could get to the bottom of the mystery of her kidnapping.

K.C. knew it was God who'd brought her to the loving sister. And in a miraculous way, K.C.'s knowledge of and love for Teresa of Ávila, and her study of this medieval woman's godly life, had brought K.C. into the safety of Sister Calandria's presence.

She had no doubt that she'd been led to the convent. The night before, just at twilight, K.C. had hobbled from the Doña María through the Plaza Mayor, not knowing where she was headed. Not caring. Only determined to find safety—and time to think about her next move, to decide whom she could trust.

Then quite suddenly, she'd recognized, from tourist book photos, the convent where Saint Teresa's house once stood.

Sister Calandria, a round-faced woman with bright, curious eyes, greeted her at the door. She had not asked a single question after K.C.'s plea for help, but had pulled her immediately into the back rooms of the convent.

She'd seen to K.C.'s needs, bringing her a large bowl of roasted lamb and vegetables and a loaf of whole-grain bread, still warm from the oven. As K.C. ate ravenously, her story spilled out.

It was when K.C. described Gav and their wedding plans that a steely glint appeared in the sweet-faced sister's eyes. After K.C. had been tucked into an iron cot in an austere guest room, she'd dared to pray—and to hope—that Sister Calandria might help her find her way through the maze.

Now K.C. let out a deep sigh and soaked up the stillness of the cathedral. "Oh, Lord," she breathed, "thank you for bringing me to the safety of this place—"

Her heart caught.

Footsteps echoed behind her, growing louder as they headed toward the chapel where she prayed. She bent her head lower, letting the drape across her head hide her face. Eyes closed, she tried to ignore her racing heart. The footsteps stopped just short of the chapel's iron gate.

She sent up a silent prayer of thanks for having had the forethought to grab her contact lenses before fleeing the hotel room. At least without the oversized glasses that always seemed to be sliding down her nose, she had one less thing to give her away.

For one wild second she tried to remember whether she'd locked the chapel after she entered. She inched her toes beneath the habit's hem, hoping the running shoes, shoelaces and all, were well hidden.

For several heartbeats, the footsteps fell silent outside the chapel. Someone was staring, perhaps studying her. She swallowed hard, but kept praying. Finally, the person moved on, slowly, deliberately, across the marble floor. K.C. drew in a deep breath of relief.

She wanted to turn, to find out if the footsteps belonged to Arabella or Wyatt, though they did seem more masculine than feminine. But she kept her head bowed and sat utterly still.

Gav found some solace in the quiet of the cathedral. He walked the length of the nave, stopping here and there to take in the beauty of the open chapels, their individual altars and crypts.

Then he strolled toward the carved wooden choir stalls near the transept, gazed up at the hundreds of brass pipes above the organ, then turned to study the enormous altar.

He slid into a wooden pew and stared up at the gold-and-jewel-encrusted edifice in front of him. He thought about the artisans who'd worked on it centuries before. Had they known that their artistry would survive this long? Probably not.

He'd heard that generations of stonemasons and artists had worked on the cathedrals of Spain. Decades of a man's life, his entire working career, might be spent working on one column or wall or part of an ornate gothic arch. The mason's son would take over where his father left off, then his son, and so on. Odd that while they were working, none of them had any idea what the final product would look like, how their portion would fit together with the rest. They never saw the splendor of the cathedral when it was completed.

It occurred to Gav that God's work with him was like that. Only the Lord knew how his life fit together with K.C.'s or anyone else's to achieve a kingdom purpose.

The mystery of K.C. canceling their wedding plans was in God's hands. Both of their lives belonged to him. Gav couldn't see beyond today, any more than the stonemason who worked on the pillar in front of him knew what the cathedral would look like after completion.

He leaned forward, his face in his hands. K.C.'s image appeared before his mind's eye, and he lifted his heart in prayer for her, for whatever she was going through, for her safety wherever she was.

K.C. moved silently from the chapel on the right of the transept. She slipped along the marble tiles, taking small purposeful steps and keeping her head bowed.

She wanted to see who had watched her in the chapel. It was long past visitors' hours, and the only reason she was there was because Sister Calandria had convinced the guard that it was part of her personal Easter Week Passion.

Skirting along in the floor-length robe, she glanced sideways every few steps to spot the other visitor. She moved from pillar to pillar, peering around. After circling the interior of the new cathedral, she decided to head to the old section, thinking she might feel safer in the depths of its catacombs. But a movement near the altar caught her attention.

Not daring to breathe, she moved silently to peer out from behind a wide column. She blinked once. Twice. Then she stood back, heart hammering. After a moment she peered around the pillar again to be certain.

Gav sat in a pew about halfway back from the altar, his face in his hands. She could have wept at the disheveled look of him.

Oh, how she ached to run to him, to gather him into her arms, to assure him of her love! No matter what was said to her in the Valley of the Dead, she had to warn him. Tell him to stay away from her. Tell him to go to the police. To the American consulate! Anything!

She glanced around, her heart pounding. If she could tiptoe closer, slip in beside him, and whisper the warning, maybe they could both be saved.

She held her breath, took one step forward.

Then the heavy cathedral doors creaked open, and footsteps approached from behind her, their tapping sounds echoing through the cavernous space.

She took another silent step toward Gav, but the footsteps drew closer, and she halted, praying they would turn another direction. Perhaps turn toward the gate leading to the Old Cathedral.

But the echo continued. She heard a snatch of English being spoken.

Her heart froze. The Sterns!

She didn't dare turn to see for sure the identities of the speakers, but staring at Gav, she prayed that he would keep his head down.

She watched him through a film of tears, saw him lean forward in an attitude of prayer. Or was he weeping? She leaned against the pillar, thinking her knees might give way beneath her.

It would be too dangerous to slip in beside him now. He would surely look up to greet her. If the Sterns were anywhere near, they would see him. See them both.

And they would be in greater danger than they were now.

Heartsick, she finally turned and silently moved the length of the cathedral to the door of the most ancient part of the building, leading into what the people of Salamanca called the Old Cathedral.

The visitors' center was dead ahead, one guard behind the counter, another standing beside the ornate iron gate to her left that divided the two cathedrals. He inserted a large key into the lock, and a moment later the gate swung open.

She stepped toward an ancient archway and turned to look back, half-expecting to see the Sterns following

At just that moment, Gav stepped to the kiosk near the gate and turned toward her, frowning.

His eyes met hers, and she caught her breath at the flicker of recognition in them. She took a hesitant step forward, longing to run to him.

But again, the hushed sounds of English carried toward her

from mere yards away. She whirled before Gav could get a better look and fled into the catacombs of the Old Cathedral.

TEN

DANITA CHÁVEZ AND HER BROTHER RAÚL HEADED ACROSS THE plaza. "Do you see the others?"

She squinted into the twilight. It was difficult to see around the families milling about the Plaza Mayor, awaiting the next of the Holy Week processions that had begun earlier that day.

"We are the first." Raúl flashed a quick grin her direction as he matched her pace, stride for stride. "Just as you always prefer. First to arrive. First in line. First to be seated at a banquet table. First, first, first," he teased. "When we were small you always grabbed the best toy first." He chuckled.

Ignoring his good-natured chiding, she grumbled under her breath about the cold. A storm, made mostly of brisk wind and light sleet, had settled in during the afternoon. Her cheeks stung, and her hair blew across her face. She wished she'd worn a hat.

No matter. The meeting she and Raúl were heading to was

far more important than her physical well-being.

"This is no time to be light-hearted. Tonight it begins."

He sobered, just as she knew he would, and they walked on in silence. She lifted her chin. Raúl was instrumental to the operation, and she was proud of her younger brother. She glanced at him to see if he was angry at her reprimand. He caught her gaze and smiled, giving her that boyish, merry-eyed look she loved.

Some, including Julian, thought Raúl existed in cyberspace instead of the real world. That he had electronic pulses instead of blood coursing through his veins. But she knew better.

"This is serious," she said again. "You have been at the heart of Tres Equis. The heartbeat of this operation. Are you still there?"

His look was still teasing. "I suppose one could refer to the computer operations as the heartbeat of Tres Equis. So in that regard at least, yes, my darling Dani, I remain at the heart."

"I mean *here*—" She halted, looking up at him, and thumped her chest above her heart. "Is your passion with us?"

He shrugged and gestured dramatically with his hands. "I am but a geek, is that not what is said about me? What would I know about passion?" He laughed lightly. "Besides, my Danita, where you go, I go. What you do, I do. It can be no other way."

She gave him a playful punch in the arm, but her heart was filled with fear for him. Raúl had a stubborn streak. They both knew his disloyalty could be fatal should he turn his back on Tres Equis. With a sigh, she hooked her arm into the crook made by his elbow and again headed toward the meeting place beneath the gigantic clock in the center of the plaza's west side.

As they approached, Doc Rafael smiled and captured Danita's hand. He kissed the air near each cheek, then shook Raúl's hand. Wyatt and Arabella Stern greeted them warmly, as did the rest of the small group.

After a few minutes, Doc smiled broadly. "We have arranged for a private dining room, downstairs, at the *Caballo Rojo*. It will be private, I assure you." He paused, glancing at the promenading families in twos and threes and sometimes four abreast. "And we will fit in with the rest of the population of Salamanca who have come for dinner before the processions begin." He pulled a miniature comb from his pocket and groomed his mustache.

Soon several members of Raúl's cell were heading toward them from across the plaza: Brother Thomas from the Jesuit College; Paz, Hector, and Iago from the university faculty and staff; Quintín and Lorenzo from the Madrid *Vilanova la Geltrú* think tank.

More of Raúl's ilk, Danita thought, wondering about her brother's involvement with such antisocial intellectuals, most of whom spent their waking hours gazing into computer monitors.

It was unlikely that military and government officials—the other cells that were part of Tres Equis—would join them in so visible a place, especially this week. A quick assessment of those who'd gathered told Danita the assembled group, most of Julian's inner circle, was nearly complete.

Doc Rafael glanced up at the clock on the central tower, combed his mustache once more, then led the group, now numbering more than twenty, through one of the eight arched entrances to the Plaza Mayor.

Falling in behind, Danita stared at Doc's back. His smart wool overcoat squared his rounded shoulders, but his shoes, though expensive and boasting a permanent shine, added nothing to his short stature. The vain little man, with his long strand of hair combed over his balding head, had a bent for cruelty. Danita had seen it for the first time when he dealt with K.C. Keegan.

She shivered as she walked behind him, wondering how he would change after Tres Equis came to power. It disturbed her to consider that power corrupted even those without such an inclination.

Which led her to think of Julian. Her heart quickened. Without doubt, he was one of the most handsome and sophisticated men in all of Spain.

Julian Hernando.

Raúl caught her hand. "I saw you smile. What is it?"

"I was thinking about Julian."

Raúl narrowed his eyes. "Oh, yes. Julian." He let his gaze drift off into the distance.

Danita chuckled. "I said I was just thinking about him. That is all."

Raúl suddenly halted, almost midstride, then caught her hand and pulled her away from the rest of the group. Arabella glanced at her in concern. "I will catch up," Danita said to the older woman. She was always so watchful. Danita told herself it was out of concern, but something inside her didn't quite believe it.

"You said that you worry about me in all this, Dani. It is I who worry about you—but for completely different reasons."

"You are the one in danger, not me." She narrowed her eyes at him. "You have never had the passion in your heart and soul that the rest of us have. Many question whether you are for us or—"

He squeezed her arm. "You should not question me. You know me better than anyone."

"That is precisely why I question you, Raúl. Why I question your motives." Her voice dropped. "I know your heart."

"It is Julian who questions me the most, is it not?"

She quirked a brow. "Does he not, above all the others, have a right to?"

"You said it clearly, *above* all others. That is what disturbs me. He has lifted himself above all."

"Does he not have a right?"

"We have known Julian since we were children. How can he elevate himself this way? He has changed. Years ago he was our champion. Our protector. We looked up to him with respect."

She nodded, and her voice dropped to almost a whisper. "You are right. We both idolized him, Raúl. He stepped in more than once to save us from unfair treatment—"

His laugh was short, bitter. "Unfair?"

"You understand what I mean."

"Only too well. But *unfair* is a euphemism for what we survived. It makes me sick to refer to it with such an insipid term." For a moment neither of them spoke,. then Raúl went on, his voice passionate. "Once we all were all filled with ideas. Our thoughts and plans were noble."

"Our noble thoughts have not changed."

"But Julian has. You simply don't want to see him for how he is now. You would rather pretend he is still the Don Quixote of your childhood, your knight riding to your rescue." Raúl's expression was taut. "You still idolize him, Dani. But I see something…a darkness has entered him. You don't see it. It is that simple."

"Do not talk like that, my brother. It is dangerous. For you. For us both." She paused. "You have become blinded with hatred for Julian and you have lost sight of our goals."

He considered her for a moment, his forehead furrowed. "You are the one I fear for, my sister. I fear for your heart and soul." He was staring into her eyes. "Do not give yourself to him, no matter what he promises. No matter what he says. He is dangerous."

She felt her cheeks color.

"I know you have fancied him since we were children."

"It is not what you think."

Raúl ignored her protest. "He knows how you feel, and he will use it. Believe me."

"Are you saying that I am not lovely enough for someone to care about?"

"You know what I mean, Dani."

"Who is to say that Julian does not really care about me?" She tilted her chin. "Besides, I am an adult. I can take care of myself." She studied her brother, saw the questions in his eyes. Touching his arm, she smiled, and her voice softened. "You worry too much about me. And perhaps, I about you."

He smiled finally, and his brow relaxed. "Because there has been no one else."

"We need to think about what someday will be known as one of the greatest weeks in Spain's history. And you are a part of it, my brother. You are the genius behind Julian. Without the Chaos bug, it could not happen."

"Yes, the Chaos bug." His smile faded. "That is my worry," he said grimly. "The Chaos bug and what I am unleashing." He met her gaze, and she realized she'd been wrong. There was passion in his expression. But is was not for their cause. "Do you have any idea what my bug will do?"

She stared at him for several seconds. "You speak as though you cannot go through with it."

He didn't answer.

She glanced around at the milling crowd. No one was paying any attention. "Remember, the chaos will be short-lived. It will be considered merely pangs before birth."

Raúl snorted. "All the fears of Y2K will be nothing compared to the chaos that will take over Spain by the end of the week. This country…its leaders…its people—" he looked away from her—"the destruction that could result. Lives lost. Children and families, Dani…" His voice dropped, and he shook his head slowly.

"With the new millennium, we are ushering in a new Spain. Be proud of that, Raúl. Be proud that you and your team will do much to bring about the rebirth of our country."

He stared into her eyes for a long moment, then took her again by the elbow. "Be sure those are your own thoughts, my sister, not merely a parroting of Julian."

She felt her cheeks color. "Only because you are my brother will I let you get away with such a statement."

For a moment neither spoke, then she gave his arm a sisterly squeeze. "Enough of this. We'd better go."

He glanced down at her as they walked, and though his smile remained, his dark eyes spoke of his deep concern. Finally he nodded. "Promise me that you will take care, Dani. Be watchful of Julian."

"Of course, my brother. You worry far too much for someone so young." She laughed, but something inside her nagged that he might be right. She pushed the thought from her mind as they quickened their pace to catch the others.

Julian caught Danita's gaze the moment she entered the low-ceilinged dining room.

Her heart thudded wildly, and her face turned warm. She concentrated on maintaining a cool exterior, especially for Raúl's sake. He stood beside her, still holding her elbow.

She shrugged off her heavy coat. Raúl caught it with an audible sigh, then draped it over his arm.

Julian stood at the head of the long dinner table, a smile curving his lips as she hurried to greet him. He kissed both her cheeks, and her heart raced even faster at his touch on her hand.

"You are looking as beautiful as ever, my Dani." His voice was low and sweet. He didn't even seem to notice Raúl standing right behind her.

She sighed. "It is good to see you again, Julian."

Finally, he stuck out his hand toward Raúl. For a moment, she thought Raúl might not shake it.

"Raúl, it is good to see you."

Raúl gave him a curt nod. Again fear for him nudged Danita's heart and she cleared her throat, turning to Julian again. "All our preparations are ready?" The air remained heavy with tension.

"It might be a question better asked of Raúl." His mouth twisted unpleasantly. "Your team is aware of its duties?"

Raúl nodded. "Most of the systems are on timing devices. We just sit back and watch…"

The chaos, Danita filled in silently.

After a moment, Raúl drifted toward the corner of the room where Paz and Quintín huddled, obviously lost in animated conversation.

"I've been in Madrid for the past few weeks," Julian was saying. "Though preparations have taken every waking minute, I have missed you, Dani."

Again, her cheeks warmed, and she swallowed hard. "You did?"

"But more about that later."

She didn't know quite how to answer, so she smoothed her

hair and forced a demure smile.

Then he leaned toward her and dropped his voice. "What is this I hear about the woman?"

She glanced at the Sterns, now huddled in the corner, speaking to three members of Raúl's team. Arabella seemed to sense her scrutiny and met Danita's gaze nervously, then looked away.

"Do you mean K.C. Keegan?"

"None other."

"She escaped."

Julian's handsome face took on a chiseled and narrow look, his eyes a bitter blue. "There is no excuse. She was in the Sterns' care for a week. No problem. Then they arrive in Salamanca, and *poof*—" he flicked his well-groomed fingertips—"just like that, she disappears?"

"We have searched. She is nowhere to be found. She remains in Salamanca, no doubt. We have watched the train and bus stations—"

"She could have left by automobile."

"We have kept watch at the rental agencies as well. Nothing. We can safely say K.C. Keegan is still in Salamanca."

"Safely say?" His laugh was short. Bitter. He shook his head. "This was a mistake from the beginning."

Danita studied him for a moment. "I thought it was your idea—" As soon as she spoke, she regretted her words.

He turned to her, his eyes suddenly cold. "We must find her. There is no choice."

"You were concerned about Elliot Gavin. His inordinate interest in Tres Equis. That is, when he thought it was a cult." She swallowed hard again. "As far as we know he still considers us in that regard. Americans seem obsessed with such ideas."

"Does anyone know if he has arrived in California?"

"Our contacts have not seen him. We had him watched all the way from Granada to Madrid. He boarded the plane. That's the last we saw of him." She knew she was speaking too fast, her voice high-pitched from overworked nerves.

Julian picked up a goblet of wine from the nearby table, took a sip, his gaze never leaving her face. "Yet he did not get off the plane in San Francisco."

"No."

His lips tightened into a thin line as he set down his wineglass. "And now K.C. Keegan has disappeared."

The conclusion was obvious. Elliot Gavin must have come for her. Danita wished the young couple hadn't gotten mixed up in Tres Equis. If only they'd tended to their own business and nothing more, they'd be married and enjoying their stay in Salamanca by now.

Two more men and three women, one Danita's age and two who were older, entered the dining room. Julian started to turn from Danita, but she touched his arm.

"Julian, why are you so afraid of this Elliot Gavin? Who is to say he would not embrace our cause if he knew the truth about it?"

"Afraid?" He snorted. "I am no more afraid of him than I would be of a pesky fly. But we know that he is a law enforcement officer in California. Plans such as ours would be met with hostility. And force. We read his history. We know more about his thinking than he does. His Internet search, every file, every Web site he visited, was traced back to his e-mail address by our people. We know everything he knows. There are only a few bridges left for him to cross." His jaw worked as the corners of his mouth tightened.

"If he does come to Salamanca," Danita asked, "is there not a way to let him continue his belief that Tres Equis is an ancient mystical organization, nothing more?"

"Ancient mystical organization?" He laughed.

"We take our name from the time of the Spanish Inquisition, based on an ancient brotherhood. He might look no further. Maybe all this was unnecessary. Maybe we didn't need to go to such lengths." She did not want to consider the danger the young man would be in if he truly had returned to Salamanca. She glanced across the room at Raúl, now deep in conversation with one of the newcomers. "Raúl might be assigned to steer him off course."

Julian laughed. "If he returns, he will search for his lost lady love. And we have made arrangements for the eventuality of him finding her."

She remembered the threats made to K.C. Keegan at Valley of the Dead and tried to push the disturbing images from her mind.

"Our insurance," Julian said, "if you want to call it that, is in playing one young lover against the other. We told his young woman that if he came near her, his life would be forfeit—"

Just then Doc Rafael stepped toward them. "I delivered the message myself." He went on to describe, in great detail, what he'd said to K.C.

It was worse than Danita remembered, and her heart went out to K.C. How appalling it must have been to hear it said about oneself and the man one loved.

She shuddered, her misgivings about Doc more pronounced than ever. Her reaction didn't go unnoticed. Julian circled his arm protectively around her shoulders.

"If you don't mind," Julian said to Doc, "I would like to continue my conversation with Danita."

"Of course." With a lift of a brow, Rafael turned away and headed across the room, stopping to grab a handful of olives from the table on his way toward the Sterns.

Julian gently took hold of Danita's elbow, turning her away from the others.

"You will not allow Doc to carry out his threats—"

But Julian touched her lips with his finger. "You must trust me, Dani."

She'd known him for more than two decades. She had never thought of him as more than her protector. Until lately. Now his touch, his every glance, caused her heart to flutter. He seemed to sense her thoughts. Perhaps he felt the same in her presence. Hope warmed her heart.

"Dani, Dani," he breathed, leaning close enough for her to feel the heat of his breath. "Sometimes I wonder about your trust."

She had to clear her throat before she could speak. "I...I trust you, Julian. You know that I do."

"I would like you to meet me afterward. Something has come up that I need to clarify with you. It is important."

He was the leader of Tres Equis. The future leader of Spain. How could she resist? She smiled tentatively and gave him a shy nod.

He let his hand slide from her elbow to her fingertips, then gave them a squeeze. "Friends have provided me with a townhouse here in Salamanca for the week."

"If all goes as planned, you will need it only for the week." She couldn't help her observation. She thought of the events that would take place during Holy Week, the surprise Tres Equis would bring to the somber processions. The changes that would occur in all of Spain because of the small but powerful nucleus of young rebel leaders. She squared her shoulders, proud to be among them.

Julian looked pleased, the light back in his eyes. "Yes, yes.

And it must go as planned. That's what I want to speak with you about. It is time that you, ah, take a more active role in Tres Equis."

"Oh, Julian! Yes, of course. I am ready."

His gaze met hers. "Yes, my dear. You most definitely are ready."

Soon the group, now numbering twenty-six, seated themselves. Julian sat at the head of the table, his eyes ordering Danita to sit at his right. Raúl sat directly across from her, his expression guarded.

Dinner was served promptly at ten o'clock. As usual, Julian had insisted on the most exquisite of Salamanca's offerings: roast suckling pig, white fish in a succulent sauce, leg of lamb, and all the finest accompaniments, including a variety of *Ribeiro* and *Rioja* wines.

The conversation was lively while they ate, then immediately following the servers' departure from the room, Julian stood.

"A toast, comrades!" He lifted his wineglass. "To our success during these holiest of days."

Glasses clinked, and the room was silent as those gathered sipped the dark red wine.

Rafael stood at the opposite end of the table. "May our success be without parallel in modern history."

"May it be bloodless!" Raúl lifted his glass and stood at the same time. His chair tipped backward and clattered onto the tile floor, and there was a moment of stunned silence—more because normally quiet Raúl had spoken than because of the noise he'd caused.

"Yes, of course. None of us wants bloodshed." Julian nodded at the group and lifted his glass. They all joined him, then drank heartily.

Julian, Rafael, and Raúl seated themselves again, then the room hushed as Julian settled back into his chair with a heavy sigh.

"We have prepared for this day, my friends," he said. "Our arms have arrived. Our costumes are ready. All is in place at last. Besides those of us in this room, some three hundred highly trained troops will be joining us. They will dress as *penitentes*, just as we will." He laughed, though without humor. "Instead of carrying crosses on their shoulders, they will be carrying weapons under their robes."

He went on to describe the details. They would join the processions, day and night, all week, so their Tres Equis "fraternity" would become known. No one would question their motives as anything but solemn penitence. The same as hundreds of other *Nazarenos* who would spend the rest of the week marching throughout the medieval streets of the city to the dirge of funeral music.

They would proudly lift the banner of Tres Equis, and their gilded *pasos*, floats borne on shoulders of their troops, would be among the most beautiful, the most ornate in the week-long celebration. "We will lift our voices in song, our *saetas* glorious enough to rival the hundreds of others."

Julian's voice droned on into the early hours of the morning. Though it was not unusual for a formal dinner to last this long, Danita stifled her yawns and forced herself to pay attention.

"Saetas," she said suddenly, surprising herself.

Julian looked displeased at the interruption. Without saying a word, he lifted a brow her direction.

She sat forward. "The saetas are praise songs...to Christ. To the Virgin."

"Yes," he agreed, still frowning.

"It is a sacrilege for our soldiers to lift their voices in praise to God when they are planning something, well, so duplicitous." She realized all eyes were on her and wished she'd kept her comments to herself. "Don't you think?"

The room was silent, and still Julian stared.

Danita cleared her throat. "I, ah, thought that perhaps we should come up with our own songs having to do with Tres Equis."

His gaze turned from cold to interested. "Go on."

She leaned toward him. "We'll create our own lyrics to known songs. Patriotic songs. These lyrics will speak of nationalistic pride. Not of the government or of the king." She smiled triumphantly. She could feel the approval of those around the table. "But of Spain herself! Our love for her."

"Hear, hear!" someone called from the opposite end of the table. "Yes, perfect solution."

"I was bothered by the duplicity myself," Arabella said, casting an approving glance toward Danita.

"To Danita." Wyatt lifted his glass. "May her bright ideas continue to shine!"

She flushed with pleasure at the clinks of wineglasses all around her.

Raúl met her gaze and gave her a nod, then Julian lifted her hand and kissed her fingertips. "Yes," he said, his voice low. "And I know just the woman who can write these words. They will ring with passion."

His look embarrassed her. She tried to slip her hand from beneath his, but he held it tight, then slowly lifted it and kissed it again. The gesture seemed timed so that each person in the room could not miss its meaning. His kiss felt more like a brand than a sign of affection.

Raúl cleared his throat, breaking the tension. "I will help Dani."

"That will not be possible." Julian didn't move his gaze from Danita's face. "You will be at the university library, lost in research."

For a moment the room was quiet, then Julian smiled and turned at last away from Danita. "We are expecting the cowboy from California, the sheriff of Sugar Loaf Mountain to ride in on his horse and save his damsel in distress."

Everyone laughed, Danita included, as she pictured the handsome John Wayne or Clint Eastwood riding across America's wide-open spaces. Doc made the sound of galloping hooves on the table with his fingers, and they all laughed again.

Julian chuckled, then went on. "We expect this cowboy to first try to find his damsel, then—one way or another—head to the university to complete his research on Tres Equis."

Raúl nodded, looking more interested.

"You must see to it that only the information we want him to find is at his disposal."

"I see."

"And I want Gavin's every move watched. He will lead us to K.C. Keegan, and when he does..." He let the words hang. "Suffice it to say, she has already been warned. But I have no doubt that they will contact the authorities at the first possible moment. They must be stopped. We have no choice."

There were murmurs of agreement.

"We have spoken of casualties," he said quietly. "None of us wants them. Yet we must be willing to sacrifice lives if necessary to bring about a glorious change that is for the good of our people."

Again came affirming nods and murmurs.

"The end justifies the means...." Danita said, half to herself. Then she realized everyone was looking at her. "The end justifies the means," she repeated. She couldn't remember where she'd heard it, only that it was from someplace deep in her past.

Julian raised his chin with practiced arrogance and nodded slowly. "Yes," he said, a smile playing at the corner of his mouth. "Yes, you are right."

Danita pulled back the curtain on the window in her room and stared out at the glistening street. It was nearly three in the morning. The processions had begun, and people milled about as though it were daylight.

She sighed deeply and went to the closet for her coat. Something told her she shouldn't go to Julian's townhouse, but she shoved the nagging concerns out of her mind and slipped her arms into her coat, still wondering at her reluctance.

Stepping to a mirror, she considered her reflection as she buttoned the coat. Raúl called her dainty, said it went with her name. He also said her face was heart-shaped, then laughed and declared his own the same shape, only upside down.

Sweet Raúl. She knew he'd be angry to know where she was headed. But no matter. It was too late to change her course now. She stepped to the door, flicked out the light, then closed the door behind her.

A moment later, she headed down the slick, wet street. A sharp sting of rain hit her face. She hesitated only a moment, then, squaring her shoulders, hailed a taxi and gave Julian's location. The man raised his eyebrows, apparently recognizing an address in the wealthiest district of the city.

Sliding into the backseat, she pulled the door closed and wondered why this visit to Julian caused her heart to beat faster, to skitter with anticipation....

Or was it fear? She frowned. Fear? Why should she be afraid? Julian was her friend, her protector. And soon he would be the leader of her beloved Spain. It was what she'd worked for, longed for—what she'd spent most of her life to bring about.

No, she was not afraid of Julian. She couldn't be.

As for her trembling hands, her pounding heart, the wave of choking emotion that swept her? Well, it was excitement at the thought of spending time with one to whom she was devoted.

That was all.

ELEVEN

ICY NERVOUSNESS TWISTED AROUND HER HEART AS DANITA RANG the doorbell at the wide entrance to Julian's townhouse. The Westminster chimes had barely begun to ring when Julian's bodyguard opened the door. The heavyset man nodded, and though he'd seen her many times, there wasn't a flicker of recognition in his hazel eyes.

"Julian asked me to, ah, come...to meet him here," she stammered. "Is he in?" Suddenly, her visit seemed foolish, as if she were part of Ricky Martin's fan club. Or even one of his groupies.

"Yes." The man stepped back from the door and allowed her to move past him. "You will find him in the formal sitting room."

A chandelier burned brightly in the foyer, and she blinked in surprise as she took in the furnishings. She'd grown up in luxury, but this was opulent by anyone's standards. Polished wood floors boasted Persian rugs. French decor, from lighting to King George II tables to Bergère chairs, set off the circular entry. Matching antique lowboys with carved rosettes and cabriole legs flanked the four wooden double doors.

On facing tables, tasteful Ming vases held tall spring bouquets. On one of the other lowboys, a sterling tea and coffee service reflected the light from the chandelier. Above the fourth table, directly across from the entry doors, was what looked to Danita to be an original Velásquez.

This was no flat rented through the local newspaper. This was obviously someone's home, given to Tres Equis for the week. Fit for a king. She smiled to herself at the irony. If the coup went as planned, Julian would be the next military dictator of Spain. By the end of the week, the country's future would be decided.

She trailed the bodyguard down one of the halls into a high-ceilinged sitting room. Two of Julian's advisors sat conferring in one corner. One looked up and nodded at Danita. She recognized him from a recent Tres Equis meeting. The other was a cruel-looking man she'd never seen before.

The bodyguard nodded for her to follow and, a few moments later, rapped on a closed door at the end of the room.

"Yes, what is it?" Julian's voice was muffled. The door was opened from within by yet another armed guard.

"Your señorita is here."

Danita bristled at the insinuation.

"Send her in," Julian said.

She marched past both guards. Julian looked up from his wide desk, then gave a curt nod to the man still in the room. "You may go now." Three assistants were seated in chairs opposite Julian's desk, and he dismissed them as well. Was it her imagination, or did one of the men give her a look of displeasure as he walked past? She ignored him and moved toward Julian.

"Julian." She spoke softly, looking for a sign of caring in his face.

But he inclined his head toward a nearby chair without standing to greet her. There was no trace of her childhood champion in his expression. He sat back with a sigh and rubbed his eyes.

She settled into a chair. "It is late, Julian. Why did you need to see me now?"

He looked up and sighed again. "As I alluded to earlier, it is time for you to become more involved with leadership in Tres Equis."

She smiled. "I would like that."

He leaned forward. "Doc Rafael tells me that you got on rather well with K.C. Keegan...." He let the statement hang.

"It is true."

"Was there a reason?"

Julian knew her so well. It was best to be honest, even if it meant admitting she actually liked the enemy. "She seems a gentle person."

He quirked a brow, obviously amused. "Gentle person?"

Danita nodded. "She is innocent. She didn't ask to become part of our hostilities."

He stared at her a moment in silence. "Innocents sometimes must be sacrificed for the greater good. For the cause itself. I thought you understood that. Your training should have covered that part of your position at Tres Equis."

Danita felt it best to keep her opinion to herself. Her months of training in the rugged and isolated Tres Equis camps of the *Picos de Europa* covered combat, both covert and overt. Psychological warfare was another matter. Those courses about manipulating people and events had been unsettling to her. She'd found them far more disagreeable than crawling on her belly in fatigues and shooting at humanlike dummies.

"She is to be your assignment."

"My assignment? We cannot find her."

He gave her a half smile, and she leaned forward. "You have found her." It wasn't a question.

"We have heard rumors."

"Where is she?"

He stood, walked around his desk to her, and reached for her hand. His touch sent an electric jolt through her. "I have news of utmost importance. It is personal." He pulled up a chair beside her and sat down, still holding her fingertips. "I must tell you about some new discoveries about your family."

"My family?"

He nodded slowly. The earlier weariness in his eyes had given way to a surprising sympathy. "You have known since childhood that you were adopted, have you not?"

She took a deep breath. "Of course. Raúl and I were taken in by our first foster parents when we were quite young. Our birth parents were killed in an automobile accident."

His gaze was steady as he continued. "That is partially true. But there is more to your story. A missing piece you have never been told."

"What is it?"

Julian wrapped his warm fingers around her icy, trembling ones. "I recently had an inquiry about you that prompted me to do some research." He seemed to consider his words.

"Are you talking about my past or my present?" She had no living relatives besides Raúl. Only a variety of estranged foster parents. Several sets. She and Raúl hadn't had anything to do with any of them for years. "What is it?"

Julian looked troubled. "First of all, Raúl is not your brother."

She pulled her hand away.

"It is true."

For a heartbeat she couldn't breathe. "It cannot be." Then she laughed, feeling better as she considered the ludicrous claim. "We look alike." She smiled confidently. "People say we could be twins, even though we are not the same age." Whoever brought you this information is mistaken."

"My sources do not make mistakes." He fell silent for a moment, then cleared his throat. "There is more."

Her thoughts were whirling. "What else?"

"Long ago a young couple, comrades in arms, met and fell in love. Their passion for each other, and their sacrifice for Spain are legendary." He stood and walked to a window, pulled back the drape, and looked out at the city lights. Danita could see the spotlighted cathedral glowing as bright as a full moon against a velvet black sky.

Then he turned to her again. "You have heard of Miguel Vargas?"

"Of course. Everyone has. Franco's protégé who gave his life for our country."

Julian nodded. "He was young when he died. But he planned to make a life with his bride after his last mission."

Her heart was thudding, and she clenched her hands to calm herself as her earlier confidence ebbed. "You are about to tell me that he and his bride have something to do with me, yes?"

For a moment Julian stared at her. Finally he nodded. "Yes. Everything to do with you. Only she wasn't his bride, only his betrothed."

She frowned. "They cannot be my parents. The years do not equate."

He walked toward her again and sat down. "Miguel Vargas was your grandfather."

"My grandfather?" She shook her head in dismay. "My grandfather?"

Julian nodded. "And I have recently located your grandmother. The woman who was Miguel's fiancée."

Danita leaned back in her chair, stunned. A blood relative. After all her years of longing for the love of a family? Why now?

Then it struck her that Julian had mentioned inquiry. Of course. "Someone asked you to find me?"

"Yes."

"The woman who claims to be my grandmother?"

He nodded. "Not only claims to be. She is your grandmother."

Danita found no joy in the prospect. She only wanted the brother she knew, not a grandmother she didn't know.

"Does Raúl know?"

"I haven't told him yet."

"This was why you brought me here tonight? To hear the news about my grandmother?" She stood to go and, sensing his gaze, turned to him again. "You did say there was something else you were going to ask me to do."

Julian held up his hand, indicating that she should sit down again. "I am not finished. Please—" He inclined his head to the chair.

She slid back into the seat just as a light tap sounded at Julian's door. Instead of calling out for the visitor to either wait or enter, Julian stood and opened the door.

Arabella Stern moved silently, gracefully, into the room toward Danita.

Danita stood to greet her, then shrank backward. Affection had been meted out sparely during her childhood, and even now she was uncomfortable with this stranger's display of it. Americans tended to be overly demonstrative anyway.

Arabella held out her arms as if to a long-lost child. Again Danita stepped backward. She looked at the other woman uneasily, realizing that she'd never liked her. And now she was related to her.

The older woman shrugged one shoulder, looking embarrassed. "I'm sorry. I really don't know what to say." Her hoop earrings jangled as she tossed her hair back with a flick of her fingers.

"Neither do I."

An awkward silence followed, then Julian again took charge. "Please, both of you, sit down. I have a matter I need to discuss with you. And perhaps it will also serve to bring you together, to help you become better acquainted."

Raúl always said that Julian performed no act out of the goodness of his heart. That he manipulated, played people one against each other, dangled them like puppets on a string.

She pushed her brother's opinions of Julian from her mind. She trusted Julian. He would do her no harm.

She glanced at Arabella to see how she was taking it. "You don't look old enough to be my grandmother."

The older woman looked pleased. "I was only sixteen when I had your mother."

"You gave her away." Danita flung the accusation as quickly as it came into her mind.

Arabella flushed. "I was barely more than a child myself. I had no business trying to raise another. But I was promised my child would be given a wonderful home." She lifted her chin. "Promised by Franco himself." Then she frowned and turned back to Julian. "About my daughter. Did you uncover any information about her?"

Julian cleared his throat and glanced at his watch, obviously avoiding her eyes. "It is nearly daylight. We must get on with business. Within the last hour an informant reported that K.C. Keegan has taken shelter in the convent of Teresa of Ávila."

That was all it took to capture Danita's attention once more. "You are to become her friend. Wait outside the convent until you see her leave. Follow her and make contact. You will tell us when you have, but we will not take action. At least, not yet."

She nodded as he turned to Arabella. "You, my friend, once worked undercover for Franco."

"In the early years, yes."

"You have an apt student here in Dani. She has undergone our program's full training. Passed every phase with honors." He smiled at Danita, pride shining in his eyes. "Though you would not know it to look at her slender frame, she is a prime sharpshooter."

Arabella looked impressed.

He smiled at the women in turn. Then he began to explain exactly what he wanted them to do.

Danita saw two things as he spoke. The chill in his eyes as he told of the trap they would set, its bait, and how it would snap closed. And the flush of pride on her grandmother's face as she discussed her role in the charade.

Grandmother? She shivered. How could this be? She studied the woman's face again. It was a blend of haughtines and bitterness, framed with an abundance of thick, dark hair. This woman was tall, big boned, long legged. Danita wondered how the mix of genes had produced them both.

"Dani?" Julian pulled her attention back.

"Yes?"

"It is late, and I am certain you are tired. I need to discuss some other issues with...your grandmother. If you wouldn't mind leaving us alone." There was no question in his voice, only a tone of dismissal. "I will send for my driver to take you home." He picked up the phone.

Danita stood. "Of course. It has been a long day."

She hesitated, unsure what to say to Arabella. Finally, she stuck out her hand American-style, and smiled gently. "I shall see you tomorrow."

"Yes," Arabella said, taking Danita's hand in her own. "Until then."

Danita moved across the room and reached for the door handle, but turned once more toward Arabella Stern.

She was staring after Danita. Their gazes met, and quite surprisingly, Danita felt a rush of pity for the older woman who seemed so sad. Quickly, Danita headed through the doorway, unwilling to look a moment longer into the woman's dark, needy eyes.

"Now that we are alone we can discuss the other issue." Julian smiled slowly.

"The contribution."

"Yes, your contribution to our cause." He leaned forward earnestly. "You and Wyatt have been more than generous. Your commitment to our efforts has been the heart and soul of Tres Equis."

She nodded, knowing he was about to launch into another fund-raising speech. "You can save it, Julian, for another time. Another donor. You've already said all the right words, done all the right things. We wouldn't support you if we didn't believe in furthering the cause we began all those years ago."

"Thank you," he said simply.

"Franco was an extraordinary man. You can be even greater.

You've got youth on your side. Good looks. Charm."

He stared at her in that unblinking way of his, then a smile curved the corner of his mouth. She relaxed and leaned back in her chair. "You do have proof of Danita's bloodline."

"Of course."

"It did not take you long to obtain it."

"Your generous donation allowed me to cut through the red tape."

"I see."

He reached into a valise near his desk and pulled out a large manila envelope with her name written neatly on the front. He handed it across the desk, and as she felt its weight, she resisted the urge to examine the contents on the spot. There would be time for that later.

She stood.

"Do you not care to see the papers?"

"Don't you think I trust you?"

He laughed nervously. Surprising, for one so confident. "You still have not presented me with—with the contribution." He looked too anxious, and for the first time since he had told her about Danita, doubts pricked Arabella.

She kept her voice firm. "Your draft will be wired from the U.S. by morning. As usual. Don't fear, Julian. Don't fear."

The tense lines on his face relaxed. "Good." His confidence had returned.

She stood and reached across the desk to shake his hand, but he surprised her by rounding the large piece of furniture and kissing her on both cheeks.

At his sudden exuberance, she reached up to pat his cheek.

He stared into her eyes for just a moment, and in that split second, she again saw the reason for her passionate willingness to help Tres Equis. Julian reminded her of Miguel Vargas.

Unfortunately, Julian knew it and he used it as a weapon. To her surprise, she didn't mind.

She gathered the large envelope and reached for her purse. "You may send for another car."

He gave her a boyish grin. "No need, Arabella. I'll drive you myself."

Just as he always did. She nodded and smiled as he took her arm to escort her to the door.

TWELVE

GAV DUCKED INTO AN ARCHED STONE DOORWAY AS K.C. FLOATED by him in her novice's robe. Her head was bowed, the drape of the hood nearly covering her face, her hands piously hidden from sight, each tucked in the opposite sleeve. She walked slowly and gracefully—and with only the slightest hint of her injured ankle—toward the Plaza Mayor.

He followed at a discreet distance, just as he had each morning since first spotting her in the cathedral.

Just seeing her in the robe confirmed what he needed to know. K.C. had gone into hiding. Why, he didn't know, but he was beginning to guess from *whom*.

Tres Equis. The group he had been researching. It was the only connection he could think of. It was a long shot, but his plan was to find a computer and continue his search where he'd left off back in Sugar Loaf.

As soon as K.C. had returned safely to the convent, he

would go to a cyber café—where he could log onto his e-mail and attempt to recreate the links he'd discovered weeks ago.

He'd already determined it wasn't safe to contact her. At least, not yet. She'd sent him away for a reason, either on her own accord, because of some grave danger, or because she'd been coerced.

Until he knew the facts, he would keep at a distance. At least, that's what his training in law enforcement tactics required of him. His heart urged otherwise, and he wondered how long logic would keep his emotions in check. He longed to run to her, to gather her into his arms.

But for now he would keep a vigilant watch over her. And wait.

Ahead of him, K.C. turned into the plaza through one of the south-facing arches. Crowds were beginning to gather for the day's processions. It was sunny and brisk, and families with young children were milling, enjoying the day, but also making it nearly impossible for him to keep K.C. in sight.

He quickened his pace, stretching his neck to glimpse her above the sea of heads and shoulders. In the distance—from the direction of the cathedral—the faint, slow beat of snare drums foretold the dirgelike procession that was approaching. Soon a lone trumpeter joined the drumming, the drawn-out bleats mournful and sad.

K.C. disappeared into a café, and he browsed at a newspaper kiosk, flipping through a *London Times* for the few minutes she was inside. It was warm enough that many of the cafés and restaurants circling the plaza had placed steel-mesh tables and chairs outside. K.C. found a table near the towering central clock and settled into a chair.

Café con leche. He had to smile as she lifted the ubiquitous Spanish drink to her lips. No matter K.C.'s dangerous surroundings, she'd found a way to enjoy a moment's pleasure with a newly discovered favorite drink.

He stepped back into the shadows, standing guard, enjoying the thought that she was near. And safe for now.

How he longed to let her know he was near. But if she was being watched, his approach might bring her danger. Before he made a move, he needed to know exactly who they were dealing with. Until then, he would watch. And wait.

His attention was diverted by a shopkeeper and patron exchanging harsh words. He craned for a look just as a bevy of teenage girls, chattering and laughing, jostled around him.

After they'd finally passed, he looked back to where K.C. had been sitting. She was gone. Heart pounding, Gav ran out into the plaza, but with dozens more tourists and Salamancan families entering the open area in droves, he couldn't see farther than the person next to him.

A shopkeeper shook his fist as Gav stepped onto a chair, shaded his eyes, and looked frantically for the robed K.C.

K.C. slowly walked east, enjoying the feel of the sun on her face. In a few minutes she would meet Sister Calandria and have to deal with the sister's latest findings at the university, but for now she felt a sense of reverie as the fresh spring breeze caressed her skin. She'd almost forgotten about her injured foot, which was healing nicely and hardly bothered her during her walks around the city.

After a few minutes the sun disappeared as she headed toward the river. She soon entered the darker part of the city near the university, winding through a maze of narrow cobbled streets flanked by towering medieval buildings.

Sister Calandria had suggested they meet someplace other

than the convent. Obviously sleuthing wasn't a normal part of the monastic life, and the sister probably faced a daily confession of her diversion from the usual path. Sister Calandria was young and jovial and it was clear she enjoyed her undercover work.

K.C. smiled as she walked back into a spot of sunshine between buildings. Sister Calandria had already delved into the information K.C. was looking for. Information based on Gav's research back in Sugar Loaf. And she loved the sister's heart for God. They had begun praying together each night and each morning and discussing their shared love of the works of Teresa of Ávila.

Strange, she mused as she walked, though they came from opposite ends of the world and different approaches to their Lord, they connected as his children. They both loved their heavenly Father with a bubbling joy and fierce adoration.

The river had just come into sight when K.C. heard footsteps approaching from behind. Her first thought was that Gav had found her at last. Whenever the thought hit her, as it often had since she saw him in the cathedral, her heart quickened both with hope and with dread. She could never quite forget Doc Rafael's threats.

She ducked into a small alley and waited until the footsteps passed. When she peeked out, a woman dressed in dark clothing was quickly moving away down the narrow street. There was something familiar about the figure, and briefly, K.C. thought of Arabella Stern.

But the clothing was stylishly Spanish, not quasi Native American via Santa Fe. And instead of western boots, this woman sported the high-fashion shoes of the well-dressed Salamancan. High squared heels. Slim cut, mid-calf length coat with perfectly squared padded shoulders.

She was still staring after the woman when she felt a touch on the shoulder.

K.C. spun, fist clenched.

"K.C.," Danita said softly. "It is my friend K.C. I had hoped it was you I followed."

K.C.'s heart dropped. "Danita." The young woman stood there looking completely harmless. The girl next door, with her perfect, heart-shaped face, her gleaming shoulder-length bob. Her pretty smile.

"Do not fear." Danita touched K.C.'s arm. "I have come as your friend. This time only as your friend."

"No one who was party to holding me captive can be considered my friend."

The girl's face fell, and she nibbled at her lower lip. Then she nodded. "You are right to be angry with me."

K.C. almost felt sorry for her, then she caught herself. "You've been sent to find me. To take me back to the Sterns. To the officials at Tres Equis." Her voice rose. "You come under the guise of friendship." She glanced around, but the street was empty. "But the others—Doc, Wyatt, Arabella—are waiting for me, aren't they?"

"No."

"You expect me to believe that?"

Danita gave her a pretty shrug. "You can believe it or not believe it, K.C. But it is the truth. They are not waiting."

"How did you find me?" K.C. looked down at the novice's robe, then back to the young woman. "How did you know?"

Danita didn't answer. Instead she raised a brow and gave K.C. a half smile. "You see, I asked myself what I would do—in your circumstances, that is. Where would I run for shelter? For comfort?"

"If you haven't come on behalf of Tres Equis, then why?

Why have you searched for me?"

"Shall we walk? I see you are heading to the river. Let us walk and I will tell you."

K.C. nodded, wondering if she had a choice. She still expected Doc Rafael—whose cynical voice and ghostly presence filled her nightmares—to jump from an alley. Or the silver and turquoise bejeweled Sterns to step out of a shop door.

"And I have something to show you. It's on the way."

"Ha! I bet you do."

Danita looked up at her, almost shyly. "It is not what you think." Then as the two women continued slowly toward the river, she stopped. "Oh, I had nearly forgotten about your foot. How is it? Would you like me to hire a cab?"

"So this is how you will abduct me this time? Tres Equis likes to take me where I don't want to go in motorized vehicles."

Danita looked confused, and without giving her gesture any thought, K.C. touched the girl's forearm to reassure her. "Never mind. No, let's walk. I'm fine. Really."

They approached a steep, cobbled street that snaked down to the river. But just as they arrived at the first switchback, Danita pointed to a squat, tile-roofed building. Above the arched doorway were the words: *Museo de la Antiqüedad*.

Danita reached into her pocket, then produced a key. "Would you like to see inside?"

"Do I have a choice?"

"Sí. Yes, you do." She nodded vigorously as if to emphasize the point.

For some reason, K.C. believed her. She looked into the girl's eyes, wondering what deception lay beneath their sparkling depths. "All right," she said finally. "Yes. I'll see what it is you want to show me."

"Thank you, K.C. Follow me." The key turned easily, and the door swung open.

Danita stepped aside and let K.C. enter first.

The foyer was small. Plain. A scarred wooden table with a guest book stood to one side. A visitor's desk on the other, though no one waited behind it. Closed metal shutters covered the two windows that flanked the door. The room smelled musty. Old.

Danita seemed to read K.C.'s thoughts. "We're here before opening time."

Another closed door was on the far side of the entrance. Danita nodded toward it. "This is what I brought you here to see." Then she produced yet another key and headed for the door, and a moment later it swung open.

K.C. caught her breath in surprise.

It was a place of worship, but not of God. The room was swathed in black and red fabric, cascading, curtainlike, down the four walls. Lances and spears and ancient paintings of fierce and realistic-looking dragons with the heads of goats covered every open space.

The air was frigid, almost abnormally so. A shudder traveled up K.C.'s spine. She started to back out of the room, then her attention was caught by three large Greek crosses, each transverse beam at least six feet long, propped up in St. Andrew's fashion at the back of a small stage, one in front of another about two feet apart. They formed three perfect X's.

A painting of a horned goat dressed in a royal purple robe looked down on the crosses, a human look of scorn on its hideous bearded face. The painting was in black, except for the whitish gray of the goat and the purple of royalty. Its eyes were like two burning coal that seemed to look straight into K.C.'s soul.

"I—I can't stay in here."

Danita looked at her in surprise. "It is a museum. Nothing

to be afraid of, K.C. I have much to explain about it. About Tres Equis."

K.C. shook her head. "No. You'll have to tell me about it somewhere else. Not here."

"But the brotherhood, Tres Equis, began here centuries ago. During the Inquisition. We are proud of the gathering of relics having to do with our brotherhood's beginnings." The younger woman turned as if to enter the place again. "This is where the ancients met. On this very spot. In this building. They worshipped here—"

K.C. grabbed her hand. "No, Danita. Please don't go back in there."

Danita met K.C.'s gaze. "I do not understand." But she allowed herself to be pulled back into the foyer and finally out into the sunlit street.

She locked the door and dropped the key back into her pocket. "I thought you would be pleased to see the museum. To see the origins of Tres Equis."

They began walking to the river again and finally, K.C. could draw a deep breath. "Tell me, Danita—"

"Please, call me Dani."

"All right, Dani. Tell me. Does your brotherhood—Tres Equis—adhere to the ceremonies, the worship of—the, ah—" She struggled with how much to say to the girl. She stopped, and beside her, Dani stopped too. "Do members of Tres Equis worship the figures, the goat figures, I saw in that museum?" Her mind was flying with possibilities.

Had Gav stumbled onto a cult unlike any they'd seen in all his research, one with roots in Satanism? Perhaps the government connection was a cover, rather than the other way around, as he had suspected.

Dani stared at her, looking dumbfounded. "Of course not!

It is what the ancients did, and we respect that. But ours is merely a brotherhood. Nothing more."

"What does that mean? A *brotherhood?*"

They were walking again, and Danita's voice was light, as if glad to explain something to a newfound friend. "When Franco came to power, he understood the history of the brotherhoods. He encouraged them to be studied and the rules set down by our ancestors followed again. A brotherhood is no more than what Americans might call a—" she seemed to be searching for the right word—"a club. Only more important than that. I'm sorry, I cannot think of the word. There are other organizations. They are international. Some go back for centuries." She frowned again.

"Such as the Masons?"

"Sí. Yes, yes. They are one such group. They, too, have their rules."

"Rules such as...?"

"Some worship as the ancients did. They use the same secret handshakes. And chants. And secret ceremonies. But they also do good works. They help the poor. They bring about change. Change for the good. Sometimes in communities. Sometimes on a larger scale."

"And Tres Equis? Is this a group looking to bring change?"

Danita didn't answer.

They reached an overlook above the river, which flowed below in a silver-blue ribbon, stretching as far as K.C. could see. A stone stairway led down a steep embankment to a small park by the thousand-year-old Roman bridge, another of Salamanca's famous landmarks.

But before they started down the stone steps, K.C. hesitated, studying Danita's face. "Dani, are you a believer? I mean, do you believe in God?"

The girl frowned. "Well, of course I do. I grew up going to mass every Sunday. Sometimes more often."

"I don't mean that. In your heart of hearts, do you belong to God?"

Danita tilted her head, still frowning. "Belong to him? Of course, we are all his children."

"Belong to him in a way that is different than sitting in a pew on Sunday mornings. Or belonging to a certain church just because your parents do."

At the mention of her parents, a harsh look flickered in Danita's expression. She tossed her hair with a quick tilt of her chin. "I don't know what you mean." Her tone said she didn't care.

"Dani, God waits for us to come to him. He wants us to give him our hearts. He is our father, but he wants us to call him Papá."

"Papá?" Her eyes filled with pain and longing. But she shook her head and shrugged one shoulder. "That is not possible."

"It *is* possible."

A beat of silence followed. The sounds of lapping water carried toward them from one direction, and from the other the funeral dirge of one more Holy Week procession of brotherhoods.

Brotherhoods. Sister Calandria had said that many, though not all, of the processions, the hordes of people dressed in KKK-like garb, were called brotherhoods. An ancient practice brought into popularity by Franco.

She frowned. Tres Equis might be participating in one of the hundreds of processions this week.

But before she could ask about it, Danita spoke. "I must go now. I'm sorry I disturbed you with the museum."

K.C. reached for her hand. “Dani. You didn’t disturb me. It was the—sacrilege of the crosses, the symbols of a triumphant Satan with the goats’ heads that disturbed me. More than disturbed. They made me feel…” She had no words to explain the chill, the cold spirit in the place. Instead, she took a deep breath and began again. “Something tells me that there’s a deeper meaning to Tres Equis than what you’ve been led to believe.”

For a moment, Danita stared into her eyes. “I must go,” the girl finally repeated with another toss of her head. Then she turned to walk away.

“Dani—”

She swung around.

“You’ll come talk to me again?”

Danita looked surprised, then pleased. She seemed to want to say more. But she held her silence for just a heartbeat and stepped away from the overlook.

“I will see you again, K.C.,” she tossed over her shoulder. “I will.”

For nearly an hour, Gav scanned the crowds around the Plaza Mayor. Finally he decided he could only wait near the place he’d last seen K.C., hoping that she might return for another café con leche.

He found a cyber café near the coffeehouse and took a place near the window. An unoccupied computer terminal was nearby. He motioned to a server, paid him for a cash card, and slid it through the scanner to log on, all the while keeping a lookout for K.C.

The familiar chimes sounded as the machine booted and loaded, then he typed in his screen name. If K.C. didn’t return soon, he might have enough time to revisit a few of the Web sites that constituted much of his research on Tres Equis.

He studied the screen, then let out an exasperated sigh. Though this was an American-made computer, every bit of text, every instruction, every menu, was in Spanish. He could read the language better than he could speak it, but even so, it was going to make it much more difficult to find the Web sites. It would be a long and tedious process, not a quick search to pass the time while awaiting K.C.

Frowning in concentration, he tried to find a pop-up menu that might change the computer's language configuration. After a moment he looked up to again scan the plaza. The open area was as crowded as before, and he looked back to the computer screen to continue his search.

Then something struck him about a woman he'd just seen approaching the coffee shop.

He stared at her, recognizing her features, but not her manner or dress. She reminded him of Arabella Stern, but he couldn't be sure. She looked, well, too Spanish. Even her hair was different. Perfectly coiffed, instead of the wild, au naturel look he'd noticed in Granada.

A younger woman accompanied her. Both their expressions were solemn, and they seemed lost in conversation as they entered the shop. Gav picked up a newspaper that had been left on a nearby table and snapped it open to hide behind. He couldn't put his finger on his reasoning, but if it was Arabella, he didn't want to be spotted. For the first time, he wondered if Arabella and Wyatt might have had something to do with K.C.'s disappearance.

The women ordered their coffees and seated themselves at a table near him, close to the window, facing the plaza.

If Arabella was in on this, he reasoned, she might also be

waiting for K.C. His heartbeat quickened.

What if K.C. returned? Before he could complete the thought, another patron entered the shop. This time there was no mistaking the identity. Wyatt Stern strode in, looking as faux intellectual and artistic as ever. The only addition to his customary attire was a black leather jacket, draped over his shoulders. An affectation that somehow suited him.

Gav slid further down into his chair and raised his paper a few more inches as Stern moved by.

The man had just seated himself when a familiar draped figure moved slowly, gracefully past the window, novice's robe swinging, hands piously tucked inside the sleeves.

Gav caught his breath. Within a half second K.C. would step into the coffeehouse.

He bolted for the door.

THIRTEEN

GAV GRABBED THE ROBED AND HOODED FIGURE, PROPELLING HER in one fluid motion through the door of the shop next to the coffeehouse. The place was empty except for a scowling, middle-aged woman behind a counter of chorizo, cheeses, and large vats of olives. She shouted something at him in Spanish.

Gav drew his arm protectively around the small shoulders at his side. "It's all right, Kace. I'm here," he murmured, leaning his cheek against her hooded head. But instead of relaxing against him, the figure stiffened.

He turned her gently to look into her face. At last.

There was a moment of stunned silence. Even the woman behind the counter stopped her screeching.

The novice wasn't K.C.

"Oh, dear. Oh, my. I'm sorry!" He backed up three steps. Waves of heat washed over his face. "Oh, I'm so sorry."

The plain-faced woman, who so closely matched K.C.'s

height and build, just peered up at him with confused and frightened eyes.

"I'm so sorry," he repeated.

She obviously didn't understand English, and in his embarrassment Gav couldn't recall even a smidgen of the conversational Spanish he once knew.

The woman behind the counter reached for a telephone and, while picking up where she'd left off yelling at Gav, was obviously dialing the Salamancan equivalent of 911.

Gav glanced into the frightened novice's face one last time, apologized again, then sprinted out the door. He followed the row of shops to the nearest exit from the plaza.

Without stopping to look over his shoulder, he jogged through the arched exit and headed down the narrow Rúa Meléndez. Another procession was heading toward him. The crowds parted reverently for black-robed penitentes and the drummers and trumpeters who followed them. Bobbing on the shoulders of at least two dozen robed men was a gilded float of the Virgin Mary bowing at the feet of the crucified Christ. The entire edifice was framed with fresh flowers.

Without stopping to admire it, he moved in and out of the crowds at the side of the street. But the mood was so solemn, so quiet and reverent, that even his slow sidling brought too much attention to himself.

He ventured a glance behind him. Was that Wyatt Stern moving through the crowd, following him? He ducked into a doorway, waited for the procession to pass, then peered out again. No one resembling Stern was in sight.

Relieved, he continued moving down the street, mingling with the rapidly dispersing crowd. At the end, he spotted an imposing centuries-old building he didn't remember from the tour books. He broke into a jog and headed toward it. Maybe this place would grant him sanctuary for at least a few minutes, give him time to gather his thoughts.

He took the steep steps of the massive building two at a time, and, without stopping to look around, pulled open the ancient wooden doors at the entrance and stepped inside.

He stopped and looked around in surprise. Instead of a church, he'd entered a modern office building. Computers hummed behind a glass partition. Its modern setup reminded him of the university office, though he didn't think they were connected. He glanced about for a sign telling him where he was.

A series of old photographs graced the walls near the entrance. They showed the building in various stages of reconstruction, gutted and restored. Finally he found a framed, written history of the building. As he pieced together a few snatches of Spanish phrasing, a slow grin spread across his face.

Perfect. *Real Colegio del Espíritu Santo.* The Jesuit College, founded in 1611—from what he could understand—by Philip III and Margaret of Austria. This was no johnny-come-lately. Judging from the offices behind the glass windows and doors, the place was well equipped. And considering the phone lines heading to every terminal, nicely connected to the electronic age.

Bless old King Philip III's heart.

Gav strode across the tile floor toward the first office on his right. A lean, dark-haired man in a Jesuit robe met him, sliding open the heavy glass above the counter.

"Do you speak English?"

"Sí," the man replied. "Yes, I do. May I be of some assistance?"

"I need to work on a computer for several hours at a time. I am looking for a quiet, private place where I won't be disturbed."

The robed man held up his hand, shaking his head. "I am sorry, but if you are asking for time on one of our computers, I am afraid it is impossible." He followed Gav's gaze as he took in the smoothly running office. "These are for official use only."

"You are a college. The Jesuit College, correct?"

The man nodded. "We are."

"Do you have computers for the students? Other computers elsewhere, I mean?"

The brother nodded again. "Yes, we do. Many of our students are working in tandem with the library across the street."

"The computers are there, at the library?"

"No. They are here, but connected to the library's archives. Also to the archives of the University of Salamanca." The Jesuit gave him a proud smile. "We are probably the greatest storehouse of ancient, medieval, and modern history in all of Spain."

Gav leaned forward. "Would it be possible to rent one of the student computers? I will pay for any time I spend on the Internet. I am involved in some extremely important research on Spanish history, particularly that of cults founded during the Inquisition."

The Jesuit raised an interested brow. "I will need to speak with my superiors, but I do not think it will be a problem." He turned to converse with an older Jesuit who was leaning over a copy machine at the back of the room, then returned to Gav.

"He is not opposed to your request. His only concern is that you not use any computer when our students are in need of it. And that you leave us a deposit of ten thousand pesetas for the Internet use. You will receive a refund for unused time, of course, at the conclusion of your rental agreement."

"Thank you," Gav said. "When may I begin?"

"Would you like to start now?"

"Yes. Very much."

"This is a good time, because our students are out of school for the Holy Week observance. Keep in mind, however, some may want to use the computer rooms for research for term papers." He reached into a drawer for some forms, handed them to Gav to fill out, and after a few minutes took them back along with two 5,000-peseta notes.

"I understand."

"Follow me." The Jesuit stepped to the glass door, opened it silently, and joined Gav in the hall. They moved briskly around a corner and up a flight of marble stairs. The Jesuit glanced at Gav as they reached the top. "What is the name of the cult you are investigating?"

"Tres Equis. Do you know it?"

A flicker of recognition lit the man's face. "Yes. It is an ancient brotherhood. The same as many others in Spain. Its members gather for political reasons rather than for anything of meaning."

Gav nodded slowly. "I see."

The man glanced at him again as they turned another corner. "You have come all this way to investigate, to study, this group?"

Gav figured it was idle conversation, but he couldn't be sure, so he merely shrugged. "I was coming to Salamanca anyway. Just figured I would check into the organization while I'm here." He looked around and shrugged again. "And what better place than this?"

The Jesuit smiled benignly as he stopped in front of a door, and, swinging it open, stood back so that Gav could enter. Then he reached to flip on the lights. A row of computers lined three walls of the room. "Would you prefer a Macintosh or a PC?"

Gav's grin was wider than before. "God has indeed blessed

me. I'll take a Mac." He'd never thought it possible. "Can you set it up in English for me?"

"Of course." The robed brother headed to the opposite side of the room, sat, and flipped on the computer in one swift movement. Within seconds, the machine was booted up with the familiar Apple smile.

Gav could have kissed the screen.

"Godspeed as you surf the 'net."

Gav laughed as the man headed to the door.

The Jesuit halted midway and turned. "If you need any help, let me know. I have made a study of Spanish brotherhoods. I have also forced myself to become computer literate." He shrugged. "In today's world, I fear these machines are a necessary evil. I would be happy to give you what little information I have gathered—about either subject."

"Have you studied Tres Equis?"

"Here, we feel the group is more political than religious, or quasi religious, I should say. I have not felt compelled to delve into a study of it."

Gav was disappointed, but something nagged at him about the man's demeanor. He wondered if he was telling him the whole truth. "I see." He turned back to the terminal.

"My name is Brother Thomas, should you need anything." He seemed to be hesitating.

"Thank you," Gav said absently, already tapping his screen name and password into his international e-mail server.

Within a few minutes, Gav was staring at the monitor, oblivious to everything but the e-mail post he'd just opened. It was from Duncan MacGowan.

Gav,

By now you are probably back in the States. But some-

thing has come up that I think you should be aware of. You are too distant to help us by your physical presence, but I write to you because I know you will pray for us. That may be the greatest help of all in this.

Pray hard, my brother, as I make my way to Salamanca on behalf of our friends Marta and Alfredo Aznar.

They have received another letter from Salamanca. It also is anonymous, but the writer reveals something more of himself, or herself, than before.

The writer touts himself as a computer expert. Someone who knows the ins and outs of the Internet, ways of digging deep to find information others can't know exists. He explains this is how his trail led to them.

He (or she) also revealed—and this is the most astounding news of all—that Marta and Alfredo's daughter is involved in Tres Equis, the same group I remember you had planned to investigate. Not only that, but also that she (he or she says nothing about their son) is in grave danger. Immediate danger.

That, my friend, was the end of the letter. As you can imagine, Marta and Alfredo are distraught. They begged me to intervene, and I would have it no other way—even if they hadn't asked.

God is bigger than this. I must do his bidding, aware that he alone knows the outcome—whether it be one of mourning or joy. But the outcome doesn't matter. Success, by our standards, doesn't matter. Only obedience. I think it was Mother Teresa of Calcutta who once said, "God has not called me to be successful. He has called me to be obedient."

You are in my prayers, my friend, and have been since last we spoke. I trust you have by now talked to your beloved K.C. and straightened out the misunderstanding between you. If she did indeed go on to Salamanca without you, I shall look her up at the university, once I am there.

Keep me in prayer as I head back to Spain. I leave today, Palm Sunday, and will stay through Easter. I don't know where to begin my search, but pray for me, my brother, as I follow our Lord in this. I sense that it will be a journey with no small measure of danger.

Blessings abundant, my friend. "I thank my God every time I remember you. I always pray with joy because of your partnership in the gospel...."

Duncan MacGowan

Duncan, here in Salamanca! Gav could scarcely believe it. By now he'd been here for a couple of days. But how would Gav find him?

He pondered the question, then his thoughts turned to Marta and Alfredo, their tragic history, and now this....

Before leaving the computer room, he typed several hurried messages. The first was an answer to Duncan's post, and he prayed as it went that the young minister had brought his laptop and would check his e-mail soon. He clicked *send* and quickly composed the others, to law enforcement friends in California, asking for help with research. The latter messages were a long shot, because most of the people he wrote checked their e-mail only sporadically, if they remembered to at all.

When he left the computer room a few minutes later, he'd made another decision. No matter the danger, he needed to see K.C., to speak with her, as quickly as possible.

Dusk had just deepened to a moonless night when K.C. moved to her room's single window and looked out over the arched, double-galleried cloister of the convent. A fountain bubbled in the center courtyard, and the lush growth of vines and flowering plants tumbled in careful disarray around it.

Her thoughts turned to Gav, to her longing for him. She wondered if he might still be in Salamanca and lifted her heart in a silent supplication for his safety.

After a moment, she knelt by her small cot to pray.

Her room had become a sanctuary of peace, even in the uncertainties and fears that whirled within her heart. And now, as she poured out her thoughts to her Lord, she felt his touch, and a still small voice reassuring her that she wasn't alone.

She looked up at the cross that hung above the iron headboard of her bed. It was Celtic, a surprise to her when she first saw it, at least until Sister Calandria explained that Celtic influence had been strong in Northern Spain centuries ago. The sister also told her that it had been brought by worshipers on a pilgrimage to León in the sixteenth century. At least that was the legend.

She stood to run her fingers over the ancient carvings on the transepts, thinking about the person who carved the worn symbols. Could that same person have been the one who carried it from Ireland, Wales, or Scotland all the way to Spain?

Why not? God was the same then as he was today. The followers who worshiped him—sometimes facing great peril for their beliefs—followed him a day at a time. No matter their journey, no matter their peril, they simply kept their eyes on him.

Teresa of Ávila had been tried for crimes against God during the Inquisition. And she had been cast into prison. Yet she had kept her eyes on her Lord, and he had done great things through her.

K.C. smiled and touched the cross again, wondering if Teresa had ever done the same.

The young Teresa, even as she grew older, couldn't have known the impact she would have on her own generation. And wouldn't she have been surprised that so many centuries later, people were still being blessed by her meditations about God.

K.C. had just turned to ready herself for bed when there was a light tap on the door.

It was too late for visitors. Since her arrival, the sisters had been careful to give K.C. privacy. Curious, she headed for the door.

It was Sister Calandria, her expression solemn. "You are wanted in the cloister gardens. Please follow me."

Fourteen

Her robe tassel-ties swinging, K.C. followed Sister Calandria through the double doorway leading to the lower gallery of the cloister. A row of dim lights framed the marble-columned Gothic arches around the entire courtyard. The glow filled the gardens with a contrast of pale golden light and deep purple shadows. The pungent fragrance of rosemary surrounded K.C. as sounds of the trickling fountain floated toward her on the breeze.

K.C. quickened her pace to match Sister Calandria's as they headed down the flat stone walkway of the gallery. "Can't you tell me who is waiting?"

The nun smiled gently. "You will see soon enough, child." Then she stopped at the center arch and nodded toward the fountain. "It is there your visitor awaits. Go to him."

K.C. let her gaze travel the pebbled path into the dimly lit area, but saw no one. She stepped down three stone steps and onto the gravel path. The air held a chill, and she shivered both with the cold and with worry. She had almost reached center courtyard when a figure stepped out from behind the tiered fountain.

For a moment she couldn't speak, couldn't move. She just stared as a warmth as sweet as honey filled her heart.

"K.C." Gav held open his arms.

With a small cry, she ran to him. Suddenly, his arms were around her, clutching her as if he'd never let go again. Quick tears filled her eyes. She let them spill down her face and drip onto his jacket, unwilling to release him even long enough to get a tissue from her pocket.

They stood in silence, holding each other, K.C. with her cheek against the thud of Gav's heart, Gav with his head resting against the top of hers.

After a moment, she sniffled and pulled back just enough to look into his eyes. "Gav..." she whispered, then started to cry again.

He smiled and gently rubbed the tears from her cheeks with his thumbs.

"How did you find me?"

"I saw you at the cathedral."

She couldn't help the small giggle that escaped. "I thought I was protected in my disguise. I saw you, but I felt the danger was too great to approach you."

He laughed softly. "It was your sore ankle that gave you away—and the reflecting tape on your running shoe showing under your robe." He pulled her close again. "I've been only steps away since I found you."

But she stepped backward out of his embrace. She wanted every shadow of doubt between them erased. "Gav, that letter I was forced to write—"

He raised a brow. "You'll need to explain exactly how that happened. Though I've got a pretty good idea."

"These people are desperate to get you off their trail. They thought they could do it by sending you away."

"*They* who, Kace?"

"Tres Equis."

So, he was right. "I figured they might be behind this. But who exactly? Do you know?"

K.C. took a deep breath. "Remember the doctor in Granada?"

"Doctor Rafael, wasn't it?"

She nodded. "He goes by Doc. Fancies himself a throwback from the American West. I was told he watches *Gunsmoke* reruns constantly, though Wyatt Earp's Doc Holliday might be a more fitting comparison."

"Doc Rafael is part of this?" Gav frowned, obviously attempting to put some of the puzzle pieces together. "You met him because of your fall. Did he plan that?"

"The Sterns did."

"Arabella and Wyatt?" Again his brow was creased in thought. "How could they have arranged any of this?"

"I don't know how they arranged it or if my fall was just a coincidence they used to their advantage. But their targeting us is no coincidence. They know about your study of Tres Equis. And there's something involving the cult that they don't want you to discover. Apparently, you've gotten too close for comfort."

Gav nodded gravely. "I've been so worried about you, K.C." Then he hesitated, dropping his eyes.

"What is it?"

"I believed the letter. I thought you'd changed your mind…about marrying me. That you'd done the same thing to me I once did to you."

K.C. sighed and reached for his hand, turned it over, and rubbed the pad of his thumb. "I was afraid you'd think that."

"How did they know? That was why I believed you'd written it. How could anyone know what happened to us before?

K.C. brought his hand to her face and laid her cheek against it. He gathered her into his arms again, and snuggled her against the curve of his shoulder. "They've got information-gathering capabilities far beyond what we can guess, Gav. Rafael alluded to details they've found out about us that would make your hair stand on end. They know about our undercover work in the Angels of Fellowship, about the rescue efforts on behalf of kids caught up in cults. They've got details. Names, places."

She shook her head slightly against him. "I've met only the peripheral players in this, but I know they've got some sort of a political network set up that rivals anything we've ever come across."

"Who have you met? How many?" He pulled back enough to see her upturned face.

"Diego Rafael, of course. And I mentioned Arabella and Wyatt Stern. They were obviously sent to Granada to intercept us."

He shook his head slowly. "How did they know we were going there? Only our friends knew, Father Max and Theo."

"I don't know how, Gav. But I do know this. They snatched me right out from under your nose." She swallowed hard. "And Rafael told me that if you came for me here, both our lives would be in danger. It was too easy for them to take me the first time.

"He said that if you came for me, I am to send you packing or I would live to regret it." She began to shake as fearful images built in her mind. "But now that you're here, that's the last thing I can do...." Her voice broke, and she turned away from him.

"Kace?" He placed one hand on each shoulder and turned her back to face him. "I can't, I *won't*—leave you. We're in this together. We'll figure it out."

"Gav, these people are dangerous."

"I know. But I'm not leaving you just to save my own skin."

"What can we do?"

"There's more involved than even what you've told me—or what I discovered during my research back home. It's hard to know where to start unraveling the tangle."

"What do you mean?"

"I've just heard from Duncan. By e-mail. Marta and Alfredo have received another letter about their children."

She frowned, chiding herself for forgetting, amid her own troubles, about the Anzars' plea for help. "What did it say?"

"Apparently, their daughter is in great danger. And it has to do with Tres Equis."

K.C. was stunned. "Do we know if it's an idle threat...or if it's real?"

"It's too much of a coincidence, I think, to be a mere threat." He paused, frowning in thought. "Have you met anyone else in Tres Equis? A female, say, in her late twenties?" He shook his head. "I know it's a long shot, but I thought I'd—"

"There *is* one. Yes. A beautiful girl named Danita Chávez. She goes by Dani."

"Does she have a brother?"

"No. At least not that I'm aware of." She gave him a short laugh. "Of course, they haven't exactly allowed me a look at their membership roster."

"It's still a needle in a haystack, Kace." He let out a sigh and looked across the courtyard. "We don't know her identity, plus we have no idea what danger she's facing."

"Where do we go from here?"

"I need to stay hidden. And as far away from you as possible."

She nodded. "It will be difficult. They seem to be everywhere. I thought I'd fooled them here in my convent hideaway, but just today, Danita approached me. She took me to the strangest place."

He looked alarmed. "You escaped from her?"

"No, she didn't try to hold me against my will. Strangely, she just wanted to talk. Show me a museum having to do with the brotherhood of Tres Equis."

"I saw Arabella Stern today from a distance. Also Wyatt. There was a young woman with them. Maybe it was your Danita."

"Probably so." She paused. "As hard as it is to say this, Gav, you shouldn't come here again. After Dani's visit with me today, I'm certain I'm being watched. If there's any indication that you are here—or especially that we've met—our lives may be in danger."

He slammed a fist into his open palm. "We should go to the local police! Get an escort out of here, fly home right now."

A slow grin spread across her face. "You don't want to do that any more than I do, Gav. What would we say? That we suspect something's going on with one of the Holy Week brotherhoods?"

"You were kidnapped, Kace." His tone and eyes hardened, and K.C. was glad he was on her side. Gav was not a man to make angry. "We could bring charges."

"I was kidnapped by Americans. I'm not sure the Spanish government wants to get involved with something like that."

"Threats were made against your life. Against mine."

"My word against the good doctor's. I wonder if the police would believe me." She studied him thoughtfully, knowing they'd both already reached the same conclusion. "We need to see this through, Gav. Find out what's going on."

He was smiling, obviously having thought this through himself, though deep concern remained in his eyes. "We can't walk away from this, can we?"

She shook her head. "No." Then she touched his hand. "Remember? It's our calling."

Someone flicked the lights off and on, and Gav grinned. "I think they're trying to tell us something."

She reached for his hand, wanting to hold it for a moment longer. "You mentioned the letter from Duncan. Are Marta and Alfredo coming to Salamanca?"

Gav circled his arm around her shoulders, and she leaned against him, a sense of warmth and peace surging through her, as they turned up the gravel path to head into the gallery. "No. They're too distraught over all this. They asked Duncan to head here from Porto. Nose around a bit."

She stopped and tilted her head to look up at him. "Duncan is here?"

"He's probably already arrived. The problem is finding him. I've sent him a return e-mail, hoping that he checks his account from here. If he doesn't..."He shrugged as they continued on up the steps.

"Did he say anything about where he'd be staying or going?"

Gav frowned. "He did say he would try to find you at the university—he was still under the impression that you broke off our engagement." He smiled gently. "Said he would put in a good word for me." He halted and turned her so that he was gazing into her eyes. A smile touched the corners of his mouth.

"Oh, Gav..." But her words were lost as Gav reached over to touch her lips with his.

The lights flicked on and off again. Twice. Three times. Gav chuckled. "I'd better go."

Holding her hand, he headed for the door into the convent. He gave her another quick kiss, then turned to leave.

"Wait! Gav—"

He turned.

"Ask at the university office if anyone has come by for me. Maybe Duncan left word about where he's staying."

He gave her a quick nod, turned to take a few steps, then stopped and looked back. "Kace—?"

"I'm here," she whispered, knowing the lights would be flipped again at any minute.

"Try to get close to Danita. Maybe she's the key to all this...."

"I will. I was thinking the same thing."

"Good." He walked closer, and, gazing into her eyes, bent to kiss her again.

The lights flickered again, furiously. They both giggled as Gav planted one more soft peck on her lips, then turned to hurry down the corridor.

K.C. reached for the door handle, but Gav's loud whisper drew her attention back to him, standing in the shadows at the end of the gallery.

"Remember, I'm only a heartbeat away."

"I love you, Gav."

"I love you, Kace." And then he was gone.

Danita stood outside the convent of St. Teresa of Ávila, just as she'd been instructed. She'd earlier seen a man enter at the street entrance. Not many men, if any, ever visited this convent.

Or any other. All of Tres Equis was on the lookout for the American lawman, Elliot Gavin. So when a man had arrived—strong-shouldered, dressed in blue jeans, plaid shirt, and a windbreaker—rung the bell, and gained admittance after conversing with one of the sisters, Danita knew it could be no one but the American lawman. The same man K.C. Keegan had planned to marry in Granada.

Danita's eyes misted as she imagined them running toward each other, arms outstretched. She knew the deception Julian had orchestrated, that Diego Rafael and the Sterns had carried out. But love was love, and when deep and sacred, no one, no outside force could destroy it.

She sighed at the thought, wondering if such a love would ever come her way.

Julian Hernando entered her mind, almost uninvited. She sensed that his interest in her was more than just a leftover friendship from her childhood. The news about Arabella, Miguel Vargas and his martyrdom, also had seemed to spark a troubling new interest when he looked at her.

She didn't understand it. Perhaps she never would. Nonetheless, it caused a small, unpleasant knot in her stomach. A warning, perhaps? Or simply an overactive imagination? Just as Raúl always said she had.

Oh, sweet Raúl. Her spirits fell as she considered her younger brother. She sighed again, still keeping an eye on the convent. Arabella advised her not to tell Raúl quite yet that they were not siblings, not true blood relatives.

Arabella had obviously been given charge over her, to train her as a more involved member of Tres Equis. Perhaps even as a leader. The older woman made it clear that this was Julian's desire.

No, more than that. It was his direct order.

But in the mere hours since she'd taken charge over her granddaughter, the woman had become too chummy, too bossy. She deified the man who had died for the cause, the man who was supposedly Danita's grandfather. Everything was suddenly Miguel Vargas this, Miguel Vargas that.

Danita had bit her tongue to keep from spouting off that she resented the woman's intrusion into her life. And that she had no intention of moving into a relationship with Arabella Stern any closer than that of comrades in arms.

A movement from a side door caught her attention. The distant glow of streetlights and her excellent night vision allowed her to make out the figure of a man moving stealthily through the surrounding foliage.

Elliot Gavin. Of course.

Julian would be angry if she didn't report that she'd seen him. Julian's anger always resulted in a swift reprisal to fit the crime against Tres Equis. He had studied the ancient rules of the brotherhood, and many of his ideas for punishment were medieval. Though, of course, he never administered them himself. He left that to those around him.

He'd never turned on her. Still, knowing his passions, she questioned whether their relationship would count for much if she was brought before him on charges of betraying Tres Equis.

Sometimes she had a difficult time reconciling the Julian who had been her youthful champion with the Julian who led Tres Equis.

She shivered in the damp cold and, keeping her eyes on the retreating figure, wondered what she should do. She stared bleakly into the dark night. Was there anywhere she could turn? Was there anyone who would pull her into love and acceptance without any strings attached? An ache had carved a place in her heart so deep that she thought it would never be filled with anything but unmet expectations.

Surprisingly, her eyes filled, and the man striding down the street almost disappeared in the veil of unshed tears. She blinked them away, almost angrily. She was not a coward. She was not a quitter. She was not a betrayer of friends and comrades.

She was part of Tres Equis. It was in her blood.

She was no sniveling child. She was a young woman on a mission that would change the whole country by week's end.

She wiped away her tears and set out down the street, following her prey at a discreet distance, just as she had been told to do.

FIFTEEN

BEFORE DAWN THE FOLLOWING MORNING, GAV WALKED OUT TO the narrow second-floor balcony of his *pensión*. From his vantage point, he could see the medieval section of the city, the twin towers of the cathedral in one direction, the Plaza Mayor in the other.

He stretched and leaned his arms against the iron railing, gazing down at the fresh-scrubbed Rúa Mayor, the glow of streetlights reflecting in the shallow puddles. It had already become obvious to him that Salamanca never slept. By the time the whooping, boisterous students had given up their pub and tapas-bar hopping at 4 A.M., the sweepers moved down the myriad streets like a small, precision army, brushes scrubbing, engines whining, backup chimes ringing out into the night air.

Gav yawned and stretched again. Even if he closed the floor-to-ceiling double windows and suffered through the night without needed ventilation, the incessant squeal of the elevator next to his room would keep him awake.

He scratched one side of his back, then moseyed into his room, flopped on his bed, and stared up at the stained ceiling.

He'd slept better last night—even with the cacophony of Salamanca's nightlife roaring outside his room—than he had in almost two weeks.

Because of K.C.

He smiled. Just one look in her eyes…the confirmation of love he'd seen there had brought him back to life. He pictured her in that novice's robe, hood over her head, looking up at him with trust and passion and determination all rolled together. He longed to go to her this morning, insist that they get out of Salamanca on the first train heading to Madrid, get out of Spain on the first flight to London.

Holy Week in Salamanca wasn't safe.

He was beginning to piece together the odd-fitting puzzle shapes, and a surprising picture was forming in his mind. A picture that he tried to reason away, tried to set aside as impossible. But it kept returning. Nagging at him.

Nothing fit together completely. Not conclusively.

Tres Equis was a medieval brotherhood, or in today's vernacular, a cult. His research had led him to their ancient practices, their secret rituals, their strange KKK-like garb, their twisting of Scripture to elevate man higher than God.

None of that was particularly unusual for a cult, even one with roots in the Inquisition.

The Inquisition. It had been mobilized to deal with people accused of being unfaithful to the Church. It also had been an excuse for Spain to expel Jews and Moors. Or to kill them. The equivalent of ethnic cleansing.

Some of the most spiritual and godly men in Spain were brought to trial. And condemned. The Inquisition judges were afraid of any opposition, even from the most pious believers.

The purging had lasted longer in Spain than in any other country. Had Tres Equis become stronger because of it? Or had it died out, then begun again after Franco came to power?

The dictator had used all the ancient brotherhoods to build a stronger sense of nationalism.

Tres Equis had not been persecuted during the Inquistion. Instead, they became watchdogs. Bounty hunters who piously spied on their neighbors, friends, political and religious leaders for any sign of opposition to church teachings.

Gav moved to the balcony once more and looked out across the pearl gray sky of dawn. Leaning against the railing, he considered the remaining facts he'd pulled together.

Tres Equis: political watchdogs to the point of fanaticism.

Members he knew so far: Wyatt and Arabella Stern, Danita last-name-unknown, and the *Gunsmoke*-loving Doc Rafael.

Locale: Far reaching, perhaps computer based, which would give the group a global network. Computer expertise evident.

Leaders: unknown.

Mission: unknown.

Tres Equis: Three crosses, each of the crossbeams identical in length, each placed one behind the other on its side, rather than upright. When he'd seen the symbol on a Web site, the first thing that occurred to him was its similarity to a swastika. A black square cross times three.

He looked out over the cathedral towers unable to enjoy the Salamancan sunrise. Words and phrases tumbled together as he tried to make sense of them.

Inquisition. Persecution of races. Racial purity. Ethnic cleansing. Watchdog. Spies. Secret ceremonies. Swastika. Tres Equis. Triple crosses. Double cross. Triple cross.

And why Salamanca, when the headquarters was in Madrid? Why this week? The holiest of weeks in Christendom?

Troubled, Gav let it all sink in for a few minutes before shaking his head. Maybe he was wrong. Perhaps none had anything to do with the others.

As he grabbed a towel and a bottle of shampoo and headed for the shower down the hall, he considered that he might be making something out of nothing.

Except for the nagging thought that K.C. had been kidnapped to keep him out of Salamanca. This week.

Which could only mean someone didn't want him to discover something important.

But what?

He tried to turn his thoughts to the next steps in his morning—conducting more research at the Jesuit College. Finding Duncan MacGowan. But in the back of his mind, the nagging conviction stayed with him: he was overlooking the obvious.

He just didn't know what it was.

Danita emerged from an alley across the street from the pensión and glanced up at the room she'd seen Elliot Gavin enter the night before.

Moments earlier, she'd been relieved to see him leaning against the balcony. The truth was—she'd concluded while tossing in her bed during the night—she didn't fear for herself nearly as much as she did for the American couple.

Julian had made it clear they would disappear without trace if they got in the way of Tres Equis this week. And their presence guaranteed they *would* get in the way. Since the couple had talked last night, Danita figured they'd concluded who and what was behind K.C.'s abduction. That made them even more dangerous to Tres Equis than before.

A robed figure moved across Gavin's room, and Danita stepped backward, hiding in the doorway of a souvenir shop. Then the room's shutters closed, and she breathed a little easier.

A half hour later, Elliot Gavin pulled back one of the pensión's double-glass doors and stepped onto the Rúa Mayor. Danita remained in the shadows as he headed first to the *telebanco* machine two doors down, slid his card through, and retrieved some cash. Then glancing up and down the nearly empty street, he headed toward *Calle de la Compañía* and turned right.

Danita trailed just far enough behind to keep from drawing attention to herself. She thought he might be heading for the public library in the *Casa de las Conches*, or House of Shells, but he surprised her when he sprinted instead up the steps to the Jesuit College.

She waited until he was inside, then made her way up the stairs, nodding at the few people who were exiting the college. At the wide stone entrance, she stopped for a moment to catch her breath. Then, almost timidly, she pulled open the heavy wooden door.

Elliot Gavin blocked her way.

She gasped and stepped back, frantically calculating her escape. But before she could act, he grasped her arm and propelled her down a long hallway.

He moved her around a corner, into an alcove near a classroom. She bit her lip to keep from crying out.

Finally the man stopped and swung her around to face him. His eyes were cold, the corners of his mouth tight. "Why are you following me?"

Her stomach knotted, and she stiffened under his withering glare. She tried to speak but nothing came out. Besides, she didn't know what to say. She cleared her throat, then licked her dry lips. "I—I, ah..."

He squeezed her arm tighter, and tears filled her eyes. "I am sorry. I do not know what you are talking about. You are frightening me. Please, let go of my arm."

Studying her with barely controlled anger, he seemed to be considering the truth of her words. Finally, he let go, his jaw still working. He stared at her for a full minute before speaking. "I know who you are—"

She started to protest, but he shushed her and continued. "I saw you last night after I left the convent. You followed me to my hostel. And now here you are again. I would say that's more than a coincidence, wouldn't you?"

She swallowed hard and bit back her tears.

His expression softened somewhat. "You've got some explaining to do."

Danita remained silent.

"K.C. thought you might be different than the others."

"K.C. told you about me?"

He met her gaze with renewed interest, then nodded slowly. "Yes. She did."

Danita studied him for a minute. His eyes now reflected a surprising glint of warmth. But she had seen the profile Tres Equis had gathered about the man. He was a law officer. He would adopt the right demeanor to disarm his enemy.

"How would she know anything about me?" She tilted her chin as she almost spat the challenge.

"She knows people. She studies them, especially those she likes."

Another ploy. Straight from the training manual at the camps. "I do not have time to discuss K.C.'s feelings about people. That is not what I am here for."

"Then what are you here for, Danita?"

"You know my name?"

"K.C. told me."

It made her uncomfortable that she had been important enough to them to discuss. Especially in light of what she knew her duty must be. "I am here to warn you."

He raised a brow. "You were sent to warn me…warn us?"

She hesitated. "I was not sent. But I have come anyway." She was going against Julian's direct orders, going against Arabella's intricately woven plans, and her heart raced with the danger of it. "You and K.C. must leave this place now. Before it is too late."

He stepped closer. "What are you talking about?"

"I cannot say."

He grabbed her arm. "Tell me."

But she backed away from him, shaking her arm free.

He followed. "You must tell me. Then perhaps we will leave."

She bit her bottom lip. She had already said too much, and that frightened her. He was the enemy. So was K.C. Why couldn't she remember that? "Please, take K.C. and go back to America. Leave us. Leave this place."

He stared at her, the corners of his mouth tight.

She tried again. "None of this has anything to do with you. Please go."

"We're leaving at the end of the week anyway." He seemed to be baiting her. "Why should we leave now? What has Tres Equis planned for Holy Week?"

She felt herself go pale, and there was a sudden flicker of triumph in his gaze, as though he'd hit upon something he had been seeking for a long time.

She'd been wrong. Terribly wrong to follow him. Why

hadn't she simply reported his whereabouts as she had been instructed? And now it was too late. And now her stupidity might jeopardize Tres Equis's carefully crafted plans.

And instead of saving the Americans from danger, she might have drawn them closer to it.

She stared at him, hot tears springing to her eyes, her voice a harsh whisper. "Leave now!"

Then she turned and fled, the clicking of her heels on the tile floor echoing through the halls.

She pushed through the doors and out into the morning sun. But the warmth did little to stave off the chill that overtook her when one of Julian's cars slowed to a stop in front of the college steps. A bodyguard stepped out and held the back door open, his gaze fixed on hers.

There was no doubt about the man's meaning when he jerked his head toward the open door. Julian had sent for her.

She drew in a troubled breath. So Julian had been watching her all along. Testing her, more than likely. She'd really never had a choice about the Americans. And she had failed the test.

She hung her head and slowly walked down the stairs to the waiting car.

Gav signed in with Brother Thomas, then sprinted up the stairs to the empty classroom. Sitting down at the Macintosh, he logged on.

Within minutes, he'd signed onto his e-mail account, and checked his new mail.

Gav saw the screen name of the sender and felt a burden lift from his shoulders. They could arrange a meeting after all. Possibly even today.

He scrolled down the post. Duncan said to meet him by the

cathedral at nine. Gav glanced at his watch. Just enough time to check some of the Web sources for more information on Tres Equis.

Then, frowning, he decided to read through Duncan's message about the Aznar children once more to make sure he had the details right.

A tap sounded at the door. "Come in," he called absently, still scrolling through Duncan's message.

"Excuse me for bothering you." It was Brother Thomas.

Gav looked up. "No bother—"

A younger man stepped into the room with Brother Thomas.

"Yes?" Gav stood to shake hands.

"I took the liberty of telling one of my friends about your project," Brother Thomas said, escorting the other man forward. "He too is interested in brotherhoods, in cults. Especially in Tres Equis."

Too late Gav realized that he'd left the e-mail from Duncan on the large screen, easily read from several feet away. He sidled toward the monitor to block it.

But he was too late. The young man's gaze had already left Gav's face and was openly studying the screen.

"Raúl," Brother Thomas said, "I would like you to meet Elliot Gavin."

The young man turned back to Gav, a surprising intensity burning in his eyes. "Yes?"

"Elliot Gavin," Brother Thomas repeated. "From America."

The younger man stepped forward and shook Gav's hand. "It is a pleasure to make your acquaintance."

"Raúl Chávez," Brother Thomas said proudly. "One of the brightest minds in Salamanca. Also a friend."

Gav nodded. "It's good to meet you."

"If there's anything you want—or need—to know about the inner working of the computer, Raúl is the one to ask. He knows anything and everything about these machines. I've called on him more than once." Smiling, Brother Thomas patted the Macintosh.

Raúl's gaze drifted to the screen again. This time when he shifted his attention back to Gav, his knowing expression confirmed he'd seen and somehow understood the content of the e-mail post.

"Actually, maybe we can visit—exchange information about our studies—another time." Gav turned and flipped off the Mac. "Perhaps we can meet here again. Soon. I'm very sorry, I have an appointment."

Raul nodded. "Yes, of course. I understand."

Gav glanced at his watch. "I really need to be going." With a hurried good-bye to both men, he made a quick exit.

As he hurried down the steps, he thought about the e-mail, attempting to recall exactly which paragraphs had been on the screen when Raúl Chávez so rudely read the post. The post had contained the names of Marta and Alfredo, and a quick mention of the latest letter from Salamanca about their children. That was all. And perhaps even those key paragraphs had remained hidden from sight.

He breathed easier as he turned the corner and headed for the cathedral, trying to brush away his growing uneasiness.

He shook his head slowly. He needed to quit thinking like a lawman all the time. Raúl Chávez was young, a computer geek who'd probably spent too much time in cyberspace instead of learning social graces. Such as not reading over someone's shoulder without being invited. Especially not reading someone's private mail.

He was still considering the young man's behavior when he

saw the welcome figure of Duncan MacGowan on the cathedral steps.

Even from a distance, the pastor's grin and friendly wave were a balm to Gav's troubled spirits.

Sixteen

As soon as Danita arrived at the suite, she was ushered into Julian's office. He dismissed his personal assistants, and they were left alone. She sat across from him and met his stare without flinching as he steepled his hands on his desk.

The morning sun through the window beside him revealed crags and lines in his face that she hadn't noticed before. Instead of angry, he looked tired, haggard, and strangely disappointed.

How long had it been since he'd slept? No matter the man's cold treatment of others, no matter his dogged pursuit of those who opposed him, she still remembered the young man who had befriended her, had been her protector—and Raúl's—when they were children.

"What have you discovered?" His bloodshot gaze refused to release hers.

Perspiration pearled on her upper lip. She had known the

question was coming, and during the short drive from the Jesuit College she'd practiced how she would answer. She measured his expression. How much did he know?

"Your assignment was clear. You were to report your findings back to Arabella."

"And she thinks I am withholding information?" She slid into an indignant tone, tilting her chin upward, hoping the tiny beads of perspiration wouldn't give away her nervousness. "She is not pleased with the way I am handling the assignment?"

"She feels you are not being candid with your findings, yes."

Danita gave him a short laugh. "She is an overzealous new grandmother." She laughed again, then leaned forward, looking into his eyes, still smiling.

The courses in psychological warfare she'd barely heard at the Picos camps came back to her now. Direct confrontation. Unblinking stares. Womanly wiles. Sometimes soft, sometimes tough. She'd never thought she would have to use the training—especially not on Julian.

"I do not like this woman, Julian. I admit I do not want to report every detail of my findings to her. I have always reported directly to you. I liked it that way."

His expression softened. She'd made the point she'd intended. Now to solidify it. "She is determined to make me into the sixteen-year-old girl *she* once was. A starry-eyed rebel with a cause. She wants to teach me the art of spying." She shook her head slowly. "Turn me into a female version of James Bond."

He didn't smile this time. "You do not like Arabella Stern?"

"She claims to be my grandmother, but I have seen no proof."

"You did not answer me. Besides, your words and your expression tell me you do not trust something. What? That I researched her claim?"

He was on the defensive, good. "It has occurred to me that

the Sterns are donors to Tres Equis. I have to wonder if she paid for the research you did."

Julian wasn't amused. "You are suggesting that she bought the relationship? Those are serious charges—"

"I am not accusing you. Your assistants were probably given this task. If a mistake was made, it is likely due to their errors, not yours. I simply want to see what they discovered. Is that too much to ask? My history has always been a mystery. You of all people know how Raúl and I were shuffled from family to family, always longing for roots, longing for someone to love us. Not someone who simply cared for us—outwardly—out of loyalty to Franco."

He leaned back in his chair, studying her.

She cleared her throat. "There's something else."

"Go on." He lifted a brow.

"You said that Raúl is not my real brother, that we were adopted from separate families."

"Yes."

"I remember being brought to our first family together. I don't remember much before that. My memory is hazy. But I do remember him as a baby."

"You were too young to know whether he was always with you."

"Still, I know he was always a part of my life."

Julian stood and walked to the window, looking down at the street below. He didn't turn to face her when he spoke. "Do you think I wanted to hurt you with this news, Dani?"

She remained silent.

He lifted a file folder and slapped it onto the gleaming surface of the desk. "This will answer your questions. Take it with you. Read it thoroughly. Believe me, you will be as convinced as I am."

Then he turned and walked over to her, leaned back against the edge of his desk, and crossed his long legs at the ankles. He was such a handsome man. As leader of the new Spain, he would provide an image his people could be proud of. Another young and handsome Tony Blair. Charismatic. Charming. And with a passion for Tres Equis.

Oh yes, far better than Tony Blair.

"It is important to me to know your feelings."

She glanced up, surprised by the tenderness in his voice.

The earlier twisted look at the corners of his mouth had disappeared. "Dani, I want you by my side…when all this is finished."

She caught her breath and let a moment of stunned silence pass before answering. "By…your side?" Lately she had glimpsed Julian's dark side; it had frightened her. But now, looking into his face, seeing his tender expression, she was moved. And she saw the side of him that drew her, and others, to him.

She drew in a deep breath. "Julian…I don't know what to say."

He stepped closer and reached for her hand, pulling her to her feet. Then he crooked a finger under her chin and lifted her face. "I need you, Dani."

She swallowed hard and managed a feeble answer. "You do?"

He regarded her for a moment, a hint of a smile curling his lips. "I need to know your allegiance to me. To Tres Equis."

"I—I thought you meant something else." She felt a blush warm her face as her childish daydreams burst like a bubble in her mind.

But his smile widened, and, stepping closer, he moved his hands to either side of her face. "Such as?"

She flinched and retreated a step. "You said you want me by your side when…when Spain falls into your hands."

"Yes."

She held her breath, wondering if he might kiss her. He looked at her mouth, then let his deep gaze slide back to her eyes.

"Do you mean—?" *As your wife?* She bit her bottom lip to keep from saying the words.

He laughed, seeming to read her thoughts. "Maybe I need to test your loyalties, Dani. Maybe that's all I mean." He let his hands drop from her face.

Disappointment flooded through her. How long she had dreamed of hearing those words! *I need you, Dani. I love you.* Impulsively, she caught his hand and brought it to her lips, kissed his palm, willing him to go on.

"Tell me," he said after a moment, "what you have observed during the past two days. I sense that Arabella is right about you. That perhaps you are having second thoughts about the Americans, about the danger in which they have placed our movement. You once said that the American woman is innocent. It strikes me that you are acting as her judge. That you are not allowing Tres Equis—or me—to give judgment on this matter."

Unable to look into his eyes, she moved a few steps away from him, toward the window. But Julian reached out, grabbed her arm, and spun her around to face him.

"I need to look into your eyes, Dani. I need to know you are not lying."

"You're hurting me, Julian." He didn't loosen his grasp, and quick tears filled her eyes. "Please!"

She backed away from him. If ever she'd needed what she learned at the Picos camps, it was now.

Gav clasped Duncan's hand and shook it vigorously. Then the pastor gave him a bear hug, pounding him on the back before releasing him and looking into his face with a wide grin.

"You look fit for all you've been through." The words rolled off his tongue in a thick Scottish brogue.

Gav didn't think the world contained a more beautiful music than the sound of a friend's voice in a foreign land. Above them the sun hung bright in a cloudless sky, and from the towers of the cathedral and university, storks in their massive nests gazed down upon the tourists and processions with their usual perplexed expressions.

Gav told Duncan everything.

After a time, almost without conscious decision, they began to slowly walk down the Rúa Mayor toward the *Río Tormé*. They reached an overlook, then headed down the crumbling stone stairway leading to the Roman bridge.

Once out of the medieval part of the city, Gav breathed easier. He doubted that anyone would search for him on this ancient chariot route, now a picturesque footpath for tourists.

"I know something is planned for this week. Something of major consequence. Possibly an uprising, perhaps a student revolution." Gav shook his head slowly as they walked. "It has to do with Tres Equis, obviously, and my research was getting too close for comfort."

Duncan glanced over at him. "Of consequence enough to cause a kidnapping. It strikes me that they could have come after you. But they didn't. They took K.C. instead."

"And if, as K.C. says, they knew about my research in the U.S., why didn't they simply stop us from coming here in the first place?"

They stepped onto the stone bridge and stopped to lean against the thick wall. The Tormé pooled into a lake beneath the massive arches, then continued into a series of shallow waterfalls. A breeze murmured through a stand of birch trees, and the tall spring grasses near the water's edge swayed gracefully.

Duncan laughed. "Ah, my lad. I've a feeling they thought you'd scare off once you were here. It seems to me they're a wily bunch. They were betting you'd both shake in your boots with each new threat." He paused, his eyes narrowed in thought. "Have you told K.C. to stay put? I don't think they would bother a woman sheltered in a convent. But on the other hand, they've proved themselves ruthless once, and they might prove themselves worse in the future."

Gav leaned against the stone wall, propping himself with his elbows, and nodded slowly. "I'll tell her. But knowing Kace, her curiosity and strong will, it might not be such an easy assignment."

Duncan looked out across the river, sparkling in the morning sun. "You mentioned the threats against your life, and hers."

"Yes."

Duncan turned to him again, his blue eyes startling in their intensity. "It also seems to me that time is running out. We've both concluded that this is the week they didn't want you here."

They watched the river for a moment. "I think we should pray," Duncan said. "Let's turn this over to God. Ask for his guidance." Then he lifted his voice heavenward, his baritone brogue lowered in reverence as he addressed their heavenly Father.

A great peace washed over Gav as he listened to the music of Duncan's voice speaking to his closest Friend.

Leaning over the counter in the convent's kitchen, K.C. pounded the bread dough, turned it, and pressed her palms into the warm lump for what surely was the hundredth time.

Sister Calandria grinned at her."You have flour on your nose, child."

K.C. sighed and lifted the corner of her apron to wipe the spot. "Do you think this is about ready?" She gave the lump a tentative poke. Small, sticky globs clung to her finger.

"Yesterday's loaf fell like a stone. When I said count to one hundred, I believe you counted by fives or tens instead of ones." Though she frowned, the nun's eyes sparkled. "Keep going, child. This time *I* will determine when your loaf is ready to rise."

K.C. had asked the Mother Superior if she could help wherever she was needed, thinking they could surely welcome her talents in the gift shop. She had even suggested writing a new brochure or booklet about the life of Teresa of Ávila.

Instead, with what K.C. thought surely was a mischievous sparkle in her eye, Mother Superior had assigned K.C. to the kitchen. She smiled as she let K.C. know that in addition to cooking, she would have the privilege of scrubbing the courtyard walkway and marble gallery floors and columns, just as all the sisters did. Kitchen duty in the morning, cleaning and scrubbing in the afternoon.

The only problem was that K.C. had always been a disaster in the kitchen. It wasn't her gift or her calling, she always joked to Gav. And now here she was, pounding loaves of bread and grinding wheat flour before daybreak.

She sighed and continued kneading the warm lump, mindful of Sister Calandria's delighted grin…and God's sense of humor. She had to wonder if Gav had been praying for her to become acquainted with a kitchen before their marriage.

All this wouldn't have been so bad if her first efforts the day before hadn't brought tittering among the sisters as they attempted to *break* bread at suppertime. Truly, they needed hammers to break the loaves they'd been served.

Sister Calandria came over and tested the dough for elasticity. With a small sigh, she sprinkled a bit more flour on the cloth, turned the lumpy loaf, and smoothed the top.

K.C. had just stuck her fists into the lump again when Sister Josefina stepped to the kitchen doorway. The older nun bit her lip, barely stifling a smile as her gaze took in K.C.'s messy work area and the sifting of flour that covered her apron, the floor, and, most surely, her face.

Lifting the corner of her apron, K.C. dabbed at her nose again.

"It is on your cheek," Sister Calandria said.

"And your shin." Sister Josefina's English wasn't as easily understood as Sister Calandria's. She had to repeat her words twice. "Your shin," she said as she tapped her chin.

The two seemed to be valiantly trying not to exchange glances. Finally, Sister Josefina cleared her throat. "You have, how you say? Visitor, yes? *En el jardín.* Garden, yes?"

K.C. reached to untie her apron, then stopped, looking at Sister Calandria.

"Go ahead, child. I'll finish the bread." She didn't seem sorry to take over the kneading. When K.C. looked uncertain, she repeated, "Go," and shooed her with her hands.

K.C. followed the sister from the kitchen, through the dining room, and out the side door leading into the lower gallery and courtyard. She expected Gav, maybe Duncan with him, and stopped with a small gasp when her visitor turned toward her.

It was Danita, her faced streaked with tears, her hair mussed, her clothing disheveled. "K.C...." she whispered.

K.C. ran to her, reaching for the girl's hands. "What has happened?"

Danita lifted her red-rimmed eyes. "I—I cannot go on," she managed. "Julian..." Her voice faltered, and she gulped before starting again. "I did not know where else to come." She buried her face in her hands, and K.C. slipped her arm around the younger woman's shoulders.

She led Danita toward the fountain, where they seated themselves on a stone bench. She fished a tissue out of her pocket. The young woman took it gratefully, blew her nose, then took a deep breath and closed her eyes.

"Tell me what happened. Are you hurt?"

The girl shook her head. "No." When she opened her eyes, K.C. could see pain and confusion in their chocolate depths.

"Who is Julian?"

Danita swallowed hard, as if tying to decide how much to say. "He is our leader. The head of Tres Equis."

"And what did he do to you?"

"I was sent to watch you, to watch for Elliot Gavin. He was expected to make contact with you. And he did. I saw him here last night."

"And you were to report back if he did." K.C. briefly considered whether she could trust Danita. It occurred to her that this visit might be a ploy to find out if indeed Gav was in Salamanca.

She nodded. "Yes. That was my assignment."

Oh, Lord, help me here. I don't know whether she's telling me the truth. I want to trust her, but am I being foolish? Our lives may depend on Gav remaining hidden. How much should I say?

She waited for Danita to go on. The young woman seemed

to be struggling with what to say.

K.C. laid her hand over Danita's. "You can trust me, Dani. You can tell me what happened."

The girl's eyes filled once more, and she bit her trembling lower lip to keep from crying. She stared straight ahead at the fountain as she began to speak.

"Long ago my brother and I were orphaned and brought to Madrid to live with a foster family. This family was cold toward us, and later—when we were older—we figured out that they took us in only because they wanted to stay in Franco's good graces. Another family was part of Franco's inner circle. The Hernandos. They had a son, Julian. He was probably eighteen or nineteen years then. That's how we came to know him."

"How old were you?"

She drew in a shaky breath. "When we first came to the family, I was three years. Though I heard later that no one knew my exact birthday. I could have been four years old."

"And your brother?"

"Raúl was little more than a baby. Barely walking. I remember him holding one of my fingers for support while he teetered across the floor. He might have been somewhere between one and two." She blew her nose again. "Probably two."

"What happened to your parents, your real parents?"

"They were killed in an auto crash."

"Do you know that for certain?"

Danita's expression changed as she considered the question. "We were told what happened, I suppose. I don't remember the actual words, but neither do I remember a time I did not know it to be the truth." Then she turned her dark-eyed gaze on K.C. "Why do you ask these questions?"

"Because I care." K.C. patted Danita's hand. "Tell me what

you were going to say about Julian Hernando."

Danita drew in a deep breath, seeming to gather her courage. "All right. He became our only friend in this cold family, in this strange cold world. He seemed to take great delight in bringing us little presents. Sometimes even taking us places. To a cartoon show. Or to the corner grocer's for ice cream."

She wiped at her eyes again. "Even after we were passed to another of Franco's inner circle families a few years later, he visited us often. He was at university then and really hadn't the time for two lost children." She laughed lightly. "Not lost literally. But still lost in the cold presence of a family that ignored us."

"I'm so sorry for what you had to go through." K.C.'s heart pounded, and she had to fight to keep herself from pulling the girl into her arms. Danita had to be María Aznar! There could be no doubt!

But what if she was wrong? What if she raised the girl's hopes, only to have them dashed? Dani had endured enough heartache for a lifetime. K.C. didn't want to add more.

And what about the letter to the Aznars, alluding to their daughter being in danger? Who had sent it? Could it be someone close to her, worried about her? Julian Hernando, perhaps? Or her brother? Julian had been her champion. But the girl's brother might have uncovered information about their birth parents, facts that Dani obviously didn't know. The question was, why would he have kept the information from her?

Danita was staring at the fountain, lost in her own thoughts, her eyes once again brimming with tears. Without prompting, she began to speak again, her voice dropping to a monotone. "When Julian went away to university, he joined Tres Equis, a group, or brotherhood, believing in the supremacy of..." her voice faltered, and she flushed slightly, "...of certain peoples."

"Similar to an Aryan brotherhood?"

Danita cringed, a deep flush crossing her face like a shadow. "It was a group sanctioned by Franco's people. Along with the other brotherhoods he encouraged. We never knew if Franco himself was part of it, but those around him were. When he died and King Juan Carlos took over, he decreed that all such groups be disbanded. Not outlawed, necessarily, but it was understood that membership in such a group could cause problems."

"So Tres Equis went underground."

"Yes. And those who'd been part of the Franco regime became the leaders."

"Julian was one of those? He seems young to have been given that kind of responsibility."

"He was chosen to be groomed by those more experienced. For ten years he trained, not only in this country, but also in South America. Trained in survival tactics, warfare, paramilitary action, weapons, revolution. Nothing was left out of his education."

K.C. caught Danita's gaze and held it. "Then what?"

"He returned to Spain and began to gather all the old guard, those who had quietly moved to the suburbs, but who still had passion in their hearts for Franco. When it became known that Julian had been chosen as heir to the dictatorship, they rallied behind him."

K.C. fought the quaking that had begun inside her. This could only mean one thing: revolution. Standing, she moved to the fountain, then turned to face Danita. For a moment she didn't speak, she just studied the girl's face. "So Julian spent the past years gathering supporters and—what else, Dani?"

"Training them and new recruits in camps at a place called Picos de Europa."

"How many?"

"Hundreds. They became the elite of the elite. Highly skilled at weaponry. And guerrilla tactics. Even high-tech computer sabotage." She drew herself up with a strange sense of embarrassed pride. "I went through the camps myself. I and my brother."

"So it was Julian who brought you in." It was a statement, not a question.

Danita's laugh was filled with irony. "Yes, but he's been disappointed in us. We haven't taken to the training with quite the enthusiasm he expected. I enjoyed the marksmanship training as a sport only, refusing to aim for human shaped targets." She smiled. "But I could hit a Coke can tossed in the air every time."

"What happened today? I mean, you named Julian when you first arrived here."

"He made threats. It was as if he did not even know me. As if he had never cared for me. He did not believe I had given a full report." Her voice broke, and for a moment she couldn't go on. "He roughed me up, shook me, and slammed me against a wall."

K.C. recognized the look of love's utter disappointment etched into fresh lines on Danita's face. Her feminine instincts told her what had happened to Dani's heart, why the young woman couldn't turn against her one-time protector completely.

"He has given me one more chance to redeem myself." Her lower lip trembled, and she fought to maintain control. Her dark eyes met K.C.'s. "I am to find your Elliot Gavin and turn him in. I have six hours to give a full report."

K.C. glanced at her watch, praying silently for Gav to stay away from the convent. "I see." She changed the subject. "And your brother? What was his training?"

"Computers. He took to it as if he had been born with a

motherboard instead of a heart." Dani's smile returned. "That is not quite correct. Actually, he has a warm and caring heart." She laughed lightly. "He was not made for revolution either."

"Why are you disillusioned now, Dani? After your training, your obvious affection for Julian Hernando, why do you seek me out and tell me your story?"

"Tres Equis—Julian actually—has been our family. They brought us in, paid for a university education for both Raúl and me. All of the people who are part of this care for us. I trained at the camps and I have known what Holy Week in this new millennium means for Spain. I have known what I was training for—" she tapped her forehead—"up here, but not down here." She placed her hand on her heart.

Her face tilted downward, and she glanced up at K.C. "I went along with the plan to stop you and your sheriff from discovering Tres Equis's true motives. I saw the plan on paper. Two people who would be stopped with gradually escalating pressure. First the kidnapping. If that didn't stop you..."

A look of tired sadness shadowed her face. "If those measures didn't stop you, then the next steps were in place. Doc's threats would become reality."

K.C. waited, her heart pounding. This girl could still betray them. Doc's threats would be carried out, swiftly, decisively. But there was something about Danita's face that told her the young woman had indeed had a change of heart. She thought now she understood why.

"Meeting me, the flesh-and-blood person behind the name on paper, when I was a captive at Valley of the Dead...is that what made a difference?"

Danita sighed. "Yes. We are not much different, in age, in caring about life and living. You had harmed no one. Neither had your Elliot Gavin. You love each other. You were taken from him on the eve of your wedding." She shook her head slowly. "I am so sorry."

K.C. sat down beside her on the stone bench and let out a long, deep breath. "You need to tell me what's planned this week. We need to stop it."

Danita shook her head. "No. I cannot go that far. I cannot. These are my friends. Julian…all he has been to me. To my brother. How can I turn against him?"

"But you've just said you can no longer go along with what they have planned. And he was abusive to you, Dani."

"I cannot turn them in."

"Then why did you tell me? Don't you know that I will go to the authorities? You've even given me Julian's name."

There was a bolder look in Danita's eyes as she met K.C.'s gaze. "I did not give you specifics. You do not know what we have planned. Or when. I doubt that you would be believed."

K.C. let a few moments pass, shooting a quick, silent prayer heavenward before she spoke again. "Is there something else, Dani?"

This time Danita stood and moved to the fountain, trailing her fingers in the water for a moment. Then she turned back to K.C. "I told you that I was sent to watch for your Elliot Gavin."

"Yes." K.C. kept her face passive, not wanting to give away Gav's visit the night before. "You told me."

"I saw him here."

K.C. didn't acknowledge her statement as true or untrue.

"I followed him to his pensión. I left for the night, then returned this morning at dawn, to see him rise and come out to the street. I followed him to the Jesuit College."

"Go on."

"There, he spoke to me, asked why I was following. I ran from him—only to find Julian's car awaiting me at the curb. I was brought before Julian and accused of everything from disrespecting my grandmother to undermining the revolution."

"Your…grandmother?"

Danita's lips tightened into a straight line. "A woman who *claims* to be my grandmother. But I have seen the proof and know that it is true."

K.C.'s hopes fell. If Danita had a grandmother, she wasn't related to the Aznars after all. "Who is she? Why didn't she claim this before now, before you were passed around from house to house, parent to parent?"

"It was her daughter, my mother, who was killed in the auto wreck. My grandmother had given her away as an infant years before. She didn't know about me until recently."

"You don't seem too happy about finding a blood relative."

"I think we are enough alike for you to understand when you know her identity." She paused. "My grandmother's name is Arabella Stern."

K.C. nearly slid off the stone bench. *"Arabella Stern?"*

Danita laughed—a short, hurt sound. "Of all the women in the world I would have chosen to be related to, she would be at the bottom of the list." She looked heavenward, biting her lip as tears again filled her eyes. "The greatest disappointment, though, is finding that Raúl is not my brother by blood."

"But you've referred to him as such…just a few minutes ago."

Her voice was soft when she spoke again. "I will always consider him my brother, blood or not."

K.C. was fighting her disappointment about Danita not belonging to the Aznars when Sister Josefina appeared, seeming to float along the gravel path.

When she reached them, she raised a brow and let out a pointedly disapproving sigh. "You have two more visitors,

Señorita Keegan. Male visitors." She tightened her lips into the shape of a withered rosebud and floated along the path to the opposite side of the courtyard.

K.C. and Danita glanced at each other, then turned as Gav and Duncan made their way down the long gallery and stepped onto the stone path leading to the fountain.

SEVENTEEN

K.C.'S HEART FELL AS GAV AND DUNCAN MOVED NEARER. SHE STILL didn't know whether Danita could be trusted, whether she would turn them in. The confused young woman herself probably didn't know for certain which direction she would go.

Danita had been on K.C.'s heart since they met. The only thing K.C. knew for certain was that God had placed the young woman in her path. For a reason. This was the time to step out in blind faith.

She had asked God to keep Gav from coming to the convent, yet here he was. Vulnerable. They both were. All in God's timing. Nonetheless, her heart pounded wildly.

Gav gave K.C. a quick hug, then turned to Danita. "It's good to see you again." He smiled gently.

Then he introduced Duncan, who, after greeting Danita with a kiss on each cheek, kissed K.C.'s as well, and squeezed her hand warmly. "You have no idea how glad I am to see you."

"Thank you, Duncan." Thoughts of the last time they'd been together whirled through her mind. It had been the day he'd prayed for their coming marriage in the gardens of the Alhambra. Then she'd been driven away, out of their lives...at least temporarily.

"Are you all right?" Duncan's concern showed in his eyes.

She grinned, glancing at Gav. "The sisters are taking good care of me. I'm even learning to bake bread." She laughed. "You don't want to hear what happened to my first attempt."

K.C. and Danita sat down again on the bench, and Gav and Duncan half-sat and half-leaned against the wide stone wall that circled the fountain. The midday sun was now high, and because the courtyard was sheltered from any wind, it seemed abnormally warm for spring.

Behind them, Sister Josefina, on hands and knees, scrubbed the gallery's marble floor with a brush and a pungent pine cleaner. She kept the foursome in sight as she moved along the floor, and her brush scratched a staccato counterpoint to their voices.

K.C. began, after asking Danita if it was all right to do so, by telling Duncan and Gav about Danita's and her brother's roles in Tres Equis. Danita broke in from time to time, explaining or clarifying. Finally, K.C. asked Danita to tell the rest, hoping that the young woman would get into more detail about the group's plans for Holy Week.

But Danita told the men no more than she had already divulged.

More than once as the group talked, Gav met K.C.'s gaze, and she could see he was as puzzled as she about Danita's motives, about whether or not to trust her.

After several minutes, Duncan leaned forward and fixed his blue eyes on Danita's face. "I think God led you to us. And that he is continuing to draw you to us and away from Tres Equis."

K.C. smiled at Gav. Leave it to Duncan to get right to the point.

Danita shifted on the bench. "What do you mean?"

"Has K.C. told you about the Aznars?"

K.C. groaned inside and lightly touched Duncan on the arm. "Maybe we should wait to tell Danita about them." Ignoring his surprised look, she hurried on. "We haven't told you yet about Dani's grandmother—"

Danita looked puzzled. "Wait, please. I do not want to talk about my grandmother. What about the Aznars? Who are they?"

K.C. hesitated, then after exchanging another glance with both Duncan and Gav, chose her words carefully. "Dani, we have information about a couple looking for their daughter and son. The children were taken from them twenty-five years ago."

The color drained from Danita's face. "And you think my brother and I…?" Her voice caught, and she brought a trembling hand to her face.

K.C. nodded slowly. "It doesn't matter about that now, Dani. You just told me about your grandmother finding you and that Raúl isn't really your brother—by blood, I mean. I wanted to spare you the pain of another disappointment."

But Danita had already recovered her composure. She leaned forward, her gaze intent on K.C.'s face. "Please tell me."

"Duncan knows the family. Maybe he should be the one to tell you their story." She glanced at him, and he gave her a nod of affirmation. Then she stood so he could sit next to the young woman. He let out a deep sigh as he moved toward the bench and settled onto it. Running the fingers of both hands through his sandy hair, his eyes closed for a few seconds, almost as if in prayer. Then he began.

For a half hour he talked, his Scottish brogue musical in his earnestness. Behind them, Sister Josefina continued her scrubbing, just a few feet from where she'd begun.

When Duncan had finished, he held Danita's gaze. "Tell me, child, have you examined the legal documentation supporting your grandmother's claim?"

"I have. The papers are in order, official government seals on each. Blood types. Birth certificates. Everything." She frowned in thought, falling silent for a moment. "Are there pictures of the children—the Aznar children?"

Duncan shook his head. "No. The Aznars lost all personal effects when they were arrested. They have nothing but memories."

"What were the children's names?"

"María and José."

"And ages?"

"Three and two. María is the elder."

Danita let out a pent-up breath. "I had hoped I might recognize the names." She shrugged one shoulder. "But there is nothing. No memories. Nothing."

Duncan took her hand. "Don't give up hope, child. God is your Father. He is watching over you." His face softened. "Every day, perhaps even this hour, Marta Aznar prays for her lost daughter and son. She knows they aren't lost to God, that their heavenly Father is with them even now. That he has been through the years."

She stared at him, her lower lip trembling. "Oh, how I wish that lost child could be me," she whispered.

"You aren't lost to God," Duncan said.

Her eyes again shimmered with tears. "Sometimes I feel there is a place inside me so empty that it never can be filled. I was robbed of something precious when I lost my parents. A mother's love. A chance to be the treasured little girl of a doting papá. The chance to know my mother and father as an adult."

"God can be a father to you. A papá."

Danita looked up at K.C., giving her a slight nod. K.C. had said as much earlier.

Duncan went on. "He loves you. There's never been a moment that you've been out of his thoughts. Your name is engraved on his hand. You have never been lost to him."

Danita watched his face intently as he spoke. "If he loves me with this kind of intensity, why did he let this happen, let my parents die?"

"I don't have the answer. Maybe none of us ever will. But I do know that no matter what's happened to you—the tragic and the good—through all of it, he's been with you. Maybe all this happened so that you might come to know how precious you are to him. Beloved enough for him to sacrifice his own Son for you—as if you were the only one in the world to love."

Danita seemed to be considering his words. Finally, she nodded. "There have been times that I felt a presence. I used to daydream that it was an angel my mother sent from heaven to watch over me."

Duncan didn't answer right away, and K.C. and Gav waited. Only the music of the fountain and the scratch of the scrub-brush were heard. Finally, he said, "I can't tell you much about angels and their presence. I can tell you, though, that our Lord is with you every moment of your days."

Suddenly, Danita shrugged and stood up. "I do not know about all this. All I know is that I have learned to count on myself alone. I need no one else. I have had no one else to help me—help Raúl and me—through these years. Only me." She raised her chin, but her eyes were sad. "If God has been with me, perhaps it is he who taught me to be self-reliant, just to get through life."

When Duncan didn't answer, she added, "I must be going now."

"What will you do?" K.C. stepped toward the younger woman. "You said that Julian is giving you one more chance to prove your loyalty to Tres Equis. He wants you to turn in Gav and me. You know what that will mean."

"Work with us, Dani," Gav said. "Help us stop Tres Equis. People, families, and little children might be killed or hurt if you let the plans continue."

She folded her arms across her chest and met his eyes without flinching. "The people in Tres Equis are my family."

Gav moved to stand beside her. "They might be killed as well, Dani. Think about it. Only you can tell us the plans, the extent of the weaponry, and the abilities of the group members."

K.C. knelt in front of the younger woman and looked into her face imploringly, searching for the lost little girl inside, for the compassion she knew was in her heart. "You told me that while the plan was on paper only, you could go along with it. Then you met me—the person behind the name on the paper—and you had second thoughts about the motives of Tres Equis."

"That is true."

"Think about what Gav just said. About the families who might get caught in the crossfire. They're real people. Not just nameless, faceless crowds."

When she spoke, Danita's voice was little more than a whisper. "I have thought about that."

"Dani," Gav said, "you've been trained in covert tactics, yes?"

"Yes."

"Can you work with us? I mean, go to Julian with just

enough information to keep him from suspecting you. Let him believe he's got your loyalty, just as always?"

She leaned back looking from one to the other as if searching each of their faces for an answer, then nodded slowly. "You want me to work for you. Play the part of a double agent."

"Work *with* us," Gav said gently. "Do the right thing by bringing this operation to justice. Save innocent lives."

She stood and walked to the fountain, her back to them. She stared into the spilling water.

K.C. moved to stand beside Danita, and after a moment, circled her arm around her waist. "We'll be with you every step of the way."

"You'll have to play a dangerous role." Duncan stepped to Danita's other side. "Pretending to be loyal while finding out everything you can, the names of those involved, from the highest government official to the person supplying weapons."

Danita turned and leaned against the fountain wall. "There really has been no question about what I needed to do. I have known for a long time. Carrying it out is another matter." She let out a deep breath as if releasing her fears—her future—into their hands.

Duncan stepped forward, took Danita's hand in one of his, K.C.'s in the other. Gav joined hands with them, and, heads bowed, Duncan entreated God to help them. When he was finished, Danita kept her head down for a few seconds, her shoulders trembling.

When she looked up, K.C.'s heart went out to her. Never had she seen such desperate longing in anyone's face.

Julian was just stepping into his chauffeur-driven car when Danita arrived at his townhouse.

His face was an expressionless mask as she approached the car. When they had parted earlier this morning, he'd been angry, so angry she'd feared he might take action against her before she could leave his presence.

Now he waited at the car door, eyes piercing and cold, shoulders squared and stiff.

"We need to talk," she said quickly before she lost her nerve.

He nodded. "Get in."

She complied, sliding onto the luxurious leather seat. He got in beside her, and the chauffeur closed the door. After raising the glass privacy partition between the driver's and passengers' seat, Julian turned to her as the car pulled smoothly away from the curb. "You have something to report?"

"First, I want to apologize for the childish way I have been behaving."

His expression softened, and he reached for her hand.

"When you questioned my motives this morning," she said, "I was hurt. You have always believed me, trusted me."

"That I have, Dani." He raised her hand and kissed her palm. "That is why your actions recently have puzzled me. I have given you opportunities other young women only dream of."

"I know that, Julian." Her voice was soft.

"Before you go on with your report about the Americans, there is something I have wanted to say to you for some time." His voice was husky, and the expression on his handsome face was the same she'd seen in her daydreams. Her heart pounded as he kissed her fingertips, then laid her hand against his jaw, covering it with his hand.

"What is it?"

"I want you with me when I at last take my rightful place.

You have heard me say this before, but you need to hear it now, again."

Her breath caught. "You need to be clear about your meaning." This time there could be no mistake. "Are you talking about marriage?"

His face broke into a devilish grin. So boyish. So lovable. The Julian of her dreams. "Are you proposing to me, my little Dani?"

Her cheeks warmed with a blush. "I just want to know your intentions."

He circled his arm around her shoulders and bent over her, kissing her as she had never been kissed before. When he moved away, she almost forgot to breathe. Eyes closed, she waited several heartbeats to compose herself. How many years she had waited for this moment. This exact moment.

"That, my sweet Dani," he said, his voice low and hoarse, his lips close to her ear, "should tell you a lot about my intentions." And he kissed her thoroughly again.

Pulling back slightly, she looked up at him. "But are your intentions honorable?"

He threw back his head and laughed out loud. "Oh, my dear, dear, sweet child." He placed his fingertips under her chin, and tilted her face toward his. "I want to marry you. And I will not take no for an answer."

She stared at him, her mind a dark whirl of confusion. This man, the same who had occupied her daydreams, her dreams of love and family, for years, was offering her what she'd always wanted. Someone to call her own. He was her childhood champion. The only one who'd seemed to care.

The one she was about to betray.

She let out a shuddering breath.

He was watching her intently. "Something tells me you are not pleased—though your kiss would tell me otherwise."

She moved away from him. "I need time to think about it." For a moment she fixed her gaze on the passing traffic, then looked back to him, her resolve strengthening.

"I told you I will not take no for an answer." He narrowed his gaze suspiciously, and she saw her mistake.

Reaching for his hand, she brought it to her lips and kissed his fingers. "Darling Julian, I have dreamed of this moment. But think about what we have ahead of us this week. That is why I hesitate. Should we not wait until all this is over?"

He laughed again. "I did not mean we would plan a wedding before Friday."

"Of course not."

"But consider yourself mine, my little Dani, from this moment on." He held her gaze with his, almost as if searching for something within her soul. "The marriage can wait. But our betrothal cannot."

She nodded. "It cannot."

"Now, tell me what you have discovered about our American friends."

Danita took a deep breath. Outside the car window, the medieval cityscape changed to rural landscape. They had crossed the river and were now heading toward the flat plains outside Salamanca. "I have spoken with the woman twice."

"She is still in the convent?" He moved closer, his eyes intent on hers.

"Yes. Though once I followed her as she headed toward the river, showed her the Museum of Antiquities, as Arabella instructed."

"Yes, Arabella has already given me a report about that visit. I take it the visit was not successful."

She ignored the comment. "Today I met with Señorita Keegan at the convent."

"Did you find out if Elliot Gavin has arrived in Salamanca?"

She felt perspiration bead on her upper lip and for a second considered her training at the camps. She did not want to lie, but knew there was no other way. Not if she was to save K.C. and Elliot Gavin's lives.

Smiling, she looked him straight in the eye. "There have been no reports that he is in Salamanca."

"Did you ask her if he is here?"

"Do you think she would tell me?"

The car slowed to turn onto a dirt road. Julian looked out the window, his jaw working in annoyance. "I thought he would have arrived by now. Are you certain?"

"She loves Elliot Gavin. I am certain she will protect him with her life if need be." When he didn't comment, she changed the subject. "Where are we going?"

"This is a command post you have not seen before." He glanced at his watch. "We will be meeting with Raúl and some of the others in his cell. Most should be here by now."

The car rolled to a stop near a tile-roofed, whitewashed farmhouse. It looked deserted except for three other vehicles parked near a fence in back.

Moments later, they were ushered inside. The entire house had been gutted and turned into what appeared to Danita to be a giant computer command post.

It looked sophisticated enough to launch a rocket.

As Danita and Julian stepped into the main room, chairs scraped across the tile floor, and the computer and electronics experts that Raúl had assembled stood to greet them.

Julian held up a hand, and the group sat again in front of their computers, though still turned to face their leader.

Danita slipped into a chair near Raúl.

Julian spoke about their plans, asking questions about the

cell's readiness. Brother Thomas spoke almost reverently in vague terms about the outcome, about the new world that would be theirs at the end of the week.

Danita wondered, as he spoke, what exactly lay in his heart. The Jesuit College was filled with young men bound together by a common religious persuasion. She had always assumed them all to be holy, but now she listened to this man's ramblings, about the call of the ancients, the traditions Tres Equis would uphold.

She couldn't help comparing his talk of the universe's spiritual forces to the personal friend that Duncan MacGowan had spoken about. The God who wanted her to call him Papá. She couldn't judge all the students and workers at the Jesuit College, but this man was as far from God as night was from day.

As Thomas spoke, Julian reached across Raúl's desk and picked up a brass paperweight—a giant cockroach. He stroked its head, almost seeming to caress its antennae with the tips of his fingers. A shiver traveled up Danita's spine.

Brother Thomas finally quit his droning, and a few of the others spoke briefly about their areas' readiness. Raúl then stood and gave a full report of the bug called Chaos—of the computer system's internal timing device—that would set in motion chaos unlike anything the country had seen before. Spain would be cut off from the rest of the world for six hours—just long enough for Tres Equis to take control. The timing device was set for noon on Good Friday, the precise time the paramilitary cell would march in the Holy Week processional.

A deep ache settled into Danita's heart. Good Friday. She hadn't given it much thought. Of course she'd been taught the rudiments of her Catholic faith, both in catechism as a young girl and by simply paying attention as an adult. Churches were filled with statues of the suffering Christ. Perhaps she'd been made unfeeling by their sheer numbers.

But now, for the first tirne ever, she considered a personal God who sent his beloved Son to die for her. Duncan had said that he loved her as if she was the only one in the world to love. Could he have sent his only Son just for her?

Sitting there, in the most unlikely of places, in a farmhouse listening to the droning of men speaking like gods, she felt a stirring deep inside her heart. A sting of tears threatened.

These men were talking about killing others to elevate themselves on the day that commemorated Jesus Christ's death on the cross. They plotted evil and destruction at the precise hour that the sky darkened, thunder rolled, and life ebbed out of her Savior's body.

Her Savior?

K.C.'s words came back to her again, softly whispering as if from some unseen Spirit within her. *He wants you to call him Papá.*

Papá!

The room almost seemed to disappear, and a warmth crept into her heart. Around her, the voices were now a mere hum, and the sense of darkness that earlier seemed to fill the place was now a shimmer of light. Only it was around her like a shield, within her like fire.

God's touch—and she knew that's what it was—happened in the space between heartbeats, or in a suspension of time that could have lasted an eternity. It had nothing to do with her surroundings.

She was in the presence of the almighty God, and it was holy and intimate at the same time. It was as if no one else existed in this moment of time. Only her Lord and Savior and his daughter Dani.

Papá!

Julian was speaking now, and when he mentioned her name, she was pulled back into the small farmhouse, into the presence of those who continued to plot their evil.

"Danita," Julian said, frowning, "are you feeling all right?"

She stared at him for a moment, unable to speak.

"Your face...there is something wrong with it. As if something has come over you. Are you certain you are not ill?"

The others were studying her now. She glanced toward Raúl, who was glaring at her.

She frowned. Why would Raúl look at her like that? "Yes, yes. Of course I am well." Then she looked back to Julian. "I'm sorry I didn't hear what you said. Could you repeat it?"

"I just announced that you have agreed to marry me."

Her heart stopped in dismay. "Oh, Julian—!"

Raúl jumped up, his chair clattering behind him as it fell. With a look that spoke volumes—of alarm, anger, hurt, and betrayal—he hurried from the house. A few minutes later, his car rumbled down the dirt road, a cloud of dust rising behind it.

Julian laughed, a short, harsh sound. "Temperamental scientist. They are all the same." His voicéd turned to ice as he continued. "As a warning for the rest of you, I determine when a meeting has ended, no one else." He stared through the window at the dust still suspended in the air.

The practice processional began at midnight. The members of Tres Equis met near the open-air market by the Plaza Mayor. The funeral sounds of dirges played by drums and trumpeters floated all around them.

Other marchers, dressed in robes of purple and royal blue, red and black, filed slowly, somberly along the rúa. Little children carried crosses; older women walked without shoes, some dragging chains clasped around a bare ankle. Suffering to honor Christ's torturous walk with the cross on his way to death.

Danita donned her black robe and placed the tall, conical hat on her head. She adjusted the face cloth so that she could see through the eye openings. Some of the members had strapped on firearms beneath their robes and wore belts with rounds of ammunition. But Danita refused to wear either. The reality of the plan was almost too much to bear.

This was different than those glory days of talking about the dream of revolution, of infusing Spain with new life through new leadership. Words! It had all begun with words.

And now? She watched the mourners walking by. Their faces were masked by cloth; she couldn't see their expressions or know their feelings. Did any of them feel as she now did? Did they concentrate on their crucified Lord? Or did they march with a brotherhood, a godless group who marched out of habit, or worse…as did Tres Equis?

She fell into formation with the others.

"Danita?"

She turned as Arabella Stern, hat under one arm, headed toward her. Danita groaned silently. She should have donned the headpiece and mask sooner. Her grandmother was the last person she wanted to see, but she nodded toward the woman as she fell into formation beside her.

Arabella gave her a friendly smile. "Did you finish the song you planned to write for us?"

The *saetas.* She had forgotten her promise. "I will have it written by the week's end. The melody, the words, have not yet come to me."

Arabella studied her for a moment. "You have had a lot on

your mind. Julian told me about your betrothal."

Danita drew in a sharp breath. It didn't go unnoticed, even behind the dark veil. Arabella reached for her hand. "Is everything all right, Dani?"

"Yes, of course. Why do you ask?"

"Since our news—I mean, the news of our relationship—you have seemed distant. It's as if you don't want to have anything to do with me."

Danita let go of Arabella's hand and removed her heavy headpiece. For the first time, she considered the older woman's feelings of hurt and longing. She was sorry she'd been so brusque.

She smiled. "I have had a lot on my mind. This week..." She could hardly mention the week without the horror of what might lie ahead washing over her. "This week is difficult. There are things about to happen that I am unsure of. I have not meant to ignore you or to keep myself from being around you. It is just that I am concentrating on my task ahead. I must carry out my duties, those things I feel passionately about."

Arabella would take her meaning to be those things connected with Tres Equis. Just as Danita intended.

"I understand, Dani."

"Thank you."

For a moment neither woman spoke.

"How is it that Julian proposed and you accepted?" Arabella was staring at her with knowing eyes.

Danita held her gaze steady. "I have fancied myself in love with Julian since I was a girl."

"Fancying yourself in love and really loving someone are two very different emotions."

Danita smiled at Arabella's intuitive thoughts. Maybe they were related after all.

"Do you feel you have a choice in the matter?"

"What do you mean?"

"Do you feel you somehow owe him?"

"That is strange for you to say."

Arabella's attention drifted to a passing procession. Danita followed her gaze. This group was dressed in light purple, carrying a float depicting the Last Supper. Then Arabella turned again to Danita. "Now that I've found you, I want to be part of your life. Available to give advice. Or just to listen, if you just need to talk."

"Thank you."

"I hope you will confide in me."

Confide in her? Danita almost laughed at the idea. If Arabella knew Danita's heart, she would run directly to Julian. "I will remember that. Thank you." She placed the hat on her head and adjusted it into place, letting the silken mask drop once more over her face.

Behind them, the drums began their slow beat, the trumpets blasted the low, dark tones of mourning, and slowly Tres Equis began to move toward the plaza to take their place in line.

If she listened carefully, shutting out the drums and trumpeters, Danita could hear the soft thud of weapons as they hit against the bodies of the marchers. A soft, rhythmic beat of death.

She shuddered and renewed her determination to see this senseless game halted.

An hour later, Tres Equis moved into the wide plaza outside the cathedral where they disbanded. Her conical hat and mask still in place, Danita was anonymous to those around her. She spotted Julian and Arabella, hats removed, deep in conversation. She sidled closer.

"Do not let her out of your sight." Julian's words were low and intense.

"I have already begun my vigil," Arabella answered.

Danita knew they were talking about her.

EIGHTEEN

THE NEXT DAY DAWNED BRIGHT AND CLEAR, BUT BY MIDMORNING a brisk wind had kicked up and dark clouds were building on the eastern horizon. Danita hurried down the Rúa Mayor toward the university, holding her coat close against the chill.

Taking the three steps with quick energy, she headed into the main entrance, past reception, and down the long outer corridor leading to the small room where Raúl worked in the computer laboratory.

Brother Thomas looked up from Raúl's normal place behind the computer when she stepped to the door. She was surprised to see him. Though he and Raúl were friends, the man normally didn't venture far from the Jesuit college. His only greeting was a slight tilt of the head.

She wasted no time getting to the point. "Where is my brother?"

"He had some errands to run for Julian. He should be back any minute."

Small talk with Brother Thomas was never easy. He was at best uncomfortable with women, rude at worst.

There was an awkward silence between them, then both began to speak at once. He blushed, then told her to go ahead.

She shifted uncomfortably. "I was about to ask you what you are working on. I would think all preparations have been made. For the Chaos bug, I mean."

He met her gaze with a quizzical look as if expecting her to understand without explanation. "Your brother and I are interested in genealogy. We are working on studies that go back centuries. I thought he had told you."

She smiled, shaking her head slightly. "I did not know that Raúl was interested in such things. Our own family history is..." She let the sentence drop, unwilling to divulge any information, no matter how benign the hearer.

But Brother Thomas had turned again to the computer. "For instance, did you know that Julian's family history can be traced to the Visigoths?"

"That does not surprise me." She pictured hoards of his barbarian ancestors invading Spain. "It doesn't surprise me at all." She *was* surprised, however, at how quickly her romantic vision of Julian was disappearing.

She leaned closer, peering over Brother Thomas's shoulder to get a better look at the screen. He clicked the mouse on a menu of names. It opened with a list of files. "Here is mine," he said proudly. "My family name is Ramírez. We go back to—"

Cutting him off midsentence, she grabbed the mouse and swiftly moved the arrow to the top of the list, to the file name Aznar, Alfredo.

Just then the door opened.

"What do you think you are doing?" Raúl's face was a mask of rage.

She spun around before reading a single word. "Raúl—"

"We have nothing to discuss."

His words were as powerful, as hurtful, as a slap on her face. For a moment she couldn't speak. She just stared at him.

"I have nothing to say to you. And I would prefer it if you would leave us now."

"But Raúl, surely we can talk. I need to tell you something. Something important."

"I have nothing to say to you." He spun and left the room, the door banging after him.

"Raúl, wait!" She started after him, but Brother Thomas called to her, and she turned.

"He thinks you have sold out, you know." The Jesuit brother was still looking at the computer.

"Sold out?" She wondered how he could possibly know her heart, know what she was doing for the Americans.

"Julian."

"Julian?" For a moment, she didn't know what he meant. Then she sank into a nearby chair, and put her head in her hands. Of course. Raúl thought she'd sold out—to Julian. He had warned her about getting pulled into their leader's web. He had feared for her if she did.

Then their sham of an engagement was announced, without warning, without explanation to Raúl.

She would have to find her brother. Make him listen. But she knew him well. He was as stubborn as she.

After a moment she stood and headed again to the computer. "The file on Alfredo Aznar. I want to read it."

"There is no such file."

"I saw it."

He shook his head. "I know the files well. There is nothing by that name."

She looked over his shoulder again, but he had closed the genealogy files. A weather forecast was on the screen. Gray clouds over Salamanca. Animated squiggles of lightning and rain.

She let out an exasperated sigh. "I know what I saw. I opened the file right before Raúl came in."

Brother Thomas shrugged. "You must have imagined it. There is nothing here. See for yourself." He pulled up the original folder and clicked the mouse to open it.

He was right. The name Aznar was missing. Her lips in a straight line, she turned away from him and walked slowly from the room.

She stepped out into the waning sunlight, her emotions in turmoil. The wind was whipping wildly now, and with a small shudder Danita hurried along the Rúa Mayor. She checked her brother's favorite coffeehouse, but he wasn't there. She headed to the library in the House of Shells, raced up the steps, and slammed through the double doors. A quick look through the stacks told her Raúl wasn't hiding from her there.

Once she was back on the street, she stopped, the wind stinging her cheeks, and wondered where she should try next.

If she didn't warn him that she was working with the Americans, he would be in danger. The time was close. Only three days until Tres Equis would strike.

She spun around, looking among the milling students and families awaiting the next procession, due to begin at noon.

Raúl, where are you?

There was so much to tell him, about Arabella's claims, about the Aznars…the possibility that they might have parents who lived and searched for them.

The Aznar file. She stopped still. Why would her brother have that particular file on his computer? If he did know something about them he surely would have told her.

Perhaps it was just a coincidence?

No, it couldn't be. She dismissed the idea as quickly as it entered her mind. That name in his files was no coincidence.

How she needed to talk with him, to plead with him to drop his work with Tres Equis and help her and the Americans stop the deadly Good Friday plans.

Without conscious thought, she breathed a prayer, surprised at how natural it seemed. It was so new, this idea of a God who cared for her as much as a father cares for a treasured child.

She lifted her heart to her newfound Lord. "Father, help me." The words were simple, but she was new at prayer and hoped he understood.

Around her the crowds still hurried by on their way to see the processions, the winds still stung her cheeks and chilled her to the bone, but a tangible presence washed over her, filled her, enveloped her, with a love so precious she could scarcely take in its meaning. It was as if she were alone with someone who loved her completely, a father-love, mother-love, friend-love, all wrapped up together and holding her in an embrace that took her breath away.

Tears trailed down her cheeks, and she stood completely still beside the rúa, barely conscious of the jostles and shoves as people hurried by. "Lord Jesus," she breathed in awe, "no matter what lies ahead, be with me. Never let me be far from your presence."

Fear not, beloved. I have called you by name. You are mine. As a mother comforts her child, so I will comfort you. Forever, my little one. Never will I let you go.

"I do not know where to turn now, what to do."

Give it to me.

"I need to act quickly. Undo my mistakes. So much is at risk. How can it be changed, undone?" Tears again streamed, this time in grief for all she had done in ignorance and pride. In need.

Give it to me, beloved.

She started to walk back toward Tres Equis headquarters, still pondering her choices. The lie was over. No longer could she go along with Julian and Tres Equis, even if it meant endangering Raúl. How she'd wanted to warn him to get out, too, before the authorities swarmed into the headquarters and made their arrests.

It was easy to imagine their swift and deadly action once she told the Americans the details. Without doubt, Sheriff Elliot Gavin—or Gav, as his friends called him—would immediately contact the American ambassador, who would pass along the information to the proper officials.

Give it to me, my child.

Suddenly, she turned and headed to the pensión where Elliot Gavin was registered. At the front desk she asked the receptionist to call Señor Gavin and ask him to meet Danita Chávez in the lobby.

The girl picked up the telephone and dialed the room. After a moment, she shook her head. "I am sorry. There is no answer."

Danita was about to head out the door when Duncan MacGowan and Gav burst in, almost as if with a gust of wind, from the street.

Their expressions were worried, the intensity only lifting slightly as they strode toward her. "We were hoping to find you." Duncan clutched her hand in both of his.

Gav's face reflected his concern. "You look pale. Are you all right?"

"I managed to avoid telling Julian your whereabouts."

Duncan's face lost some of its worry, but deep concern remained in his eyes as he listened.

"I have information for you." Danita watched their faces. "I know the times, the places…even the Chaos bug that is set to disrupt every detail of life in Spain."

Gavin put his hand under her elbow and, with Duncan following, escorted her to the lobby. "Tell us everything," he said as they sat down.

She opened her mouth, then closed it again. She couldn't. Not until she found Raúl and convinced him to get out of Tres Equis…but not before he reprogrammed the computers so the implanted bug could not be unleashed.

Gav tapped his pen against a notepad as he waited. Duncan watched her expectantly, his gaze never leaving her face.

"I am sorry," she finally said. "I have details, times, events, names to name. Everything. And in here—" she touched her chest above her heart—"I am ready to tell you." Then with a heavy sigh, she inclined her head. "But I cannot. The time is not yet right. I will come to you—here—again. Maybe tonight—to tell you all you need to know. Then you can go to your ambassador to ask for help."

The men exchanged glances, the import of her words obvious in their stricken faces. "There is not much time," Gav said. "Please give us something to go on, some way of stopping this."

An image of a handcuffed Raúl came to her mind, her brother being arrested for treason and led away in shame. She had to warn him first. There was no other way. "I cannot tell you anything now."

Duncan seemed to have guessed that some sort of emotional

dilemma whirled inside her. "You must do what you must, child. God will be with you."

"I must go," she said. "But before I leave, I need to tell you about someone I have met." Unable to keep the wonder, the awe, from her voice—or the tears from her eyes—she told them what had happened.

Across the street from the pensión, Arabella watched the shadowy figures sitting in the lobby. She wasn't sure of their identity, other than they were two men and her granddaughter. One appeared to be American, judging from his dreadful Levi's and sweatshirt; she couldn't guess the other's country of origin and identity. But she had no doubt that the American was Elliot Gavin.

Standing in the doorway of the bank, she melted back into a recessed archway, her gaze never leaving the trio, a mere dozen yards away.

Her patience was rewarded several minutes later when the two men accompanied Danita to the door. Her granddaughter looked pale, her face tear stained even from this distance.

The men were obviously tense, shoulders taut even as they gave her granddaughter a quick embrace.

Danita hurried on down the rúa, and, heartsick, Arabella knew what duty called on her to do. She had to report what she'd seen. As soon as the younger woman was out of sight, Arabella hailed a taxicab.

She gave the cabby the address, then settled back into her seat, determined to keep her mind on her obligation to Julian, distasteful as it would be.

Six hours later, she stood with Julian as his bodyguards—one on either side of the blindfolded, bound girl—shoved her into an opaque-windowed sedan. The driver moved the vehicle slowly away from the curb and it soon disappeared from sight.

Julian looked grim, his jaw working as he turned to escort Arabella back into his townhouse. She tried not to think of the sadness in her granddaughter's face when she discovered who had betrayed her.

Instead, Arabella glanced at Julian's handsome profile, thinking how much he reminded her of Miguel Vargas.

Nineteen

The expression on Danita's face when he left her standing in the computer room plagued Raúl for hours.

Now he sat in front of his monitor, unable to let go of the thought that she seemed to have had something she wanted—no, *needed*—to tell him. And he hadn't stayed long enough to hear what it was. He raked his figers through his hair. He had warned her about Julian, and now it seemed she was giving in to her girlhood fantasy.

But, was that all there was to it? This was no make-believe story he and Dani were involved in. It was real life with far-reaching consequences. That's what bothered him. Those consequences.

He had made a mistake in dismissing her without hearing what she had come to tell him. Had she come with a warning? Or to tell him he'd overlooked some detail? Or maybe that he'd upset Julian by running out of the meeting at the farmhouse, and

Julian's anger was about to explode into some sort of retaliation?

He shrugged, then pressed the switch to turn on the computer. What Julian did or didn't do was becoming less significant by the hour.

His attention was diverted by the folder opening on the monitor. In alphabetical order, the Aznar file was back in place at the top of the lists. He clicked on the icon, and the file opened.

He skimmed through those items he had placed in it from Web sites he'd visited over the past three years. It was all coming into focus in his mind, especially since his last letter had been answered by Marta Aznar.

He pulled it from a manila folder by the keyboard, unfolded it, and read.

Dear writer,

I do not know what you hope to gain by your anonymous letters to my husband and me. You have not asked for money—as so many impostors have through the years—so I cannot help but think you are sincerely looking for our lost children. Or perhaps, it would be more appropriate to say, you think you have found my daughter and my son.

You warn against our daughter being in danger because of a group she is involved in, Tres Equis, a medieval brotherhood. If it is my daughter—and that is a very big IF—I cannot help but wonder if you are her brother, or fancy yourself to be. Why else would you care about what happens to this young woman?

You have not given us your name or the name of the woman you say is our daughter. You may or may not know my children's real names. I see no harm in telling you. My daughter, María, would be twenty-eight years old now. She was nearly four when she was taken. My son, José, would be twenty-seven.

We have no legal records of their birth. Our copies, as well as the hospital and government records, have disappeared. Franco's forces took everything from us, as I am sure you must know. Even our treasured family photographs were destroyed. I found only ashes and small segments of the pictures in our fireplace when I returned from questioning after my husband was arrested.

So you see, we have no proof our children ever existed. But they live on in our hearts and will forever.

My husband, Alfredo, sang a song to our little ones each night at bedtime. He composed his own words to a lilting bedtime lullaby written by Schumann, part of the composer's Kinderszenen collection for children. The words went something like this:

Sleep, my child, as angels attend thee.
Sleep in heaven's peace.
Sleep as God himself watches o'er thee.
Sleep in his strong and gentle arms.

Wake, my child, to his rosy dawn.
Wake to his promise of love.
Wake as God himself watches o'er thee.
Wake in his strong and gentle arms.

Neither of us has told anyone about this lullaby. I am not certain why I tell you now. Perhaps it is in the desperate hope that you know my children, or are my son and might recognize the words, or that the Schumann melody might unlock some distant memory. Of course I also run the risk that you might say you do to prove something untrue for your own purposes.

I sense you mean us no harm through your communications. You have said my daughter was in grave danger. I thank you for telling me because, though I already pray for her daily, I will seek God's intervention in her life, in whatever it is she faces.

You will remain in my prayers. If by some miracle you are my son, I welcome you home with arms wide open—with strong and gentle arms of love.

Raúl let out a pent-up breath, just as he did every time he read the missive. He didn't know what Marta Aznar looked like, didn't know anything about her, only that his computer search had matched certain details about when and where she lost her children. The words to some little song meant nothing to him—only that the Aznars' children had been desperately loved. And they jogged nothing in his memory.

If he was the Aznars' son, he'd have been only two at the time of the abduction, much too young to remember anything.

But Dani might.

Dani. He folded the letter and placed it in his pocket. He couldn't put it off any longer. He would go to her, listen to what she'd wanted to tell him, and give her a piece of his mind about her engagement to a man Raúl knew meant them—and all of Spain—evil, not good.

He flipped off the computer and headed out the door. More than likely Dani was with Julian. Inwardly he cringed at the thought, and once he was on the Rúa Mayor, stepped up his pace to the taxi stand near the plaza.

Minutes later, he pulled up beside Julian's townhouse and

headed inside. Julian's armed guards, a couple of men he hadn't seen before, didn't hesitate when he gave them his name, but ushered him into Julian's presence.

Arabella and Wyatt Stern were seated nearest Julian's desk, with Doc Rafael and three other advisors seated opposite the American couple.

Raúl wasted no time with pleasantries. "I need to speak with you about my sister." He looked directly at Julian.

Julian's face was an emotionless mask, even at the mention of his fiancée's name. There was a pregnant silence in the room.

"I need to speak with my sister."

Arabella Wyatt was the first to acknowledge Raúl, her voice a low confident drawl. "First of all, you should know that Danita is not your sister."

"Second," Julian said calmly, "Danita is unable to meet with you."

Raúl, still standing, held up a hand toward Julian, then turned to the American woman. "What did you say?"

She tilted her chin slightly and gave him a tight smile. "I said Danita is not your sister. At least not by blood."

He frowned, dumbfounded by her words. "Of course she is. What would make you think otherwise?"

"Not *think*, Raúl. *Know*." Julian leaned back, steepling his fingers, watching Raúl's reaction.

Raúl sank into a nearby chair. "What are you talking about?"

Arabella laughed. "You're having the same reaction Danita did when she found out."

"Found what out?"

"I suspected she might be my granddaughter and had Julian do some research. He was able to trace beyond her first foster placement back to her birth mother, the daughter I gave away when I was sixteen." She went on to explain the circumstances of Dani's mother's birth.

Disquieting thoughts raced through his mind as she spoke. He didn't trust any of them. Why should he believe her story? On the other hand, what would be gained by concocting such a tale? He nodded finally. "I see." Then he asked, "Are you certain your daughter did not also have a son?"

Arabella laughed, a sound as silvery as the jingle of bracelets at her wrist. "Julian had his people check, and I'm truly sorry to report that the answer is no. There were no other children. Only Danita."

"I see." His mind reeled with the possibility that the words could be true. Then he let his head hang, trying to make sense of it, trying to sift through his swirling emotions. He looked up after a minute. "I would like to speak with Danita. We should talk about this."

Julian looked unusually grim. "It is not possible. She is unable to receive visitors at the moment."

Raúl wondered if the news had upset her as much as it had him. Perhaps that's why she had come to talk with him. And he'd sent her away in anger.

"I will tell her you stopped by." Julian stood in dismissal. The others remained seated.

Awkwardly, Raúl stood, shook hands with Julian, gave the others a nod, then abruptly left the room. The cabby hadn't waited, and there wasn't another in sight. He took off at a jog, heading back into the older section of town.

Elliot Gavin came to his mind as he ran. He'd met the man only once. At the Jesuit College through his friend Brother Thomas. He and Brother Thomas had kept Elliot Gavin's presence hidden from the others in Tres Equis. Not even Danita had guessed that Brother Thomas had met the American, had reported to Raúl, his cell leader, both of them understanding and keeping their motives for silence to themselves.

Danita's high-rise apartment building loomed on his right, and he headed toward it. Within minutes he was in the elevator on his way to the eleventh floor.

He knocked, waited, knocked again. Obviously the stop had been a waste of time. He should have known, after what Julian told him, that she wasn't here.

He glanced at his watch and waited five minutes, hoping she would rush in breathlessly with a sack of groceries in the crook of her arm. Smiling. Forgiving. Ready to talk. He leaned against the doorjamb, crossing his ankles. Ten minutes passed. Then another five. Still, no Danita. He sighed and reluctantly headed back to the elevator.

He was just stepping into the street when a taxi pulled up and a woman rolled down the window and gestured for him to approach.

It was Arabella Stern. Her husband sat beside her.

"I see you're still looking for Dani."

"Yes. I must speak with her."

"You will not see her for a very long time."

"What are you talking about?"

"Why don't you get in, ride with us? I'll tell you what happened."

Raúl considered it for a moment, then declined, sensing danger. "Just tell me what you know."

She lowered her voice. "I can't go into it here. But Danita was brought before Julian on the charge of treason."

"What—?" His knees threatened to buckle beneath him.

"Julian would have told you himself, I'm certain, but he was understandably upset by the turn of events." She was whispering so the cabby wouldn't hear, and he leaned closer as she went on. "Perhaps I shouldn't be telling you this, but I don't see the harm. You two have been close. It's only right that you should know."

"Tell me."

"She was seen with the Americans on several occasions—both Americans. K.C. Keegan and Elliot Gavin. Not only that, she kept the whereabouts of Elliot Gavin from Julian. It was her duty to report when he appeared in Salamanca." She paused. "Julian saw her actions as high treason against Tres Equis."

He couldn't breathe, but forced himself to keep calm. "Where is she?"

Arabella narrowed her eyes. "I don't know."

"He has taken her someplace? Or is she there—in the townhouse?"

She let out a short laugh. "He wanted her out of his sight as soon as possible."

"So he has taken her…" Then he paused, the tight, brittle look on Arabella's face difficult to ignore. "You told me you are her grandmother. Yet you seem not at all upset by this. Did you not try to protect her?"

There was a shadow of pain in her expression, but only for an instant. "I was loved by the great Miguel Vargas," she said, lifting her chin. "He gave his life for the good of the country. For Franco." Her mouth drooped. "This young woman, who I thought would bring me such joy, might as well have spat on her grandfather's grave. Spat on me, for all she cared."

"You turned her in. It was you who trailed her, watched her."

She shook her hair, flipping it with affectation. Bracelets jingled. "I did my duty."

He leaned closer, his voice dropping to a low growl. "If you are her grandmother, her flesh and blood, tell me where Julian has taken her. Have pity on her. When I think what he might do…" He couldn't go on.

"She is a traitor. Be glad she is not your flesh and blood after all." She started to raise the window, then paused, her fingers resting on the top of the glass. "Julian sent an armed guard to pick up Elliot Gavin. Also K.C. Keegan. They'll both be apprehended within the hour." She smiled. "And we'll find out exactly how much Mr. Gavin knows and what he's done about it. Julian has his ways of finding these things out. That will be all that's needed to nail shut Dani's coffin."

Before he could respond, the window slid up as silently as it had come down minutes earlier. And the taxi pulled into traffic.

Stunned, Raúl stood as rigidly still as if made of concrete. Only, his heart wasn't made of stone. It was flesh and blood, and it threatened to break for Dani.

K.C. was in the kitchen of the convent with Sister Calandria. Her back and shoulders ached from another day of working to prepare for the coming Easter Sunday meal. The sisters were determined that she learn how to fix the greatest delicacy known to Salamancans, roast suckling pig.

She had ridden with Sister Calandria and Sister Josefina that morning to a farm on the outskirts of town. There, they picked out a dozen piglets, and watched as the farmer took them, one by one, from the nursing sow and tossed the squealing little animals into a wheelbarrow.

Now looking at the pale pink, dead piglets, lined up in a row on the counter, she thought it wise that she'd asked to be excused from the slaughter and entrails cleaning. This was bad enough.

She pulled on some rubber gloves, slipping them up over her elbows. A pot of boiling water was in the sink in front of her. Sister Josefina pulled stray bristles from the hides, then handed each sad little carcass to K.C. to plunge into the steaming water and scrub it inside and out with a soft brush.

The movie *Babe* came to mind with each piglet she was handed. K.C. was so tired, she was borderline hysterical, ready to either cry or laugh or both. *Ba-a-abe,* each little pig seemed to say as it was handed to her, its snout so perfect, and little ears perky even in death, its long lashes lying curly and cute against its piglet cheeks.

She scrubbed harder, head down, willing herself not to giggle. *Ba-a-abe.* She pressed her lips together as Sister Calandria explained the seasonings that would be used and how they would need to leave the convent once more to head out to another part of the country to pick rosemary and bay leaves. Only the freshest spices could be used on such an occasion. And—she looked pointedly at K.C.—no mistakes could be made preparing this meal. The Cardinal would be joining them, also other church dignitaries after the Easter Sunday morning service. Everything had to be perfect.

Piglet number four. Number five. Still she fought the giggles. Number nine. Ten. Eleven.

Sister Calandria was writing down directions to the farmhouse since she wouldn't be accompanying K.C. and Sister Josefina. Then she looked up, a twinkle in her eye. "Did you ever see the video movie *Babe?*"

Before K.C. could answer, Sister Josefina made a little noise. It could have been the real Babe. *"Ba-a-abe,"* the nun said with a grin.

The three women exploded with laughter, all of them making identical talking pig sounds as they placed the freshly scrubbed piglets into the refrigerator.

Raúl almost sprinted down the Rúa Mayor. If Elliot Gavin was in the student computer room at the Jesuit College, he would be safe. He hoped that's where he'd find him.

Another procession was heading toward him. And another behind it. Hundreds of costumed marchers moved in dirgelike rhythm along the street. Visible above them were the floats carried on the shoulders of dozens of men behind the penitentes. He ducked and dodged as they came nearer.

As far as he knew no one else was aware of Gavin's use of the computers at the college—except Brother Thomas. The cathedral loomed in the distance, the university across from it, the college just around the corner.

He wasn't a praying man, but he sent up a prayer anyway, hoping that Gavin had gone to the student computer room. Reaching the college, he took the stairs in seconds and burst through the tall, wooden doors and into the foyer. Beyond him, as usual, the office staff was busily working.

Brother Thomas looked up and nodded, then moved to the window partition.

"Much has happened," Raúl said. "I will explain later, but right now I am looking for Elliot Gavin. Is he here?"

Brother Thomas nodded. "Yes. He came in more than an hour ago. I have not seen him leave." He glanced at the sign-in board. "Yes, he is still here."

"Come up when you can get away from the office. We have much to discuss."

"I can take a break in a few minutes."

"It is important, my friend."

"It sounds like the time is nearly here."

Brother Thomas didn't need to explain. Raúl understood perfectly. "Yes," he said. "It is."

He ran up the stairs, taking two and three steps at a time. He burst through the door, startling Gavin, who sat calmly at the computer terminal. A ruddy-faced man sat beside him, equally startled.

"I met you once," Raúl said, nearly out of breath from his run. "Here in this room. My friend Brother Thomas introduced us."

Gavin and the other man were both standing now. "This is Duncan MacGowan." He didn't explain who he was, but it didn't matter.

Raúl shook his hand. "I'm glad to meet you." Then he looked back to Gavin. "We need to talk. Privately."

"Duncan is aware of what's going on here, if that's what you mean. And I trust him to hear anything you might have to tell me."

Raúl was surprised at how candid the man was. He nodded. "All right, then, please sit down. I have asked Brother Thomas to join us in a few minutes. But I will start.

"There is a coup d'état planned in Salamanca before week's end." He paused while Gavin and MacGowan exchanged glances, obviously surprised by his words. He could see that it wasn't the event itself that surprised them. It was the fact that he had told them.

"I know you have been researching Tres Equis since you were in the States. I tracked every move you made on the Internet. Every hit. Every time you logged on, I knew. I read your e-mails. I knew exactly how close you were to discovering that Tres Equis wasn't a brotherhood at all—or cult, as you would say—but that it had a much different, much more ambitious mission."

Gavin nodded, his intense gaze never leaving Raúl's. There were questions behind those eyes, but Raúl figured the lawman in him wanted to hear everything he had to say first.

"I also knew that when Julian Hernando devised the kidnapping plan to divert you, it wouldn't keep you from going right back to where you started."

Gavin leaned forward, frowning, but still he didn't speak.

"And I have been following your inquiries here, on this Macintosh." He nodded to the computer behind Gavin. "I know whom you've contacted—your law enforcement friend, those government officials you thought might help—everyone. New sites on the Internet dedicated to insurrection rumors. Tres Equis research. Every night I have come in and logged on, and checked your cache—and your findings.

Another quick glance was exchanged with Duncan MacGowan, but still Gavin held his silence.

Raúl smiled. "You are good, Señor Gavin. Very good."

"What do you want from us?" Gavin asked. "Hasn't this gone on long enough?"

Raúl considered for a moment how much to tell, but decided his vows of silence had to remain just that. Silence.

"I am not at liberty to say."

"You are not *with* them?"

He didn't answer.

"Why have you told us, then, what you've discovered about us?"

"I need your help. And I will help you."

Gavin narrow his eyes. "You will help us? How?"

"Julian Hernando has dispatched armed guards to find both you and K.C. Keegan."

Gavin stood, the chair banging over behind him. "Then let's go! Why did you wait so long to tell me—?"

Raúl held up one hand. "Not so fast. She is temporarily safe. I telephoned the convent as soon as I knew what was planned. I know the Mother there, and I told her that K.C. is in danger. They have made arrangements to keep her away from the convent, away from Salamanca."

He smiled. "Mother told me that K.C. is receiving cooking lessons. They have taken her to the country to gather herbs. K.C. is unused to life in a convent and never questioned why they did not simply go to the market and buy them."

Gavin seemed to study him as he spoke. Finally, he said, "Why are you helping us? You are part of this group."

Raúl didn't answer.

"You said you need our help," Duncan MacGowan said, breaking the silence.

Raúl hesitated, choosing his words carefully. No need to let them know Dani was his sister. "Danita Chávez was picked up and accused of treason by Julian earlier today."

Concern flashed across the faces of both men. It was evident they knew her, cared for her. Though his voice was still low-pitched, Gavin's alarm was evident when he spoke. "Do you know where she's been taken?"

"No. Arabella Stern told me only that she is being held under house arrest."

"And you need our help to find her?" Duncan MacGowan asked.

"Why us?" Gavin added.

"You are in law enforcement. And Dani was arrested for protecting you. I hoped you would want to do the proper thing by helping her."

"We will do everything we can," Duncan said.

"Do you have any idea where Julian has taken others who challenge his authority?" Gavin still watched him warily.

"You do not believe what I say?" Raúl asked Gavin.

"Can you blame me? You kidnapped my fiancée, you've just divulged that you've invaded my privacy on the computer." He laughed, a short, cynical sound. "Now you've come to us with some fantastic story about your sister that may or may not be true—"

He broke in. "My sister? How did you know that?"

MacGowan sat back in his chair. "She told us."

"Did she also tell you about Arabella Stern's claims?"

Gavin nodded. "Yes."

"If the woman is right, then Dani and I are no relation at all." He held up a hand. "Look, this is getting us nowhere. It does not matter whether Dani and I are blood relations or not; in my mind she will always be my sister. I care about her. I do not care if you believe me. I must find her—with or without your help." He stood as if to go.

This time Gavin held up a hand. "Please, don't jump to conclusions. We are willing to help." He glanced at MacGowan, who inclined his head in agreement.

Raúl took in a deep breath. "The first thing I must do is get you out of here without being seen. Brother Thomas has a car—"

Almost as if on cue, his friend stepped into the room so quickly his robe swished around his ankles. "I do indeed," he said, obviously having overheard Raúl's words.

Raúl quickly explained what had happened. Brother Thomas nodded briskly. "You have considered the Valley of the Dead?"

"Yes. Julian has used it more than once."

"Then we will head there immediately."

"Can we get to your car without detection?" Raúl asked.

"Of course," Brother Thomas said. "I have kept this

eventuality in mind when parking."

"K.C. was held there," Gav said as they left the room. "Perhaps she knows something about the layout."

K.C. had just finished picking a basket full of fragrant rosemary, when she glanced up to see a car approaching the farmhouse. It was a beat-up sedan moving slowly down the dirt road, a cloud of dust rising behind.

Sister Josefina looked alarmed. "We must hide!"

K.C. frowned, her gaze still on the vehicle.

Sister Josefina pulled at her arm. "Please, you might be in danger. Mother said to take care…"

She allowed herself to be pulled to the rear of the house. "What do you mean? What danger?"

"There was a telephone call warning us to get you away from the convent." The little woman smiled sheepishly. "Mother arranged for you to be…away."

Hidden by the foliage of a small olive tree, K.C. peered around the corner. The car crept up the road, slowed, then finally rattled to a halt. The windows were opaque, and her heart caught as she waited to see who would emerge.

Then she grinned. Gav was the first one out of the car. She didn't wait to see who was with him. Dropping the basket of rosemary, she ran into his arms.

TWENTY

K.C. SAT NEXT TO GAV IN THE BACKSEAT OF THE EXHAUST-PUFFING vehicle. It rattled along the highway, heading toward Valle de los Caídos, Valley of the Dead. She didn't know if they could trust Raúl and Brother Thomas, but it seemed that they had no choice.

At least there were no signs of weapons. No threats of any kind. But heading back to where she'd been held prisoner did not help her spirits. She had to wonder if Dani's alleged disappearance was a ruse for getting her and Gav out of the way. Again.

But the weight of the world seemed to have settled on the shoulders of Raúl Chávez, sitting in the front passenger seat. For a would-be captor, he didn't seem at all threatening. Still, she and Gav knew better than to let their guard down simply because someone appeared benign.

"We had hoped that you might help us understand the setup, especially the section where you were held," Brother Thomas called over his shoulder as he drove.

She leaned forward. "I was in a well-furnished room behind the cathedral. I moved from there to a dining area several times, and then of course into the cathedral itself. But other than that I can't tell you much."

They turned off the highway, and headed along a winding ridge for a half hour before the huge concrete cross she remembered loomed over the dark horizon. Several minutes later, they pulled into the parking lot.

"There's a side entrance—behind the coffee shop," K.C. told them, "but I'm sure it's locked. It was each time I was taken in and out of the place."

K.C. and Gav trailed behind Raúl, Thomas, and Duncan as they wound their way through groups of tourists waiting in line in front of their luxurious coaches. Some stood listening to their guide's lectures about Franco's tomb and cathedral; others stood gawking at the cross towering above them.

K.C. and the others skirted the coffee shop with its shopping tourists and headed in the direction K.C. had indicated.

She showed them the door, then Raúl used a telescoping metal pick to unlock it. He worked with quick, expert hands, causing Gav and K.C. to exchange a glance. The computer whiz was a man of hidden talents.

Seconds later, the five of them were inside, and the door locked behind them. "We don't know who we'll find guarding Dani, if she's here, that is." Raúl's love for his sister was clearly written on his face. "I do not want to place the three of you in danger, but I need K.C.'s help in finding her old room. Just maybe, Dani's there."

But the room was empty, as were those that flanked it. The

entire wing where K.C. had been held was deserted. They wound around for another hour or so before heading back to the door.

As they walked to the car, something nagged at K.C. about the place. It was as if she should remember something about it, something important, but try as she may, it wouldn't come to her.

"Gav?" she said, putting her hand on his arm. "Wait."

He held open the car door, but she didn't get in. The others stepped closer.

"There's something that we're missing," she said. "It's right here in front of us, but—" She shook her head and shrugged. "I'm sorry. It's just not coming to me."

Raúl frowned, then shook his head slowly. "We are all worried about her. Maybe it's just that. Our imaginations are grasping at anything. Everything."

"No. There's something tangible we're missing. A link we should know." She shrugged again and bent her head to enter the car, taking her place between Gav and Duncan.

She leaned against Gav, who was on her left, as the car traveled along the winding mountain road. But the nagging thought would not leave her. She whispered a prayer for Dani. If what they'd been told was true, the young woman could be in grave danger. And terrified.

The group fell silent as they traveled.

K.C. laced her fingers with Gav's. "Do you think it's safe for me to return to the convent?"

He shook his head. "No. And I can't return to the pensión."

Brother Thomas smiled. "We have already thought of that. We have some places in mind for your safekeeping."

K.C. tightened her grasp on Gav's hand. He squeezed her fingertips in return.

"Do you know the Aznars?" Raúl suddenly asked, turning in his seat to look back at them.

"Duncan knows them best." K.C. smiled at Duncan, sitting on her right.

"Yes, I know them well," Duncan said. "I have also guessed that it's you who's written to them."

A shadow crossed Raúl's face. "Yes."

Duncan nodded. "I thought so."

"I was convinced I had found our parents—and the search wasn't easy—until I found out about Arabella's claims."

"The Aznars told us about your letters, even the latest one. You had given them hope that their search was over at last."

"I was so certain. Though I do not have absolute proof, the times, dates, our ages—everything—fits together perfectly." He looked back at the road, falling into a pensive silence. "I am sorry I have brought these good people pain, opened old wounds."

Duncan reached up to place his hand on the younger man's shoulder. "It isn't the first time they've been through it, my friend. When they find out your motives were pure, though misdirected, they will forgive you. Of that I am certain."

"I received a letter from Marta Aznar just days ago," Raúl said. "If I could choose the perfect mother, I believe it would be she. I have nearly worn out the letter from the reading." He laughed lightly, but K.C. felt the pain beneath his words. "I had gone to show Dani when I got the news about Arabella's relationship to her. And that Dani had been taken."

K.C. remembered Dani's adamant belief that the documents she'd seen were legal and accurate. Her heart went out to both young people, and to the Aznars.

She wished she knew the truth...wished she could be sure Arabella's claims were false, that the Aznars were the parents these two young people had longed for.

But there was only one thing right now that she knew for sure: Raúl Chávez meant them no harm.

When they reached Salamanca, Duncan was let out at his friends' home just outside the city. He wrote down his telephone number and gave it to Gav. "Please call if there are any new developments."

The men shook hands, and Duncan stepped out and closed the door. He headed toward the small house, then turned back, as if to say something more, something important he'd just remembered. Then he smiled and shrugged, waving as the car pulled back into the street.

Several minutes later, Brother Thomas headed the car into a narrow alley behind the Jesuit College. "We have rooms here for the students," he said, glancing upward. An ancient stone façade rose four stories or so. K.C. followed his gaze, craning her neck to see the top as he went on. "There is an overflow wing where some of the penitentes have taken rooms during Holy Week. There are females here as well, so you will not stand out."

K.C. smiled. "Thank you. This will do nicely." Gav squeezed her hand.

"Before you go," Raúl said. "I cannot give you details yet, but there are certain things I...*we*—" he glanced at Brother Thomas—"know about Good Friday."

Gav's expression was searching. "Do you know enough to stop it?"

"I would tell you everything right now if I did."

"What can we do?" Gav asked, his voice somber.

Brother Thomas turned in his seat. "We will need your help, but we cannot say anything more than that right now. Too much is at risk."

"For that matter," Raúl said, "I am sorry that you got caught up in our affairs. It should never have happened." A muscle clenched along his jaw as he studied them. He seemed ready to say more. Then he waved his hand in a gesture of dismissal.

"I will meet you tomorrow morning and tell you everything. Nine o'clock." He paused, and his voice sounded tired when he continued. "When I come to you there may be a heavy price on my head. We need to take care where we meet."

Gav nodded. "Just name the place."

"When I was a child I played in the tower of the old cathedral. Only a few of us knew how to get into the place. I have often thought it is probably the most secure place to meet in all of Spain." He laughed. "If you are up to a bit of a climb, I will meet you there."

"I will be there."

"And I," said Brother Thomas. "I trust you meant to include me?" He looked pointedly at Raúl.

"By all means, my friend. Such a meeting cannot take place without you." Raúl told them how to find the passageway into the old cathedral's tower, then stuck out his hand to Gav. "Thank you, my friend."

When they had exited the car, K.C. stepped closer to Raúl. "What are you going to do about Danita?"

His face was sad. "I will do what I must to gain her release. That is why I will need to go underground immediately after." Before they could ask questions, he held up his hands and shrugged. "I cannot tell you anything more until tomorrow morning."

He kissed both of K.C.'s cheeks, then stepped into the car and closed the door. Brother Thomas ground the vehicle into gear, and it rattled and smoked its way back down the alley.

K.C. and Gav hurried through the gate and into a walled courtyard. The place looked like a fortress. They glanced at each other and shrugged.

"Will life ever get back to normal again?"

Gav chuckled. "This is a trip we'll never forget. If I weren't so worried about Good Friday, the possible bloodshed—"

"And Dani. All that she may be going through."

Gav turned to her suddenly. "Do you remember the museum you told me about—the place Dani showed you?"

"Of course. I have nightmares about it."

"I would like to see it. I *need* to see it."

"It will be dangerous. . . ."

He grinned. "When has this trip *not* been dangerous?"

"You've got a point, Sherlock." She grabbed his hand. "It's good just to be near you again."

He stared into her eyes. What she saw in his dark eyes melted away all her fear. "Have I told you recently how much I love you?"

"Not often enough," she breathed.

"I love you, K.C. Keegan."

"Enough to marry me?" She couldn't hold back her smile. "The minute all this is over?"

His chuckle was deep and warm, and it wrapped around her as he pulled her close. She grinned up at him, her heart singing with delight at the look of him.

"I thought you'd never ask." His voice broke with huskiness. He bent and kissed her tenderly.

She sighed and rested against him. "Among our many problems, there's one I should bring to your attention right now," she murmured.

"Only one?" There was tender amusement in the question.

"People are staring."

"Let 'em stare."

"I'm still wearing the robe of a novice."

He jumped back from her as though she were on fire. "Oh, honey, I forgot." He glanced around at the scowls, gave a half wave, and attempted a sorry grin. Nothing helped.

"You might get stoned for your actions, dear sir. There's probably a law against kissing a would-be nun. Methinks we'd better hightail it out of here." She giggled and gave him one last peck on the cheek.

He grabbed her hand, and they ran from the courtyard into the alley.

"Oh, sweetheart! I have missed you." He bent and kissed her again, this time with no one watching.

She circled her arms around his neck, and kissed him back. "Will we ever get home?"

"This is home, darling. Right here in your arms. I need no other home than this."

She grinned up at him and kissed the tip of his nose. "That's exactly how it should be."

The museum of antiquities was open to the public. K.C. took a breath, bracing herself for the menacing darkness inside.

A woman seated behind the visitor's desk looked up at them somberly as they stepped nearer.

"Do we need to purchase tickets?" Gav inquired.

When she didn't understand, he repeated his words, this

time using sign language as well.

She frowned as if trying to process his mix of pidgin Spanish, gestures, and English. Finally she shook her head. "No." And she gestured almost angrily for them to enter.

K.C. drew in a deep breath and grabbed hold of Gav's arm as they stepped into the ghoulish room Danita had shown her a few days before. She shivered at the sight of the three crosses, the paintings, the drapes of black and red. It was all as she remembered: the satanic symbols, the horned goat heads with the burning-coal eyes.

Gav's curiosity seemed to draw him forward. He examined every painting, going over the details. He pointed out ancient satanic symbols that modern-day cults had adopted. He found detail in the paintings that K.C. had missed. But then, she had been in a hurry to leave the place.

Gav's presence gave her courage to venture into the corners of the room. Hands clasped behind her, she wandered in silence, shuddering, yet strangely curious at the same time.

Gav had found some old photographs in a small room off to one side. He held one up. "Come look at this."

She moved closer. The faded pictures were scratched, but the identity of the man standing with a young Franco was clear. Adolf Hitler.

He set the photograph down and picked up another. It was of a shrine of some sort. A swastika was above it, two dates below.

Gav frowned at the dates. "The dates of Hitler's birth and death," he mused.

"Gav, look at the first date. Closely."

"April 20."

"Guess what tomorrow is."

"April 20." He stared at her a moment. "Raúl said a coup is planned by week's end."

"And tomorrow is the anniversary of Hitler's birth."

Gav nodded. "Are you thinking what I'm thinking?"

"Oh, Gav. Do you think Raúl knows?"

"Julian may have left many of his people purposely in the dark until the last minute."

He placed the photograph back with the others. "I think we need to meet with Raúl before tomorrow morning."

They walked toward the back of the red and black room. Gav held open the door for her, and she stepped into the foyer, then out into the fresh air. It was like walking from a dungeon into the bright light of freedom.

"How will we find him?"

"I'll go to Brother Thomas at the college and tell him we must speak to Raúl immediately."

They walked toward the cathedral, turned by the university, then into the small alley near the Jesuit College.

"What kind of game is Raúl playing?" K.C. asked as they reached the courtyard gate. "Are you sure we can trust him? That bit about the tower? That's a frightening place." She shuddered. "I can't think why he suggested it."

Gav wrapped his arm around her. "He spoke of going underground. I think he's part of the political structure trying to bring Julian down."

"Lawfully?"

He shrugged. "I've been trying to figure that out myself. I don't know. I hope so."

She entwined her fingers in his. "Should we go to the ambassador? If we left now, perhaps we could meet with him in Madrid."

"I've thought of that." He shook his head. "I'm not so sure we would be believed." He laughed, the sound full of irony. "Besides, I saw on CNN that he's out of the country. We would need to speak to an assistant." He laughed again. "Not that we wouldn't be handed off to an assistant anyway."

"Plus we have no proof."

"Which brings us back to where we started." He let his gaze drift away from her face, and she could see he was lost in thought. After a moment he turned back. "I would like to think we can trust Raúl. There's something puzzling about the way he and Brother Thomas are operating right now. Either one could have turned me in when I first arrived in Salamanca, but they didn't."

The cathedral bells tolled low and mellow in the distance, echoing through the old narrow streets. In her mind's eye she again saw the soaring heights of the tower…imagined what it would be like to peer at the ground so far below….

Shivering, she lifted his hand and kissed his knuckles. "Gav?"

"Yes, babe?"

"Promise me something?"

"Anything."

"If I ever suggest a wedding in an exotic place…"

He was grinning at her, clearly guessing what was coming.

"…don't listen. Run with me to the nearest minister in our little old hometown. Don't let me out of your sight until we both say 'I do.'"

He grabbed her and held her close enough to hear the thudding of his heart. She sighed and leaned against him, never wanting to leave the circle of his arms.

Raúl strode into Julian's office.

"We need to talk." He stared hard at the Tres Equis leader, seething with mounting rage.

Julian inclined his head slightly. "You arrived just as I was about to send for you. Come in. Sit down." It was an order, not an invitation.

"I would rather stand for what I have to say to you."

Julian lifted a brow, and the corners of his mouth hardened.

"Arabella Stern told me that you have seen fit to arrest Danita."

He didn't look surprised that Raúl knew. "Dani disobeyed orders."

"Have you no thought for who she is?"

The older man's laugh was short, bitter. "Do you mean your *sister?*" He laughed again. "Or the granddaughter of the esteemed Miguel Vargas?"

"I mean she is your friend. You practically raised us both."

To his credit, a flicker of discomfort crossed Julian's face. "That is in the past. She betrayed me; I did not betray her. She was given her orders. She disobeyed." He stared bitterly at Raúl. "It is I who have been wounded by her betrayal. Not the other way around, as you seem to think."

Anger swept him, so hot and powerful it took all his control not to put his hands around Julian's throat. When he spoke, his words were low and measured. "If you harm her, you will answer to me."

"You cannot stand up for a traitor, Raúl. No matter your personal feelings, you must pledge your allegiance to me. To Tres Equis. I have always considered you my protégé; do not disappoint me now, no matter the path Danita has chosen."

"Where have you taken her?"

"She is in safe keeping until her trial."

"Trial?"

"Yes. Once we are in power, many will be tried for acts of treason against Tres Equis." Julian paused and leaned back in his chair. Narrowing his gaze, he gave Raúl a piercing look.

Raúl forced himself to keep a hard-eyed gaze on the other man's arrogant face. He didn't speak or shift his weight. He simply stared, waiting.

Julian pursed his lips. "I was about to send for you because there is something that I require of you. Something that will test *your* loyalty. I hope you will not disappoint me."

Still Raúl didn't speak.

"The codes for the Chaos bug. I need them now."

"They are set for the time you required. There is no reason for you to need them." Raúl forced a withering stare, feigning outrage that Julian should doubt him.

Julian returned the angry look. "I want them now. Before you leave this room."

Raúl swallowed hard. The codes were his leverage, and he planned to use them. He gave Julian a look of utter disdain. "They are complicated. Not something one keeps in one's memory bank. I do not have them with me."

Julian studied him for a moment. "I will send a driver with you. I am assuming you have left them in the laboratory."

"They are encoded within my computer system. I do not carry them with me. Neither have they been printed out. They are also protected by a password."

"You have seen to their security. That is good. But now it is time for you to hand over everything. We will begin with the password." He picked up a Mont Blanc fountain pen then pulled out a sheet of paper. "Your password?"

Raúl considered his options, quickly weighing one against the other. He could bring Julian's wrath down on himself through his attempt to get to Danita. Or continue his charade of allegiance to Tres Equis, while protecting the work he and Thomas were doing for the king of Spain.

He stared at Julian for another few seconds, then finally spoke. "I will give you the password—everything you require—as soon as you take me to Danita. I need to see that she has not been harmed."

Julian nodded. "I should have expected as much."

"Take me to her."

"That is impossible."

"Then you will not have the codes." He turned to leave.

"Give us the codes, then I will see to your transport to Danita."

"No." He turned back.

"You will not leave these premises."

"And still you will not have the codes." Raúl shrugged. "Have it your way."

Julian stood and moved around the desk. "Perhaps I should put it another way. If you want to see Danita alive, you *will*—let me emphasize, *will*—give us your password and codes."

Raúl considered Julian's words. He'd figured that the man would use Danita as a pawn, so he wasn't surprised. He held up his hands in surrender, and at the same time, raised his shoulders in a nonchalant shrug. "All right, you win. I will give you the information you seek, but someone will need to come with me to the computer headquarters. It is a complicated system. I will give instruction to the person you designate."

He took a few steps closer to Julian. "However, if you need the codes to change the date or time of the Tres Equis actions, I can program the changes myself. There would be no need for a third party to take over." He paused for emphasis. "Just tell me the new day and time."

The light in Julian's eyes told Raúl the other man knew his words were nothing more than a fishing expedition. And he wasn't about to let Raúl set the hook.

Julian leaned forward, narrowing his eyes. "That will not be necessary. You will be accompanied by my personal assistants, and you will return here to await the outcome."

"And to be taken to Danita."

Julian smiled slowly. "Yes, that too."

After K.C. was safely ensconced in her plain but barren room, delighted that someone had asked Sister Calandria to bring her small traveling bag, Gav checked into his room several doors down.

It was unsafe to return to the pensión for his backpack and clothes, so he headed immediately to the corner grocer's and bought a toothbrush and package of disposable razors, then to a tourist shop to look for a plain, black hooded sweatshirt. It took him several minutes to pick through dozens with the University of Salamanca logo and dozens more with Picasso's *El Toro* splashed across the front.

He pulled on the sweatshirt as soon as it was paid for, then pulled the hood low over his forehead and tucked the small package of toiletries in his shirt pocket. Minutes later, he was dodging the growing crowds as he headed toward the Jesuit College.

Brother Thomas wasn't at his usual post behind the glass partition, but Gav stopped and signed in anyway. He took the key from the girl, then jogged along the hallway and up the stairs.

When he entered the room just seconds later, he hesitated at the door. A group of casually dressed men were sitting at the computer terminals. Some were turned toward Brother Thomas, who was standing in the center of the group with his back to the door. Others who hadn't bothered to turn when Gav stepped inside seemed lost in a program on their computer monitors.

He must have interrupted a computer class.

Then Brother Thomas turned toward him, his face a chilling, unreadable mask. "Come in, Sheriff Gavin. We have been expecting you."

TWENTY-ONE

"I WOULD LIKE TO INTRODUCE YOU TO MY COLLEAGUES," BROTHER Thomas said.

There was nothing for Gav to do but enter the room. They looked benign, but if he'd learned one thing since arriving in Spain, nothing was as it seemed.

"Hello." He kept his tone and nod casual.

The men, seven plus Brother Thomas, stood to shake his hand. There was respect in their faces, and Gav relaxed as he was introduced to each one. They all spoke English, but with varied Spanish accents.

Finally, they were seated again, and Gav settled into a chair, facing Brother Thomas.

"This is a place we can be certain is not bugged," Brother Thomas said in English. "I was just telling my colleagues about your interest—and help—with Tres Equis. We have known because of your background in law enforcement that we could trust you."

"You should have let me know sooner that I could join forces with you," Gav said. "I would have been happy to tell you all I know."

"We could not give away our role in the organization," Brother Thomas said.

"Raúl Chávez is part of—" he looked around the room—"part of your group as well?"

"Yes."

"And his sister, Danita?"

Brother Thomas shook his head. "She was pulled deep into the inner circle because of their charismatic leader. It is only recently that she has begun to doubt the work of the brotherhood. Julian Hernando's campaign, if you can call it that, to lead a bloodless coup was one that led his followers down a slippery slope. Most did not realize what he was planning until it became too late to get out."

"She is in danger," Gav said, though these men probably knew it far better than he. "Do you have any plans, any ideas for getting her out?"

"Raúl is meeting with Julian as we speak. Attempting to negotiate for her release."

"Brother Thomas—"

The man smiled. "You may call me Thomas. I am not a Jesuit brother. Actually, I am not even Spanish, but Portuguese. Brought in by Interpol. The good people here have allowed me to use their facilities, particularly because of their outstanding computer and Internet systems."

Gav grinned. "Thomas, then. You had me convinced."

Thomas nodded and returned the grin. "I will tell my wife." Some of the other men chuckled.

Gav went on. "You are working for the government? For King Carlos?"

"Both," Thomas said. "And, as I mentioned, Interpol has a hand in this as well. That is where I come in. Some of the Tres Equis support—both financial and personnel—are from other European countries."

"So instead of stopping the uprising, you've been trying to gather specific names and countries the help is coming from?"

"Yes. It is not enough to simply stop this. The group is a throwback to Nazi Germany. We want to stomp the entire organization into the ground hard enough that it does not rise again."

"Are Germans involved?"

"Yes, as are some Swiss, some Italians. A number of people in Brazil. And of course, Americans." Thomas paused. "This is a fascist group. They have brought together those who still swear by their long-ago beliefs in fascism—from countries where it existed pre-World War II."

One of the other men spoke up. "We have identified one of the key donors. A certain American couple has given millions of dollars to fund the organization." He nodded at his computer. "We have gained access to the Tres Equis accounts."

Gav didn't need to ask, but he did. "The Sterns?"

"None other," the man replied.

"When was their latest gift?"

"Just a few days ago," Thomas said. "Though they are here in Salamanca, it was wired from their bank in Santa Fe, New Mexico."

"It fits," Gav said.

Thomas frowned. "Fits what?"

"The timing of the discovery of Arabella Stern's claim that she's Danita's grandmother."

"You think she bought the relationship?" Thomas shook his head. "That doesn't make sense."

"Maybe it was never stated as a purchase—" Gav shrugged—"only funding for research." He shrugged again. "It's a long shot, I know. But I suppose I'm just looking for a happy ending for some friends."

Thomas didn't hesitate. "The Aznars?"

"Yes, and speaking of happy endings," Gav said, his voice heavy with irony, "do you know the day and time of the coup? And I'm assuming you've taken steps to counteract it."

"Our sources have informed us that it is scheduled for Good Friday at noon, precisely the time of Christ's crucifixion."

"How reliable are your sources?"

"We have people in several of the cells. Unless we find out differently, we are set to move against the group Friday morning as they gather to march in the procession."

Gav frowned. "I came across something this afternoon that might be of interest." He went on to tell them about the photographs and his thoughts regarding the dates of Hitler's birth and death.

The men leaned forward, and there wasn't a sound in the room except the voices of Gav and Thomas.

"You are bringing this up because of the dates?" Thomas frowned. "As I recall, Hitler's birth and death are in the same month." There was a slow dawning on his face. "April, is that right?"

"He was born on April 20, 1889. He died on April 30, 1945."

"Tomorrow is Hitler's birthday."

"Yes."

There was an almost audible gasp. "Tomorrow, then, is

when Tres Equis will strike." Thomas was clearly excited. "There can be no doubt."

"That is my conclusion," Gav said. "Can you move in your opposition forces that quickly?"

Thomas glanced at the other men. "Yes, but it will depend on Raúl. He is the only one, that we know of, with the codes for the Chaos bug. If someone else gets into his system, triggers the bug, even our forces will not be able to halt the chaos that will reign." He rubbed his forehead. "All our modern technology…we thought our worries about the Y2K were monumental. They pale compared to what is planned by the CB."

"Chaos bug?"

Thomas nodded. "The same. From what we've been told, it will be worse than a virus. It virtually explodes in every system it touches, wiping out memory, upsetting everything from utilities to banking systems. Police and the National Guard will be struck powerless, unable to communicate with individual officers or each other. Spain will be left without defense."

"Perfect setup for a takeover," Gav added.

Thomas rubbed his head again. "I must get to Raúl." He looked up, his face grim. "If Julian has purposely changed the date to throw off any opposition, he'll need Raúl to change the computer codes that release the virus."

"You said he's negotiating for Danita's release right now?" Gav asked.

"Yes." The leader's mouth twisted with worry.

"He may have walked into a trap. Danita was the bait."

The others exchanged alarmed glances.

Gav's heart constricted. "Has Raúl been trained to defend his country at all costs? To keep your secrets?"

One of the other men spoke up. "He has received the best of Interpol's training, also that of King Juan Carlos's private forces."

"But if he must choose between saving his sister or saving his country…" Gav studied the faces turned to him. "Which will it be?"

A sense of heaviness descended over them all. After a moment, Thomas said quietly, "Raúl Chávez has a heart. Some see it as his only weakness. Some see it as his strength. But none of us in this room doubt that his heart will determine his choice."

Gav nodded, understanding. "Then we'd better find him. And fast." He stood, glancing around the roomful of men. "I'm not sure what I can do to help, but please know I am at your disposal."

"You must remain hidden from Tres Equis. Keep your K.C. out of sight as well. You have already helped us a great deal with the information you brought to us. We thank you." Thomas shook Gav's hand.

"I would like to join you tomorrow, once your people come in force."

Thomas grinned. "Julian refers to you often as John Wayne. Perhaps it is the one thing he got right." He put his hand on Gav's shoulder. "I will make arrangements for you to join us. We need all the help we can get."

"You know where to find me."

"Yes, my friend. I made the arrangements myself—or rather, Brother Thomas did." The others laughed with him. "Being a Jesuit brother opens all kinds of doors."

"Just tell me when and where."

"We'll send word."

Gav shook hands around the room again, and, as the men bent their heads in conference, he headed back through the door.

Julian's sleek sedan halted at the farmhouse. The back door opened, and Raúl was forced out at gunpoint. Before he could resist, a meaty hand was planted against his back and he was shoved toward the front door. Julian's thugs were as impatient as they were surly. Apprehension coursed through him as he was propelled toward his computer terminal with no more courtesy than one might give an animal.

He wasn't surprised to find that one of the men, new to Julian's inner circle—a bookish-looking assistant, balding, fringe-haired—was as computer literate as he. And that was saying a lot. Raúl had been trained by the elite of the electronics world.

One of the thugs pulled out a chair and forced Raúl to sit. The bookish man sat in a chair beside him, watching every stroke of the keys. Raúl had the feeling the man didn't need to take notes but relied instead on a photographic memory, his eyes darting from keyboard to monitor and back again.

He went to the encoded files, typed in a password that Fringe-Hair didn't miss, then a series of codes that opened another file. A series of numbers and letters flashed across the screen.

Fringe-Hair moved closer, studying the monitor. His face might as well have been a stone mask. He stared at the codes without blinking, rapid eye movement his only motion.

Raúl settled back in his chair. "So what do you think?"

Fringe-Hair didn't answer, just narrowed his eyes and kept staring.

"Do I need to spell out the codes for you, or can you take it from here?" He pushed his chair back a few inches, starting to get up.

A rough hand pushed downward on his shoulder, forcing him to remain seated.

"You will stay until we have changed all the codes to my satisfaction," Fringe-Hair muttered.

Raúl drew in a deep breath and scooted the chair closer to the screen. "What is the new time?"

The man told him, and Raúl hit the appropriate numerical keys.

"The day?"

Again, the answer. Raúl keyed in the new information.

For nearly an hour they worked. Raúl knew with growing clarity that the information he had just been given was a death warrant. Julian had already made it clear that he was not to be trusted. And in Julian's world that meant only one thing.

Resigned, he typed in the final codes for the release of the Chaos bug. Unless stopped, this bug would create a new world within twenty-four hours. A world of abject darkness.

The task completed, the computer was shut down. Without another word, Raúl was escorted back to the waiting car. When they reached Salamanca, the three assistants were let out at Julian's headquarters.

The thugs—one driving, the other beside Raúl with his hand curled round a loaded pistol—drove on through town.

Within minutes the vehicle turned onto the highway leading to the Valley of the Dead.

Gav stopped by K.C.'s room just as the sun was setting. The earlier wind had died down, and the air seemed almost balmy in comparison.

She stepped to the door, and Gav relaxed into a wide grin. K.C. was beautiful. For the first time in weeks she was dressed in ordinary clothes—and it took all his self-control not to take her in his arms and kiss her senseless.

The evening already looked too glorious to miss. He was glad he had convinced K.C. that it would be safe to take a stroll if they steered away from the crowds. Even without her novice's robe to hide her hair, they could keep to the shadows and remain unseen.

"The sisters bought this for me. What do you think?" She spun in a circle. "They felt sorry for me running away from Arabella and Wyatt with only the clothes on my back."

"They've got good taste." He lifted a brow. The jeans fit perfectly, the shirt was fresh-pressed and classic, with its cuffed long sleeves and open collar.

K.C. pulled out one side of her vest and spun again, modeling her new look with feigned high drama. The vest had to be American. Western, judging from the herd of wild horses and cowboys with spinning lassos appliquéd across the front.

"This is my favorite. They bought all this at a secondhand shop. Apparently, students from all over the world leave clothing here they don't want to bother carrying home."

"Better not let Doc Rafael see the vest. He might want one for himself."

She flinched, and Gav grabbed her hand, regret piercing him. "Oh, honey, I'm sorry I mentioned him—"

"It's strange, Gav. Of all those who've come against us in this—the Sterns, Danita—it's Doc who haunts my thoughts. I wake at night with the feeling I'm being chased." She laughed nervously. "Though when I wake, I have to wonder at the strange form he takes in my nightmares. He's always in Western garb, sometimes riding a horse, other times a goat. But his eyes are those in the museum paintings—glowing like hot coals."

He could tell from her expression, the way she shifted uneasily, that just talking about it was disturbing her.

"There is something evil in him, Gav. I can feel it when I'm near him. A darkness that scares me. An absence of human emotion."

She shuddered, and Gav pulled her closer, wanting to protect her even from her nightmares. "How about a moonlight stroll by the river?"

Her smile was soft, warm, as she gazed into his eyes. "I can think of nothing I would like better."

"I'll tell you what I've discovered along the way. But you'd better grab a sweater. Did the sisters get you one of those as well?"

Shaking her head, she disappeared into her room for a moment then returned. He recognized the sweater as one of her own. "I at least had the forethought to grab this as I left that abysmal hotel room. That, and my contacts."

"I've missed your glasses." He pushed them up on her nose, and she grinned at the familiar gesture.

They walked into the courtyard and let themselves out the gate. Other visitors in Salamanca for Holy Week were hurrying out at the same time. The sounds of drums in the distance, with their slow, sad beat, carried toward them. The processions had begun again.

Gav nestled K.C.'s hand in his own as they walked. "It must have been an awful time for you, Kace."

"I won't try to pretend it wasn't." She kept her eyes straight ahead. The glow of the orange-pink sunset sky tinged her face a rosy color, and her hair seemed made of flame.

He stopped, and she turned toward him. His heart caught as he touched her face gently, then tucked a strand of hair behind her ear. "Kace, if anything had happened to you—" His voice choked, and he couldn't go on.

She reached up and put a hand on either side of his face. For a moment she didn't speak, just looked at him with that bright, soulful, gray-eyed gaze. "But nothing did, my love. God was with me, with us both, through it all." She smiled softly. "I worried about what was happening to me, to you. And I was scared much of the time. But never once did I doubt that God was with me."

He bent his head and kissed her, and she leaned into his arms. He felt her slim arms slide up to circle his neck. This woman God had chosen for him was more precious than words could express. He rested his head on top of hers and drew in a deep breath to catch the scent of her hair.

Suddenly, he chuckled. "What's that…er, *fragrance*, in your hair, Kace?"

He could feel her laughter, a wonderful light rumble against his chest. "It's a shampoo the sisters make themselves. I fear it's made with the same pine cleaner they use on the floors."

He pulled her tighter, thinking it was the most wonderful scent in the world.

"This week has been one we'll never forget." She pulled back, smiling up at him. "Think of the scrapbook we'll put together when we get home."

Taking her hand, he guided her along a back road that led to the river. "Speaking of home, Kace. I've decided it's time for us to go."

She stopped and looked up at him. "Has something else happened?" She frowned. "You talked to Brother Thomas, didn't you? What did you find out?"

He held up a hand to stop the journalist in her from taking over. Then he told her about the meeting in the Jesuit College classroom, every detail of the operation—at least what they'd divulged to him. She was stunned by the news.

"You see, Kace," he concluded, "this group has everything under control. They have no need for us now. I offered to help, but I felt they really see no need for me to be involved. Out of politeness, they said I could come along."

But she saw through his offhand comment, just as he'd feared she would. "We can't go."

"There's a possibility that the Chaos bug will be unleashed tomorrow. The coup will begin." He pulled her closer, holding both hands in his. "Kace, if we don't get out before this thing hits, we may not get out for a very long time." Flights, train schedules, every mode of transportation would certainly be affected. "Surely you can see that."

She stared at him, unblinking, her gaze unsettling in its intensity. "We can't leave Dani."

"Interpol is involved. The Spanish government..." He knew by her expression that he wasn't getting through to her.

"We can't go." She turned away from him. "I won't leave not knowing what's happened to Dani...not knowing if we could have helped."

They started walking toward the river again. Twilight was settling and the sky, so bright just minutes earlier, was now fading to pearl gray.

"We are still being sought by Julian and his thugs."

"I realize that."

"It may get much more dangerous, more so than what we've already been through." He caught her hand again, and was about to tell her every reason on God's green earth why they needed to get out of Spain tonight...until her stricken look squeezed the words right out of his mind.

"Dani was trying to help us. That's why Julian has taken her. Because of us, Gav. She was trying to protect us."

"I know. I feel the same thing—but I'm also concerned about your safety, Kace. The two of us getting picked up by Julian isn't going to help free Dani."

She looked up at him, her eyes narrowing. "You are trying your best to get me to leave. I know your tactics, Sheriff Elliot Gavin. You forget, I know them almost better than you do. You are trying to get me on the next bus to Madrid, and after that, the next flight home." She paused, a smile playing at her lips. "Then you would *accidentally* miss the bus, or the flight, and hightail it back here to play cops and robbers with the big boys."

He didn't smile or acknowledge in any way that she had hit her target. "This is no game of cops and robbers."

She touched his hand. "I didn't mean to minimize it, Gav. I just know you very well. The more dangerous the circumstances, the more casual your attempt to get me away from danger."

He let out a deep breath, closed his eyes and shook his head. "Guilty as charged, your honor."

She held his hand solidly in hers. "It's not gonna work, Sherlock."

"I had to try."

"And I love you for it. But we've got to figure out how to find Dani. You care about her as much as I do." She frowned. "But where, Gav? How can we find out where she was taken?"

The darkening sky spread across them like a blanket, and the ancient stone buildings, bathed in artificial light, shone in golden relief. The cathedral bell tower loomed above the rest of the medieval part of the city, and the incessant, slow drumbeats of the processions pounded, floating toward them through winding cobbled streets.

TWENTY-TWO

DANITA SAT ON A COT, HUDDLING IN THE DAMP COLD. SHE PULLED her thin jacket closer and shivered. The room was stark, with one dim bulb hanging from the center of the ceiling. A decades-old washbasin stood in one corner, its pipes rusted and bare. A stained toilet was in the opposite corner. The single iron cot had no mattress or blanket.

In the hours she'd been there, she'd been given nothing to eat. The only water to drink was from the faucet above the basin. The water flowed in dribbles, was the color of tea, and smelled like sulfur.

She felt like talking to God, to the One she'd come to know as Papá. But was it prayer? She wasn't sure. Finally, she bowed her head. "Papá, I cannot see beyond this moment. I cannot see tomorrow and I do not want to think of yesterday. I refuse to ask why I am here. I only want to trust that there is a reason. Only you know."

Tears filled her eyes. "I am so lonely and afraid. I would like to be brave, but I am not." She had been trained to withstand almost anything that came against her, and yet...

Dealing with loneliness was part of her training, but the reality of it was more frightening than anything she had known before. "I think I shall die here in the silence," she whispered. She had no idea where she was. Julian had made it clear he would bring her to trial for treason. If that were true, she very likely did not have long to live.

Head still bowed, she shuddered, her tears now sliding down both cheeks.

Beloved, don't be afraid. I have redeemed you.
I have called you by name, and you are mine.
You are precious and honored in my sight.
I love you, my child.

She wiped her cheeks with her fingers. "Papá, I have so much to learn about you. About your love and who you are. Teach me, even in this prison. Do not leave me, Papá!"

Lo, I am with you always....

Exhausted, she fell back onto the metal cot and, using her arm as a pillow, fell asleep.

The faint sound of voices woke Danita. She wasn't wearing a watch and had no concept of how much time had passed since she had been placed in this prison, or even how long she'd slept. But she rubbed her eyes and sat up, hoping that someone had come to release her.

The footsteps came nearer, approaching from down the dimly lit corridor. She stood and walked to the cell grate, placing her hands on the metal bars.

Still nearer, though now the voices had fallen silent.

A few more minutes passed, and she said a silent prayer for her safety. What if they were coming to take her to Julian for trial?

Perhaps the government had already fallen into Julian's hands. Perhaps—

Listen for my voice in the stillness, beloved. Listen…

The footsteps were louder, and soon they rounded the corner at the end of the corridor. She held her breath, afraid she might call out in fear. She closed her eyes, willing herself to think about the Lord who loved her, to remember his presence was always near her.

"Dani!"

Her eyes flew open.

"Dani!" Raúl's voice was joyous even as he was prodded into his own cell. The door slammed shut, the key turned noisily, and one of Julian's guards flipped the key into his pocket and sauntered back down the corridor.

"Raúl! Oh, my brother! I cannot believe it is you!" She held on to the bars, almost shaking them in her desperation to go to him.

He stared at her from across the several meters that separated them. "I had hoped they would bring me to you, lock me up in the same place." He smiled at her. "And here I am."

She drank in the look of him. "They did not harm you?"

"No, my sister, I am well."

"Why are you here? Has Julian brought charges against you?"

He gave her a gentle smile. "I tried to bargain for your release. Julian saw it as traitorous."

"Some friend, our Julian."

"Yes, some friend." He fell silent a moment. "Dani?"

"Yes?"

"That day you came to see me and I wouldn't talk...?"

"I remember."

"I am sorry."

"There is no need for apology."

"I had no reason other than my anger and dismay over Julian's announcement."

"That was a mistake. I never intended to marry him."

"I know that now." He was quiet a moment. "There is something else."

"What is it?" She leaned against the grate.

"Arabella told me about her relationship to you."

A bleak sadness settled into her spirit, replacing the earlier joy. "I do not want to believe it, but I have seen the papers."

He was silent for a few minutes. "I need to tell you something else."

"What is it?"

"I did some research of my own—without telling you. Through some genealogical Web sites, I thought I had traced our family, our real family, back to a man and woman who lost their children twenty-five years ago."

She remembered the people that Duncan MacGowan told her about—also the file name on Raúl's computer.

"They are called the Aznars."

It was the same. Curious, she thought, that the same name might come up twice in one week. "I saw Arabella's legal documents. They were in order."

"I know that."

"I cannot stand the thought that you are not my brother."

"If we belonged to the Aznars, your name would be María. Mine, José."

She smiled, delighted. "I have no memory of such a name, do you?"

"I was so young when we were taken—"

"*If* we were taken, you mean, which we weren't."

He laughed. "I know. Perhaps it is just that I would like to belong to these people. Their loss was so great. So tragic." He told her about the letters he had been writing, about Marta Aznar's replies, about the love for her children that seemed to animate her words about them.

"I wonder how it would feel to be so loved by earthly parents."

He sat on his bunk, bounced on it a couple of times. The springs jangled and clanked. "This is quite a hotel Julian has put us up in."

"Yes. Julian—" she leaned her forehead against the bars—"you were right all along."

"It is the age-old truth. Power corrupts."

"I could not see it when you first told me. But now I do. Now that it is too late."

They fell silent, and Danita settled onto her hard cot with a resounding clang. "I am glad you are here."

"I am too," he said.

"I do not know what is ahead..."

"Neither do I. It is best that we think of other things." He stretched out on his cot, which protested with another clang and squeak.

"Do we have any chance of being rescued?"

He turned to look at her, his struggle evident. He wanted to lie to shield her from the awful truth, but he couldn't. Raúl never was a good liar, even as a child. "No," he said. "No one knows where we are."

"I see." Her voice sounded small.

"I am sorry, Dani."

"So am I, little brother. But we have each other."

Her heart swelled at the truth. They had each other. It was enough.

The following morning K.C. awoke with a start, her heart pounding wildly. Her nightmare began to fade, but snatches of it remained.

Men, miners perhaps, working in a tunnel. It was dark, dank, and cold. Some had been holding lanterns, their faces smudged with granite dust, maybe explosives powder. Somehow she knew they were Spanish, though she had no idea why she would know that. And then a rider with glowing eyes of coal, riding a thundering horse toward her, toward the caves.

Horse hooves beating the ground with earthquake force. Boulders and rocks breaking loose, bouncing up from the earth. An explosion. A cave-in. Men crying out in pain and fear.

With a shudder, she swung her feet off the bed, wondering why she would dream such a thing. She checked her watch. 6:53. Gav would stop by to accompany her to breakfast at eight o'clock. Grabbing her towel and the nun's pine shampoo, she hurried to the bathroom at the end of the hall, awaited her turn at the shower and then headed back to her room to dress.

The dream stayed with her through it all, nagging at something in her memory.

She brushed her hair back and tied it with a ribbon, wishing for the hundredth time she had a blow-dryer. She smiled, remembering the expressions on Sister Calandria's and Sister Josefina's faces when she asked if anyone at the convent had one. She missed the sisters. Perhaps today she would slip out of her hiding place and take them flowers, something to show her appreciation.

Outside the wind was howling, and in the distance thunder rolled. K.C. shivered and pulled on her jeans and an extra shirt—another the sisters had purchased at a street market.

Gav knocked at her door precisely at 7:59.

Swinging it open, she arched a brow. "You're a minute early."

He grinned. "I got here early just so I could do this…" He pulled her into an embrace. "Just to feel you in my arms once more."

"A whole minute early. I would rather have had two," she teased, relaxing against him. She pulled back slightly after a moment, reached up to put a hand on either side of his face. "I love you, Señor Gavin."

A clap of thunder suddenly shook the room. Gav turned to look out the still-open door. "I was going to suggest we head to a coffeehouse across from the Jesuit College for breakfast, but we may get drenched."

"After what we've been through, what's a little rain?" She laughed.

A worried frown still creased his brows. "If we're right about Tres Equis moving up their timetable, our whereabouts might be the last thing they care about right now."

"I agree. While you're meeting with Raúl and Brother Thomas, I'll take flowers to the convent."

He paused. "Here's a better idea. Why don't you wait until I'm through with the meeting? Then we'll go together."

She gave him a playful punch in the arm. "You worry too much, Gav. I can take care of myself." She tilted her chin upward and grinned. "Look what I've been through. And I'm fine. Perfectly fine."

He shook his head slowly. "If anything happened to you, Kace..."

She touched the tip of his nose with her index finger. "Nothing will, silly. I will be careful."

But he didn't seem comforted. "I'd feel better about it if you'd wear the robe one last time. So you can blend in with the crowds."

Shrugging, she grabbed the novice's robe off a hook and slipped it on with a smile. "Aye aye, my love."

As they walked toward the courtyard she changed the subject. "Have you ever seen so many processions?"

Seeming especially vigilant, his gaze scanned the crowds as they walked toward the rúa. "I heard someplace that there are over five hundred between Palm Sunday and Easter."

"And I think we've either seen or heard every one." She chuckled, but Gav only grunted a halfhearted laugh.

The first few drops of rain fell, and Gav opened his umbrella. She caught his hand and held it between both of hers as a group of penitentes moved toward them on their way to the procession route.

Finally, Gav's spirits seemed to lift and he laughed out loud. "The fourteen-inch rule."

"What?"

"I had a friend at a Christian university where they enforced a rule requiring their male and female students to remain fourteen inches apart at all times."

She giggled. "I can't think of anything more appropriate for us today." She stepped away from him, precisely a prim fourteen inches. "Or anything I like less."

They stepped into the coffee shop just as a deluge of sleet began. The racket was deafening. K.C. seated herself near a window, and Gav went to the counter to order café con leche and rolls. He returned minutes later with two cups of steaming coffee.

She bit into the soft, sweet biscuit. "Hmm." Outside, the icy rain sheeted against the windows.

"Kace, we're both trying too hard to make light of the danger…." He paused. "But in reality, we may be facing some tough developments by this afternoon."

"I know." She took a sip of coffee, then reached for his hand. "It's been in the back of my mind."

"This Chaos bug may be set to take effect at any time today." He glanced at his watch. "We may still have time to get out of Salamanca…."

"No. Not until we do what we can for Dani."

He let out a deep sigh, shaking his head. "We don't have any idea where to begin. And we don't know—perhaps Raúl was successful in gaining her release."

She sipped her coffee, looking at him over the brim of the cup, then set it back in the saucer. "When you see Raúl—if you find that he's been successful—then I'll agree to leave."

His face relaxed, and he took another bite of his roll. "Good. I'll hold you to that." He gave his face a swipe with his napkin, then drank the rest of his coffee.

A clap of thunder hit a distance away, rattling the windows. K.C. jumped, then gave him an embarrassed laugh before taking another sip of coffee.

Gav glanced at his watch. "I'd better head over to the cathedral. I don't want to be late—have to make my way into that tower without a guide."

Suddenly, she didn't want him to go. Perhaps she was wrong to insist on being away from him, on being out on the streets alone. "Be careful, Gav. The place is centuries old, probably falling apart inside. The rain…the height of it…"

He glanced around the small room to make sure no one was watching before lifting her fingers to his lips. "I'll be fine. I promise." He stood, hesitated a moment, looking down at her. "Wait for me. If all is well with Dani, we'll leave immediately."

She gave him a soft smile. "I'm going to buy some flowers for Sister Calandria and Sister Josefina. I'll hurry back right after. I promise."

He glanced around again, then with a grin, bent to give her a chaste peck on the cheek. "I love you, Kace," he whispered.

Grabbing his hand, she held it for just an instant. "You are my life…my love, Gav."

He walked out into the rain, opened his umbrella, and stopped outside the window to wave. She blew him a kiss. Grinning, he jumped in the air to catch it. Her eyes misted as she remembered the last time he'd done the same thing. In the gardens of the Alhambra.

K.C. found a corner grocery store all of seven feet wide and twelve feet deep. After she picked out two bouquets of daffodils, a toothless little man with a hook nose took her bills of pesetas and counted out her change in Spanish.

The flowers' bright, sunny color seemed incongruous with the stormy day, and that was precisely why she chose them.

Soon she was hurrying along the rúa toward the convent, her cellophane-wrapped bouquets getting drenched. The processions continued, even in the freezing rain, the penitentes marching without umbrellas or raincoats.

Just as Gav suggested, she mixed with the crowds, weaving in and out of the groups, trying not to move too quickly so she wouldn't draw attention to herself. She skirted the Plaza Mayor, then headed down an alley near the convent. Soon the ancient building was in sight, and she breathed a sigh of relief.

When Sister Calandria answered the door, a wide smile lit her face. "Greetings, my child!"

K.C. knew the woman's vows wouldn't allow physical contact, but she clapped her hands in delight. A passable substitute for grabbing K.C. and doing a little jig—which is what Sister Calandria's eyes said she wanted to do.

Just then Sister Josefina skirted around the corner, made a *tsk-tsk* sound, and placed her hands on her hips. "Well, come in out of the rain," she said, frowning. But her eyes also told a different tale. They said she would have loved nothing more than to gather K.C. into her arms.

"I know you can't receive personal gifts," K.C. said, "so I've brought these for all the sisters to enjoy." She handed them each a cluster of daffodils, watching as the women dipped their noses into the bouquets and drew in deep breaths, smiling as if they were in heaven.

K.C. chuckled. "I knew you would like them—they reminded me of you."

Josefina scowled. "Ha! Me a daffodil?"

"It is your bright and sunny disposition she was thinking of, Sister Josefina." Sister Calandria's grin was pure mischief.

Josefina was still scowling, but a little smile played at the corners of her mouth.

"I came by to thank you both for taking me in, for sharing your hearts and love and good food."

"And teaching you to cook?" Sister Josefina quirked a teasing brow.

K.C. giggled. "Yes, and teaching me to cook."

"Come with us, child." Sister Calandria gestured for K.C. to follow. "We are making Easter pastries. Perhaps you would like to join us."

"I can't stay, but I'd love to see the kitchen one more time." She laughed. "Actually, I want to tell some of the other sisters good-bye. Especially Mother, if she isn't too busy."

Several other sisters looked up and greeted K.C. as the threesome passed through the lower gallery on the way to Mother's office, then a few minutes later, as they made their way through the dining room and into the kitchen.

The kitchen was filled with a bustle of activity and the fragrance of baking. K.C. stopped by each counter to comment on the beautiful little delicacies. Two sisters were decorating the creations with frosting, two others were rolling out dough layered with slathers of butter, then folding, slathering, and rolling again with the pin.

"Would you like to try?" Sister Calandria nodded to those bent over the counter concentrating on their decorating skills.

"Do you really think she should?" Sister Josefina commented dryly.

They spoke for a few minutes about the Easter Sunday preparations, the sisters teasing K.C. about how they needed several more weeks to teach her a few more tips about cooking. Through it all, Sister Josefina shook her head slowly, making her *tsk-tsk* sound as though to say it was a lost cause no matter how long K.C. stayed with them.

As Sister Calandria walked with K.C. to the door, she thanked K.C. again for the daffodils, then added, "This is our day to march in the processions. If you see a group pass by dressed in royal purple, you will know it is the convent of Teresa of Ávila."

The sister's words brought back the Tres Equis plans, and K.C.'s heart caught for an instant. "I will watch for you if we are still here."

"You look worried, K.C."

She briefly filled the sister in on the latest movements of Tres Equis. Sister Calandria nodded, and it was obvious from her somber expression that she understood the seriousness of the group's plans.

"Can you postpone your procession? Wait one more day…? March tomorrow?"

The sister shook her head. "No matter the heart conditions of other groups as they march during Holy Week, we do this in honor and praise of our Lord. He will be with us."

K.C. looked out into the rain as a rumble of thunder carried from the distance, then turned back to Sister Calandria. "I will pray for your safety this day. What time are you scheduled to march?"

"We will begin at eleven, but when the bell tolls twelve you will find us near the cathedral. We planned it that way." She looked pleased. "It is a place of honor on Maundy Thursday. Our cardinal will speak to those who have gathered there. I hope you can come."

K.C. winced, then attempted to calm her fears. Just because the original time was noon on Good Friday, it didn't mean that the new time set for the Chaos bug was noon today. It couldn't be. Why would it be? She forced herself to remain calm. "If Gav and I are still here at noon, we will watch for your royal purple robes and know it is you."

"Every year Sister Josefina carries a cross as tall as she is and walks with bare feet to experience a portion of our Lord's suffering. You will recognize her, but not the rest of us, with our headdresses and masks." She smiled softly. "And shoes."

K.C. left the warmth of the convent a few minutes later, sorry to say good-bye. If she and Gav did leave before noon it was likely that she wouldn't see the sisters again.

The freezing rain fell in sheets and hit at a slant, bouncing from the street and stinging K.C.'s ankles. She stayed under the shelter of awnings, hurrying from one to the next as she made her way back to the Jesuit College and its hostel.

A loud clap of thunder suddenly hit right above her.

K.C. gasped and fell back against the outer wall of a nearby shop. Her heart pounded, and she fought to draw in a deep breath, laughing at herself for her unreasonable fear.

She stepped out into the cobbled street once more…just as another rumbling, explosive clap rattled the ground.

This time she stopped dead still. The rain poured down on her, dripping from her hood and robe, soaking her through to the bone. But she was too stunned to move.

Her nightmare came back to her. The miners. The picks. The lanterns. The explosions.

Valle de los Caídos. Valley of the Dead.

It was Alfredo Aznar who had worked in the tunnels…it was he who had lived and worked there as a slave laborer for years.

If prisoners were still taken there today, he would know how to find them in the maze of tunnels.

It was a big *if*, but just maybe…

K.C. moved to the shelter of another awning and, lost in thought, walked slowly along the side of the rúa.

Julian had ordered her taken to the Valley of the Dead. Wouldn't it stand to reason that his pattern would be the same for all those in his custody?

And if he was holding political prisoners, wouldn't it follow that he would take Franco's example as his own?

She stepped up her pace, then stopped and checked her watch. It would be too long to wait for Gav's meeting to be over. No. She needed to find a telephone. And fast.

She glanced across the street, then back again. Finally, she spotted a pay phone just outside a café at the end of the block.

Gav's warning about moving in the crowds, slowly and nonchalantly, so she wouldn't draw attention to herself drifted into her mind. But she was running out of time.

As was Dani.

Picking up the edge of her sodden robe, K.C. jogged along the street, dodging puddles and paying no attention to the soaking penitentes still marching past.

She grabbed for the receiver, then frowned in irritation. It took phone cards only. With a sigh, she headed into the café and asked the proprietor if she could purchase a card from him.

He nodded, and she lifted her robe to dig into her jeans' pocket for some bills. The man was watching her with a puzzled look, and she realized too late what she'd done. She quickly dropped the robe, handed him the money, then hurried back to the telephone, belatedly adjusting her hood to conceal her hair.

A moment later she had received the Granada number from the information operator. With trembling fingers, she punched in the number and waited while it rang.

Doc Rafael, dressed in a white penitente gown and headdress, headed down the rúa toward the Jesuit College where Tres Equis would assemble within the hour. Beneath his robe, weapons were strapped on a belt at his waist. The other members were already preparing themselves in the same manner.

He held himself proud as he strode along the rúa, head high, chin up. This was the day they had all been awaiting. It was genius of the leadership to switch days and times. And how fitting that they had chosen the anniversary of Hitler's birth.

He was about to turn left onto Meléndez, which would lead him to the college, when a familiar figure caught his attention.

K.C. Keegan's slight build and red hair had given her away. She was talking on a pay telephone, gesturing, quite animated. Obviously excited about something.

He moved closer, realizing his prey had no idea who was stalking her…or even that she was being stalked. Perhaps his robe wasn't the color of the other penitentes' this day, but he was covered head to toe in the same garb as hundreds of others.

K.C. Keegan would not know he was following her every move.

As he inched close enough to hear her conversation, he reached beneath his mask to adjust his mustache, irritated that it caught on the silken material nearly every time he drew in a breath.

Suddenly, she replaced the receiver and glanced around as though sensing her vulnerability. She pulled her hood further over her hair and started down the street, obviously trying to fit into the crowd, sometimes sidling, sometimes sauntering.

He chuckled as he matched her stride, movement by movement.

TWENTY-THREE

K.C. CHECKED HER WATCH, SHELTERING IT FROM THE RAIN WITH the cuff of her robe. Gav might still be in his meeting with Brother Thomas, Raúl, and Duncan. If she hurried, she could catch them all together to tell them of her discovery. And of her hurried call to the Aznars to ask for their help in finding Dani.

She'd heard the disappointment in Alfredo's voice when she said that it was unlikely Dani and Raúl were the children they were looking for. She'd briefly explained about the grandmother who'd turned up.

Then she added, almost as an afterthought, that it was possible—in her opinion—that the documents provided to Dani could have been forged. Sadly, there was no proof either way.

But when Alfredo heard about the missing girl—and listened to K.C.'s plea for help—he said they would head to Valle de los Caídos and see what they could do.

Pulling her hood closer and shivering with the cold, K.C. headed for the cathedral. She tried to recall the directions Raúl had given them the day before. He'd mentioned a back entrance, one now used by artisans who were restoring the altarpiece of the old cathedral. Few people knew about it, and usually the door was kept unlocked, he'd explained, because the workers used that entrance to carry their materials into and out of the cathedral day and night.

Though perhaps not during Holy Week. She had observed that schools were closed, shops were dark, street workers had stopped laying cobbles and their jackhammers had fallen silent. Everything in Salamanca was shut down, it seemed, except the coffeeshops. Salamancans seemed willing to give up everything except their café con leche.

She smiled, observing still dozens more penitentes marching in the street next to her. Of course the city shut down. Everyone was dressed in robes and marching in the streets.

She rounded the corner near the Jesuit College, headed past the small fountain next to the House of Shells, around another corner, and into a narrow cobbled street. It was surprisingly deserted. Only a few tourists and penitentes. Glancing around, she noticed one who seemed to be heading the same direction as she—toward the cathedral. Not surprising. After all, many of the processions began from there.

The rain still fell steadily, but the wind had died down. She hopped over a few puddles, and continued on her way, glancing back once or twice.

Still the robed figure followed.

Gav settled into his chair in the computer room at the Jesuit College. The men he'd met earlier were seated near him, as was

Duncan. Thomas had taken his usual place in the front of the room.

A bleak atmosphere seemed to have settled over them. No one had seen Raúl since the day before.

"It can only mean one thing," Thomas said. "He's been taken by Julian's forces."

One of the other men spoke up. "Our worry, then, is if he gave away the codes. Then the timetable has indeed been moved up."

Someone else asked if it was possible Raúl could have gone to their originally planned meeting place.

Thomas shook his head. "He would know we changed our plans. The place is simply too dangerous to attempt in this kind of weather." He paused. "We have met there before, gentlemen. You know as well as I do that the dangers of reaching the tower outweigh the advantages of a completely secure location with several kilometers' visibility every direction."

He paused, his expression grim. "This means we must assume insurrection is imminent. We can no longer wait for Raúl or for further clarification about the Chaos bug. We must act. And act quickly.

"Right now, National Guard troops are moving into position in and around the city."

Someone from the back of the room spoke up. "What is the estimated time for action against Tres Equis?"

"Since the original time was noon tomorrow," Thomas said, "we are assuming that the internal device for Chaos was simply moved forward a day. We cannot know for certain, but we are planning to move our troops into the city by noon."

"What about the Chaos bug itself?" someone else asked. "Won't it affect the operations of our tanks and helicopters, as well as the communication among the troops?"

Thomas stepped back, leaning against the wall behind him. "We have spent the night developing strategies to counteract that." He gave them a weary smile. "After all, armies have operated for centuries without computerization. Perhaps we can pull from our centuries of practice—without electronics—and wage a healthy offense against this group."

He looked around the room, the dark circles under his eyes telling of his fatigue and deep concerns more than his words ever could. "I want to warn you, gentlemen. Get your loved ones off the streets today. If any of your family members are marching in the processions, especially around twelve o'clock, I cannot recommend strongly enough that you find them and pull them out. Encourage them to wait to perform their religious obligations until tomorrow."

He gave them a thin-lipped smile. "Tell them I think God will understand." Gathering together his papers, he, several of his men, and the Interpol agents all vacated the room.

Gav glanced at Duncan, whose face was taut with worry, as both men stood and headed to the door.

"They obviously don't need our help," Duncan said with a short laugh.

Gav shook his head slowly at the understatement, pulled open the door and let his friend go through first. "We still don't know what's happened to Dani. Or to Raúl."

Duncan shook his head. "I came to help the Aznars find their children—and here we are in the middle of a national emergency. And still no closer to helping my friends than I was in Porto."

Gav hung his arm over the other man's shoulders as they headed out of the college.

"Wasn't it you who said that we don't always know why God allows certain things to happen to us?"

Duncan grinned. "Aye. I believe it was."

"Think about Dani. Whether she's related to the Aznars or not—your coming here made a difference in her life. She may never find her earthly parents, but you helped her discover her heavenly Father."

"God knows better than we when we've succeeded and when we have failed." Duncan mused for a moment.

Gav grunted in assent. "He asks us to obey him, not shoot for success," rephrasing K.C.'s favorite Mother Teresa quote.

Duncan nodded. "How easily we forget." He fell silent a moment as they headed down the steps and into the street.

Crowds, even greater than before, were moving into the street that led to the cathedral. Groups of penitentes—in costumes of crimson, purple, blue, black, and white—were marching, even in the pouring rain. More of them carried life-sized crosses. One directly in front of the men was so large and heavy, the bearer dragged it in much the way Jesus himself must have done.

"Some of these people are so fervent in their desire to honor God, to honor the sacrifice of his Son on the cross," Duncan said. "Then there are the others. Those who see the processions as something to prove their religious fervor."

"Which has nothing to do with their heart relationship with their Lord."

Duncan's troubled gaze never moved from the bearer struggling with the heaviest of the crosses. "And most never give a thought to that intimate relationship with their Creator."

"My friend," Gav said as they started down the Rúa Mayor, "you said there's nothing we can do for Dani and Raúl at this point…."

"Aye, that I did."

"You are wrong. There is."

Duncan halted midstep and turned to him, a realization lighting his blue eyes before Gav could get the words out.

"You are a prayer warrior, my friend. Let's go someplace quiet and lift our hearts to God."

Duncan nodded. "How we need him this day." His gaze scanned the crowds. "Not just Dani and Raúl, but how we all need him! Aye, let's find a place to pray."

The cathedral towers rose in the distance through the shroud of rain. Gav nodded toward it. "What better place to take shelter—and share in prayer?"

Just then lightning cracked open the sky and another deluge of rain pounded the earth.

Gav laughed. "Maybe that's not such a good idea after all," he shouted above the roar of the rain. "Why don't we head back to the hostel? I need to let K.C. know the latest anyway—make sure she stays away from the processions."

Duncan nodded and they sprinted toward the place of lodging behind the Jesuit College. A clap of thunder rumbled in the distance, and suddenly Gav couldn't wait to see if K.C. was safe.

K.C. had found the door open, just as Brother Thomas had promised. She'd found her way to the cloister, passed by the ancient tombs with their carved effigies, and finally found the spiral staircase leading to the top of the tower and to the room that Brother Thomas had said was off to the side.

But one look, from where she stood at the bottom, up into the open tower itself, had made her so dizzy she had to sit on a bottom step to recover.

The steps, uneven and nearly too small for a foothold, were made of stone and built into the side of the tower itself.

Obviously the early builders of this glorious church had been hardy and nimble souls and hadn't seen the need for a railing of any kind.

Every time she ventured a look up, vertigo overwhelmed her and the entire tower seemed to spin madly.

She didn't know how long she sat there, holding her head, but it seemed like an eternity. Finally, she drew a deep breath.

"Okay, Kace, m'girl," she muttered to herself. "You can do this. You can do this. You can do this."

Then she stood, closed her eyes and prayed, swallowed hard, and moistened her dry lips.

Still, she couldn't bring herself to climb those stairs. So she sat down again, buried her head in her hands. "Dear Lord, help me! Don't let this fear conquer me. I know you are with me always—whether on the solid ground, or—" she glanced up, her heart hammering —"up there," she finished with a shudder.

There weren't many things in life that she couldn't conquer—with God's help—if she set her mind to it. She prided herself on her fearless nature.

Her terror of heights was the one exception.

She stood, feeling silly. It wasn't as though she had to climb these stairs. After all, Gav and the others would be coming down soon. It was foolish to push herself this way. In the grand scheme of things, whether or not she climbed this tower would probably not matter one iota.

Except to herself.

And maybe to Dani.

The girl's heart-shaped face came to her mind. If she was in trouble at Valley of the Dead, and if Brother Thomas—or whoever he really was—could order troops to meet the Aznars there, Dani's life might be saved. Minutes might make a difference.

Climbing this tower might matter after all.

Plus, she was determined not to let it defeat her.

"Okay, Father," she breathed. "It's just you and me."

Clenching her jaw and fighting the urge to keep her eyes closed, she put her foot on the first step, lifted the hem of her robe, and stepped onto the second.

Tentatively, she moved to the third step.

Eyes forward, she refused to look up. Or down. Especially down.

And she took one more step, gathered the edge of her robe with her right hand, and—keeping her left palm flat against the curved wall—took another.

The stone beneath her foot wobbled slightly. She bit her lip and kept going.

"Dani?" Raúl called across the space that divided them. "Are you all right?"

The sound of his voice woke her, and Danita rolled over on the squeaky cot and sat up, rubbing her eyes. "I just had a bit of a nap. Do you know what time it is?"

He checked his watch. "I have 11:30. It's Thursday morning. Time has a strange way of passing, I mean without daylight and dark to help divide the days from nights. I have been here a matter of hours, but it seems like days."

"It doesn't help that we cannot turn off our light." She stood, bent to touch her toes a few times, then stretched and yawned. "I wonder if they plan to feed us today?"

He chuckled. "Actually, last night's supper was not as terrible as I thought it would be."

She sat back on the edge of the cot. "We should talk about our rescue."

"I told you last night that there is no chance."

"Then our escape."

"This place is impregnable. Even I have figured that out."

"We are highly trained. Julian saw to that himself."

Raúl laughed, though without humor. "My blindfold was removed once I entered this place. It is a maze, Dani." He stood and moved to the locked grate, took hold of two of the bars and leaned his forehead against them. "Escape isn't an option."

"I do not give up as easily as you do, little brother." She forced a tone of challenge into her voice, but in reality, her heart sank. She knew he was correct. She too had seen the labyrinth of tunnels.

"Tell me again about the letter," she said after a few minutes, thinking it might lighten her mood.

"From the Aznars?"

"Yes."

"It may only serve to make us feel worse. Not only has Julian rejected us, we found another dead end in our own search."

"I do not accept that you are not my brother."

He nodded. "I feel the same way. No one will ever change my mind, no matter what evidence they provide."

"The letter?" she prodded. She laid back down on the cot, ignoring the corkscrews of metal tht poked into her back.

"The woman's name is Marta Aznar. I do not know what she might look like, but she writes from a heart filled to overflowing with love for children she has not seen in twenty-five years."

As Raúl talked, Danita closed her eyes, imagining the writer of such a letter.

"Her children were taken from her in the middle of the night, after she and her husband were arrested for treason against Franco."

Danita's eyes flew open. "For resisting the fascist state? Even if we were their children how could they forgive us for becoming a part of Tres Equis?"

"I do not know how we can forgive ourselves, my sister."

She fell quiet a moment. "Somehow, I have felt that you never were working for Julian...for Tres Equis." When he didn't answer, she turned on her cot, propping her head with her hand, to face him. "Am I right?"

He sat back down on his cot, put his head in his hands, his fingers fanned in his hair. He looked up after a long moment. "I suppose there is no reason to keep the truth from you now."

"What truth?"

"I have never worked for Julian."

"That is why I sensed you had no passion."

"True. I felt only abhorrence for his plans."

"You have been working for someone else, yes?"

"Yes, my sister."

"Can you tell me who?"

"It is better that I do not." His gaze locked on hers from across the space that separated them. "I do not know what Julian might do to get to the truth, to find out who I have been working for. It is for your protection that you do not know."

Staring at the ceiling, she thought about his words for a moment, then turned to look at him again. "How will he find out? You said he sent you here because of treasonous acts having to do with protecting me, finding me. How will he equate that with you working for someone else?"

Raúl drew in a deep breath and looked at his watch. "At exactly twelve o'clock today—less than a half hour from now—he will know. My ultimate betrayal of Julian, of Tres Equis, will be evident to everyone."

"What do you mean? How?"

"In exactly eighteen minutes—the Chaos bug is scheduled to explode throughout every computer system in Spain."

She gasped and sat up. "Today?"

He nodded. "Julian switched the time to throw off any move against him." He smiled with the irony of it. "To throw off moves by people planted within the organization. Like me."

"But you outsmarted him…and that is how he will discover who you really are." Suddenly her heart ached with pride and fear for her brother. "What did you do?"

He chuckled with real amusement. "I programmed the real bug to implode, to render itself benign. I also programmed an alias file in the event of my capture—that could be programmed by myself or someone else—for whatever time was chosen. An alias that is perfectly harmless." He laughed again. "When it releases, the bug will travel through cyberspace and land in a single place: Julian's e-mail."

He was smiling ear to ear. "I would love to be with him when he opens his e-mail, expecting disaster, and finds instead an animated brass-colored cockroach, waving his antennae. I have programmed this bug to do one thing. Greet Julian with a big smile, a salute, and the word *¡hola!*"

Danita laughed. "You did *not.* Surely you did not do that."

"I did." He sobered. "But you see, Dani, he will know then that I double-crossed him. I—and now you—will be in grave danger." He shook his head. "I am desperate to get us out of here. I just do not know how."

"The guards took everything from me. I have not an earring, a pen—absolutely nothing metal—to use in the lock."

"They did the same with me."

She lay back down on the cot and stared at a stain in the ceiling. Her heart pounded in fear. She tried to pray, but found the words…the thoughts, wouldn't come. "Tell me again about Marta Aznar."

He laughed. "I have told you everything. Well, except in her last letter she mentioned a song that her husband Alfredo made up for their children. The melody is from Schumann's songs for children. Do you know them?"

"No. I have never heard of them."

"She called the collection Kinderszenin."

She searched her memory. Nothing came to her. "I keep hoping I will remember something. A clue I can cling to…but it is no use. I have never heard the name before."

"Neither have I."

Hot tears filled her eyes. "I want to find our family, Raúl. I refuse to believe that you are not my brother. I also refuse to believe Arabella Stern is my grandmother."

He snorted. "I cannot blame you. She told me that she has already disowned you for your actions against Tres Equis."

"She was the one who turned me in."

"I know, Dani. I know."

She brushed her tears from her cheeks. "The sad thing about it is that I was almost getting used to the idea, and wondered if we might have a relationship after all. The night of our practice march, she came up to me as though she cared. She asked about my engagement to Julian, even advised me to be sure I loved him."

She looked across at Raúl. "It was the kind of thing a grandmother would do." She paused. "And she asked me about the saetas I told everyone I would write for our procession. There was something in her voice that sounded so proud of me, of my accomplishments."

She sniffled quietly. "It is hard for me to trust anyone who says they care, after what was done to us as children. But I was drawn to her in that moment. I actually believed that we might be related. And oh, how I wanted her to love me! Just for that instant, I wanted to know that she cared, that she was proud to call me her granddaughter."

"Then it was destroyed," Raúl said. "You act as though you do not care. But she betrayed you."

"Yes."

"Did you ever write the song?"

She laughed lightly. "Not *that* song. Something happened to me that brought new music to my heart."

He looked confused, and she laughed again. Then she told him why the only song she could possibly write was one of praise to her heavenly Father, not one of praise to her country, lifting up nationalistic pride. Raúl listened intently to every word.

The prison walls seemed to disappear as she talked about meeting her heavenly Father, the Lord who wanted her to call him Papá.

"Papá?" He didn't seem to know whether to laugh or cry or be joyful with her. "Papá?"

She gave him a decisive nod. "Papá."

They sat staring at each other in silence. Raúl's expression reflected such longing that she wondered if it stemmed from the same heart needs as hers—a yearning for the parental love they had missed.

Then Raúl pulled back his cuff and glanced at his watch. "It is almost noon."

Danita closed her eyes. Almost time for their death sentence.

TWENTY-FOUR

K.C. HAD ALMOST REACHED THE TOP OF THE BELL TOWER WHEN she heard a noise behind her.

Below her.

She didn't dare look down. If she did, the world would spin.

She would fall.

Strange that she could hear noises below her from this towering height, but she could hear nothing from above...nothing from the room at the top of the tower, where Gav was supposed to meet Brother Thomas and Duncan.

She tried to laugh at her fears. The same hardy builders who'd designed the staircase without a railing probably built their rooms with five-foot-thick stone walls. Gav had to be there...didn't he?

But the nagging concern wouldn't leave her. What if Gav and the others weren't at the top of the tower at all? Perhaps their meeting had been short.

Or—and she shuddered as she took another step—or maybe they had met with foul play.

Her heart thudded, and she drew in a deep breath, fighting the urge to cry. Here she was, nearly to the top of a stories-high tower. To find Gav. Who might not even be there. Might not be able to pull her into his arms…and help her down.

Again the sound at the bottom of the tower caught her attention.

Suddenly, she smiled. Gav!

It had to be. Perhaps the group had met, disbanded early, and now he was coming for her.

But no. Her elation died as quickly as it had sparked. Gav had no way of knowing she was here. She'd told no one.

The creak of shoes on stairs carried upward, its echo magnified as it bounced off the circular walls.

"Gav?" She held her breath, hoping above all hope to hear his warm baritone call up to her. "Gav?" Her voice sounded pitifully weak.

Still the footsteps approached, climbing more quickly than she was.

Fighting the urge to look back, she riveted her attention on the stairs left to climb. One step. Then another. Only a few more to the top.

The climber was closer now, and she knew she was being watched.

She took another step, almost tripping on her hem. For the hundredth time she wished she'd thrown off her robe at the bottom of the stairs. The stone beneath her foot crumbled. It broke off and fell, echoing and bouncing as it descended. She halted her ascent and closed her eyes to get her bearings.

"Oh, Lord, help me…."

A laugh came from behind her. "You thought I would forget, did you not, K.C. Keegan?"

Her heart froze.

Doc Rafael went on. "I told you what would happen if your Sheriff Gavin returned for you."

She moved up one more step.

"I told you back at the Valley of the Dead that my threats are never empty. You can count on my word, K.C. Keegan. Always."

Fighting to breathe, she placed her foot on another step.

"It is lucky I saw you come to this place. Otherwise my job would have been so much more difficult. As it is, you in your bungling have made this day complete." He laughed.

Only three more steps to the top. She drew in a deep breath and calculated the distance to the walkway that circled the inside of the tower. Crouching, she could scramble on all fours to reach it—and safety—within a heartbeat.

But just as she crouched and gathered her robe around her, ready to spring, his fingers wrapped around her ankle.

K.C. was not at the hostel. Scarcely pausing for breath, Gav and Duncan headed out of the hostel courtyard and turned right, toward the Rúa Mayor. The drums had begun again, the echo of their dirgelike rhythm rolling through the narrow streets. The mournful tones of trumpets and trombones carried from blocks away, accompanying the hundreds of penitentes who had stepped into formations. Dozens of processions already snaked from the plaza, heading along the rúa toward the cathedral.

A light rain was all that now fell—a dank, gray drizzle. Floats with statues of Christ—sometimes with his mother, other times with his disciples—bobbed along on the backs of the penitentes, the rain droplets causing the carvings to gleam as if newly varnished.

Some of the groups carried torches, their flames leaping into the gray mist.

Gav shot a worried look at Duncan as they headed toward the cathedral with the rest of the throng. "K.C. said she'd be right back. Her stop at the convent shouldn't have lasted this long."

Duncan frowned. "Why don't we split up? I'll head back to the convent to see if she's still there." He pointed to the cathedral steps. "From up there you might get a better look at the crowd."

Gav nodded. "Good idea. Hurry back and let me know what you find out."

Duncan sprinted away, and Gav turned to head up the stairs leading to the cathedral. Once in place, he scanned the plaza in front of him. A dais was being set up for church dignitaries, and some of the robed penitentes, who'd already finished their portion of the march, strolled by with headpieces held in the crooks of their arms.

He leaned against a flat stone wall and studied the crowds. No one resembled K.C. He knew it was a shot in the dark, but still he hoped that just by chance she might glance up at him.

Where could she be? He shuddered, refusing to think that she had been nabbed from under his nose again. The Tres Equis threats made to K.C. while she was held captive came back to him full force, mocking him for his naiveté.

Why hadn't he taken greater care?

Heart pounding, he scanned the crowds milling in front of him.

"Elliot Gavin!" called a voice from among the penitentes.

He squinted through the gray drizzle to the terraced area below.

"Señor Gavin! Señor Gavin!"

Finally he spotted two robed figures, both waving. They were dressed in dark purple, and one had a heavy cross leaning against her back. Both wore their headpieces, but had pushed aside their silken masks.

Sisters Calandria and Josefina!

He sprinted down the steps and hurried toward them.

"Where is Señorita K.C.?" Sister Calandria asked. "We thought we would find her here with you."

With that one simple question, Gav's breath caught in his throat and his heart dropped.

K.C. was in trouble.

K.C. crouched in the corner of the bell tower watching Doc Rafael stride along the walkway, peering down at the crowds. The rains had stopped completely, but a brisk wind whipped through the open arches of the tower.

"In just minutes, this will all belong to Tres Equis." He tugged at his mustache, a pleased look on his face.

The winds lifted the strand of hair that he usually kept wound around his bald head. But with the icy fear that had knotted inside her, K.C. couldn't find any humor in it.

She inched toward the walkway, pretending to adjust her back against the short stone that framed the tower. If only she could make a run for the staircase. As frightening as it would be to make her way back down, she had decided it was her best chance.

Maybe her only chance.

The room in which she'd hoped to find Gav, Thomas, and Duncan had been empty, just as she'd feared. No help there. And the little man who waited for the countdown was waving a western-style, pearl-handled revolver.

"Stand, my dear," Doc commanded. His flowing white penitente robe snapped in the wind. "I want you to see this."

She didn't move.

"I said *stand.*"

"I can't."

He turned to glare at her, holding his pocket watch so that it swayed by its gold chain. "In precisely three and a half minutes the Chaos bug will be unleashed. I want you to witness the first moments. Lights will dim, then go out. That will be our first sign."

He made a move as if to yank her to her feet, so she stood, digging her fingers into the wall, feeling her stomach drop to her toes. Her knees shook so violently that she thought he would surely notice, even beneath her robe.

Moving toward her, he jerked her around to look at the plaza below. She closed her eyes and prayed desperately for strength.

"Two minutes." His voice was triumphant. "Two minutes!"

Eyes still closed, she felt his breath in her ear as he moved his face close to hers. "You do not look well." His tone was menacing, chilling, as he continued. "Do not tell me our brave K.C. Keegan is afraid of heights."

She didn't answer.

"I have the perfect solution," he said, laughing. "Any doctor will tell you the best way to conquer your fears is to face them. You can condition yourself through exposure to those things that bring on the fear."

She trembled, her legs now as weak as cooked spaghetti.

Doc wrapped his fingers around her neck. K.C.'s eyes flew open as he pressed her against the wall. "There will be more than just the Chaos bug unleashed when the bells toll twelve.

In the excitement, no one will notice that you decided to go for a walk—" he jerked his head toward the outside of the tower "—and fell, poor little accident-prone thing."

She struggled against the grip he had on her neck, but the pressure was nearly too great to suck in a breath of air. He held up the watch with his opposite hand, smiling as it swung from its chain.

"One minute," he announced. Then he dropped the watch into his pocket. "And it's time for your walk, Señorita Keegan."

Unable to speak, she shook her head. "No," she mouthed. She couldn't bear even the thought of climbing over the ledge. "Please, no."

He laughed and waved the pistol in her face. "Now go, before I lose my patience. I do not want to miss the first inklings of chaos. Although, I must say, your performance on the ledge—or flying off it—may provide us all with the best entertainment yet."

She choked back a cry. The world spun around her, and she breathed in short, gasping breaths.

"No," she whispered hoarsely. "No...please!"

He prodded her with the barrel of the gun.

"No!" The tight knot of fear in her stomach gave way to nausea. She squeezed her eyes shut to stop the spinning sensation. "No..." she whispered again. But no sound left her lips.

"Move!" A dull metal click of the gun's hammer being cocked accompanied the word. "Now!"

Trembling violently, she whispered a prayer and hiked up her robe to swing one jeans-clad leg over the squat wall.

He gave her a shove.

She teetered precariously and grabbed for one of the tower's four arched columns. Desperation gave her strength as she wrapped her arms around it.

"Thirty seconds," he announced, "and the Chaos bug will reign!"

If there was ever a chance to make her move, it had to be now. She counted slowly to herself.

Expectation lit up Doc's face like a little boy's at Christmas. He leaned forward, absorbed in the activities below. Penitentes continued marching into the terraced area below the cathedral…the cardinal moved onto the dais…a choir shuffled into place behind him…the moaning horns and dirgelike drums fell silent.

"Now!" Doc shouted triumphantly.

From the tower on the far side of the church, a bell began to toll.

He waited.

And waited.

Then he frowned. Nothing unusual happened. Still the bell tolled. His attention remained riveted to the crowd below.

Bracing her arms, K.C. swung both legs back over the wall, away from the ledge. Her feet landed in Doc's midsection with satisfying force. There was a whoosh of air from Doc's lungs, and he staggered backward toward the open staircase.

He screamed—and then he was falling.

K.C.'s hand flew to her mouth. She could only stand and listen to the sickening sounds of the man's body bouncing off the sides of the tower.

At last, there was silence.

K.C. collapsed backward against the tower wall and drew up her knees, trembling so violently she thought she would come apart. She squeezed her eyes tight, trying not to see the expression on Doc's face when she kicked him. When he fell backward away from her.

Finally, she put her face in her hands and wept.

Danita lay back on the cot, staring heavenward. Since Raúl's confession about the Chaos bug and his deception, she'd been waiting for the guards to come for them.

She feared more for Raúl than she did for herself. He would be blamed for the failure of the Tres Equis coup. Julian would act with swift—and, in all probability, fatal—cruelty.

She shook the thought away. "What time is it?"

Raúl's voice drifted to her. "It is after twelve o'clock."

She sighed. "Julian will act swiftly once he knows of your betrayal—" She turned on her side to stare through the iron grate at her brother.

They fell quiet for a moment, then Danita sighed. "I am sorry you ended up here because of me."

He smiled at her. "I would have ended up here sooner or later."

"I doubt that. I do not know who you are working for, but from all you have told me, you—they—had every contingency covered." She sighed. "Except your love for me. Your willingness to risk your life for me."

"You would have done the same for me."

She had, in fact—when she delayed telling Duncan and Gavin all she knew—and instead fell into Julian's trap—out of the false notion that she was protecting Raúl from arrest. She chuckled. "Yes, little brother, you are right. I would have."

"And so we wait."

Danita nodded. "And pray."

Julian checked his watch as the bells from the tower tolled twelve.

He frowned. Doc Rafael should have reported in by now with the news that the Tres Equis troops were in place, armed and ready to strike.

Leaning back in his chair, Julian allowed himself a confident smile. Doc was expendable. The Chaos bug was not. All he had to do was wait—and, of course, detail the action of the troops since Doc had the audacity to be late with his report.

Reaching for his intercom, he buzzed his assistant. A new plan would be implemented, a new leader would take the place of the missing Rafael. He congratulated himself that he always insisted on backups for his people.

For his plans.

He had already seen to it that today's ushering in of New Spain would not fail!

The deaths of any who dared to thwart his plan would be swift and certain.

He thought about those who had already betrayed him, and his lips curled in a hard smile. He would see to their punishment.

Soon.

Gav craned around to see if he could find K.C. By now he was nearly frantic.

Duncan stood on one side of him; on the other were sisters Calandria and Josefina, nodding and bobbing their heads as they listened to the cardinal. From time to time, they murmured words of agreement and soft praises to their Lord.

When the cardinal was finished, the choir began a soft and mournful song. The words were in Spanish, but the snatches Gav could understand spoke of Christ's sacrifice, his love even for those who rejected him.

If Gav hadn't been so worried about K.C., he would have

delighted in the beauty of the music, in the glory of Salamanca as the sun finally came out from behind the heavy gray clouds.

Halfway through the song, Sister Calandria shaded her eyes and turned to look up at the sunbathed cathedral tower. Sister Josefina hesitated, then asked Gav to hold her cross for a moment, apparently so she could have a look at the glorious sight. She removed her tall, pointed hat and shaded her eyes as well.

The women fell silent and their expressions turned to surprise. They were obviously transfixed on something other than the sun-drenched bell tower.

Gav followed their gaze. For the second time that day, his heart twisted in fear. "That can't be…"

Josefina scowled. "Why would she climb all the way up there to see the activities? You can see them perfectly well from here." She shook her head. "Americans. Always insist on having the best."

Sister Calandria frowned. "Look, she is waving! She is in trouble! She needs us now!" The sister threw down her headpiece, and, lifting her gown, began running for the tower.

Sister Josefina raced after her. Gav leaned the cross against Duncan before he could say no and took off after the sisters.

Surprisingly, the sisters knew very well how to get inside the tower. Sister Calandria explained between pants that it had long been the playground of Salamanca's children. Even she had played there as a child.

Minutes later, the circular stairway leading to the tower came into view.

Gav was the first to spot the crumpled, robed figure on the floor beneath the stairs.

He had stepped close enough to recognize Doc Rafael when he heard a cry.

He looked up. K.C., tears streaming, was trying to make her way down the stairs. Before he could move, Sister Josefina headed up the stairs surefooted as a deer.

Within seconds, she held K.C. in her arms, then turned, so that K.C. could put her hands on Sister Josefina's shoulders and follow her down the precarious staircase. By the time they reached solid ground, K.C. managed a tremulous smile.

Seconds later, she was in Gav's embrace.

Julian waited for the Chaos bug to make its presence known. So far there was no sign of it. The lights in his office had not dimmed. The all-news station on the corner television made no mention of computer or electronic interruptions in Spain or elsewhere.

He must be patient, he supposed. Raúl had likely programmed the bug to invade the systems through electronic mail. And that would take time.

To double-check his assessment, he picked up his telephone and punched in the number of the farmhouse where the new computer genius worked at the latest command center.

The man's thin voice answered after the first ring.

Julian's words were clipped, to the point. "Why have we not seen signs of chaos?"

There was a long pause, and he thought he heard the man swallow hard. "I think you need to check your e-mail. There is...well...something that you alone need to see. I cannot describe it."

Julian frowned. "What are you trying to tell me?"

Again, an awkward silence. "Just look at your electronic posts."

"Your voice tells me this is not good news."

"You need to see for yourself."

Julian slammed down the receiver and turned to his computer. Perhaps he was reading the fool's tone incorrectly. Perhaps chaos was indeed about to reign. He refused to think otherwise.

The Chaos bug would make itself known within seconds.

He pressed the key to turn it on. The computer hummed obediently, its screen causing a glow in the darkened room.

Julian opened his e-mail server. The flag on the mailbox was waving. He had mail. Perhaps this was how it would begin. He smiled. Of course. That's how so many viruses spread throughout the world. Through e-mail.

Raúl was a genius. No matter how much he disliked the young man, he was a genius.

Julian clicked on the server to open his mail. Just as he'd thought. The subject heading read, "Chaos Reigns."

He clicked to open it, curious to see how quickly it would wipe out his system. How clever that he and all Tres Equis had backups of everything they needed for the new millennium. They'd also developed a new program that would not be affected by the bug. It had taken years to develop it, but it would be worth it now. All their efforts would finally be repaid.

Then his smile faded.

A facsimile of the brass cockroach pranced onto his screen, wiggled its tail to some honky-tonk, American jazz number. It did a little two-step, then turned to him and bowed, waggling its antennae.

"¡Hola!"

And with that, the little bug winked and continued its dance, tiny legs kicking in time with the music.

That was all.

There was no flashing of lights, no diminishing of electrical power…no chaos overtaking the area…the room…

Nothing.

Just this bug dancing across his computer monitor.

He slammed his hand onto the toggle switch. The piano jazz stopped immediately, and the screen went dark.

White-hot fury roared through his veins.

Raúl had just signed his death warrant. And that of his sister.

TWENTY-FIVE

K.C., GAV, AND DUNCAN WAITED IN THE COFFEE SHOP AT THE Valley of the Dead. K.C. had explained to Gav about her call to the Aznars, how she'd hoped for Alfredo's help in finding Danita. The three were also praying that Julian might have imprisoned both young people there.

Because it was Maundy Thursday, a single tour bus was parked in the lot, and only a sprinkling of tourists wandered about, ducking in and out of the coffee shop and snapping pictures with palm-sized cameras.

K.C. had finally stopped shaking from her fright in the tower. It helped that Gav's solid arm had been around her on the drive from Salamanca, and he had kept her close ever since.

It was midafternoon when the Aznars drove into the parking lot. K.C. was the first to spot them. She placed her cup of café con leche in the saucer with a clatter and jumped up to meet them. Gav and Duncan followed.

K.C. had not seen them since the day the gardener drove her away in the little cart.

Marta drew her into a warm embrace, holding her tightly for a moment before greeting Gav. "We are so glad to know you are well," she whispered.

"You had us worried," Alfredo said, then kissed both her cheeks. He stepped back, holding her hands. "But you are safe. We rejoice in that!"

He shook hands with Duncan and Gav, then took a deep breath. "Tell me about the young woman inside."

Marta stepped closer to her husband and hooked his arm around hers. "We cannot help but hope."

Duncan reached for her hand. "We have no proof one way or the other—no records of your children's births or even photographs. On the other hand, the leader of Tres Equis, who supplied Danita and the woman claiming to be her grandmother with papers, just may have had the documents forged." He shook his head slightly. "There was money involved in the transaction, which makes it even more suspect."

Marta looked up into her husband's eyes. "We have come to so many dead ends, experienced so many heartbreaks—" her voice broke—"I think we can survive another." She turned back to the others. "But even for a few minutes, while we search for this Danita Chávez, I will allow the hope to bubble from deep inside my heart." She smiled, then added, "But I will not allow it to overflow quite yet."

"There is something else," Gav said. "The young man, Raúl, who they both believe is Danita's brother, has disappeared as well. He was working in the underground against Julian Hernando and Tres Equis. Apparently he fell out of favor with the leader, perhaps in trying to gain Danita's release. If in fact

Danita is being held here, Raúl is too."

Alfredo turned to assess the structures before them—the concrete cross with its elevator to an observation deck, the massive basilica carved into the granite mountain. "Forty thousand civil war victims from both sides are buried inside. What a symbol of death!" He shuddered, and Marta circled her arm around his waist.

"Sixteen years to build," he went on, "and only folly resulted." He turned back to K.C., Gav, and Duncan. "The tragedy is that none of those prisoners who died while building this abhorrent memorial are honored here at all." Then he nodded toward a configuration of granite slabs and boulders to one side of the basilica. "The entrance to the tunnel is over there."

Within a few minutes, he stepped into a dark cave. The others were right behind him. He flicked on a large flashlight and, with its strong beam, surveyed the tunnel ahead.

"Let's get started," he said, and the small group headed into the bowels of the mountain.

"No one has come with food today," Danita said. "Does it strike you as odd that we have not seen or heard the guards?"

"Not unless it is because of some new orders from Julian."

Terror struck her heart. "He would not simply leave us here to die, would he?"

"No."

But her brother's short answer didn't convince her.

"I saw cruelty that I did not know existed within him—"

Raúl broke into her dismal thoughts. "Dani, do not dwell on what Julian might or might not do."

She drew in a deep breath. "You are right. It serves no purpose."

"Let us talk about something pleasant. You told me yesterday that if you could write a saeta, it would be of a new sort. One of praise to God. Tell me some of your ideas."

She smiled, feeling her heart lift at the thought. "There are some words that echo in my mind time to time. Someday I would like to set them to music—though a melody has already come to me."

"What are they?"

"So far, just snatches—phrases if you will—of incomplete thoughts. Sometimes I think it is more of a lullaby than a praise, though."

"Tell me."

She hummed a few notes, then laughed, self-consciously. "I am no musician."

"It is beautiful. Go on."

Humming again, she felt braver because of his encouragement and hummed a bit more of the music as it came to her.

"It is a comforting melody."

"You like it?"

"Very much. But you are right. It does not sound like any saeta I have heard before."

She could almost forget the dismal, frightening surroundings as she thought about her song. Closing her eyes, she began to hum the melody, once in a while murmuring words that came to her.

God watches over me...his strong and gentle arms hold me....

Throughout the afternoon, Julian met with Tres Equis leaders and discussed how they could salvage the remnants of the uprising. When they left to carry out his orders, he turned to stare again at the dark computer screen. He did not know how long he stared. It could have been minutes. It could have been hours.

Raúl had betrayed them all. And that obscene dancing bug was the final indignity.

Slowly, with an exaggerated precision, Julian reached for the telephone. He pressed the numbers to call his assistant at Valle de los Caídos.

Raúl Chávez would pay for his crime. Immediately.

Within minutes of this phone call, the arrogant and foolhardy Raúl would be yanked from his cell and eliminated.

As for the delicious Dani...well, he regretted losing her. He'd looked forward to years of enjoying her company. But clearly she was as much a traitor as her brother.

They both had to die.

Fortunately, that should require little effort. They had no real family, no history that anyone knew of. In mere moments, it would be as if they had never existed.

Julian drummed his fingers on the table, waiting as the telephone rang three times, four...seven times...

He clenched his teeth and punched down the disconnect. He dialed again.

Still no answer.

No matter. He would keep trying until he gave the order. And if that didn't work, then he would order his car brought around and accomplish the task himself!

His anger built as he punched the redial button. How he would like to be there, to savor the agony Raúl would experience as he watched his sister die. He chuckled, congratulating himself on the brilliance of his plan. For that was what he'd decided. Dear Dani would die first. Slowly, painfully, her screams echoing in her brother's ears as he faced the full cost of his foolishness.

And then, with slow precision so as to avoid freeing him from the images he'd just witnessed, Raúl would join his sister in oblivion.

Julian smiled. A fitting end to those who betrayed him.

Alfredo was still in the lead, and K.C. hoped that he knew the caves and tunnels as thoroughly as it appeared. He strode forward with confidence, every footstep echoing against the wet granite walls.

They had been in the tunnels for several minutes when they came to the first cave. It was similar to a large room, cells carved into the walls, rusted grates across each one. A desk was in the center, and chairs scattered around it, some tipped over, some upright.

"This is where trials were held," Alfredo said, and offered no more explanation as he hurried them through to the entrance of another tunnel. Soon they reached a crossroads, and he stopped to study both choices.

"There are over four hundred cells in the maze of tunnels." He shook his head slowly and let out a deep breath.

K.C.'s spirits dropped. "It could take hours to check them all!"

Marta's eyes reflected her sorrow. "I had no idea there were so many."

"Should we split up?" Gav swept his flashlight beam down one, dark corridor. "We could go in groups, taking different directions, then report back...."

Alfredo shook his head. "No, it would be too dangerous. It might take days to find anyone who got lost. We need to stay together."

Flashlight scanning the cave to his right, he seemed to

study the direction, turned, looked at the tunnel to the left. Considered it for a long moment, then shook his head. "Let us go this way."

His shoulders slumped, and K.C. wondered if it was from discouragement or bad memories.

Or if he was trying to find a way to tell them they were lost.

"Sing your song again, Dani."

Danita smiled, delighting in her brother's excitement.

She hummed for a few moments, then began to murmur the words again. *God watches over me...his strong and gentle arms hold me....*

The image of her heavenly Father came to her, and she could almost feel herself being held in his arms, as an earthly papá might hold a child cherished beyond all measure.

She opened her eyes and grinned at Raúl. "So, what do you think of my songwriting talents, little brother?"

His only answer was a silent, stunned expression.

She frowned. "Was it that bad?"

"Again." He stood and walked to the grate. "You must sing it again. Try to think of more words. Try to remember...."

There was such joy in his voice, and it pleased her. He was glad to hear her praise to God! She smiled at him, and then saw that tears had filled his eyes.

This time her voice choked as she lifted her voice in song.

Alfredo stopped as another tunnel veered off to the left. Frowning, he scratched his head. "There are so many tunnels. I had forgotten how many until now. It has been so many years...."

He looked to the tunnel on the right, and his forehead creased again. "Let us try this one."

Julian frowned as he slammed the phone in its cradle.

So, he would have to drive out and take care of the traitors himself. His fool assistant obviously had wandered away. Perhaps he would take care of that incompetent as well....

He strode toward the door, but then hesitated. What was that sound?

He rushed to the window, pulled up the blind, and peered out. The whipping, beating sounds of helicopter blades vibrated the panes of glass. Then came the sirens. Dozens of shrill, screaming sirens. The sounds assaulted Julian's ears, his entire being.

Rage, pure and punishing, surged through him as he watched police cars, lights flashing, screech to a halt on the street below the townhouse window.

Julian spun, ready to bolt, then froze where he stood.

Brother Thomas, flanked by two other men, stepped into the room.

"What are you—?"

But before Julian could finish, Brother Thomas smiled and held out a badge. "It is over."

Julian stared into the face of the other man as his dreams shattered and broke, falling about him like yesterday's refuse. Suddenly, he was conscious of only one thing: the arrogance of those who had come for him.

Did they not know who he was? Did they not know that he had been chosen to lead this nation into the new millennium? That he had been destined to great leadership since before time began? Not only of Spain, but of the entire *world*?

He drew himself up and raised his chin. If he could get to his place of worship—the place others called the Museum of Antiquities—the one and true leader of Tres Equis, his Supreme Being, would tell him what to do.

Just as always.

Yes. That was the answer! Julian pictured the dark, womb-like room with its beautiful symbols of worship and smiled, confidence sweeping him.

He was the Chosen One!

Squaring his shoulders, he stared at the circle of men who had now entered his office, weapons pointed at his chest.

He almost laughed when the handcuffs clicked around his wrists.

Did they not know men's metal shackles could not contain him?

He was the Chosen One!

And they could do nothing to stop him.

Marta stepped up to take Alfredo's hand as they walked. Then she stopped and tilted her head. "Do you hear music?"

The others stopped, standing still and craning their heads to listen.

"Music..." Marta frowned in concentration. "Do you hear it?"

All K.C. could hear was the echo of water dripping. Once in a while, the groan of a water pipe in the distance. Nothing else. She shook her head.

"Sometimes these tunnels can play tricks on you," Alfredo said solemnly. "Some say they are inhabited by the ghosts of those who died building them."

They all laughed nervously as Alfredo turned once more to

lead them deeper into the mountain.

They had walked several more minutes, when Marta halted again and put her finger to her lips. "Listen," she mouthed.

The group stood perfectly still.

A faint melody drifted to them from an entrance to still another tunnel. It almost sounded like a child singing.

K.C. frowned. Could it be Danita? Or perhaps a trick of her imagination? A quick look into the others' faces confirmed that they heard it too.

Alfredo turned to the second tunnel and picked up his pace. With a small cry, Marta followed.

K.C. exchanged puzzled glances with both Gav and Duncan, then hurried to catch up with the Aznars, who were almost running by now.

Then quite suddenly, Alfredo bellowed out, his voice off-key and choking with emotion.

"Sleep, my child as angels attend thee. Sleep in Heaven's peace."

K.C. looked at Gav, who shrugged and shook his head. Duncan was murmuring a prayer behind them. And Alfredo...

The older man was still lifting his voice in song, tears now streaming down his face.

"Sleep as God himself watches o'er thee. Sleep in his strong and gentle arms."

Danita was standing at the iron grate of her cell. In the distance the sounds of someone singing stunned her into silence.

It was the same melody she had been singing to her brother moments earlier.

Across the space that divided them, Raúl stood watching her, tears streaming down his face. "It is the song, Dani! The song I told you about. Marta Aznar wrote it in the letter. Our father sang it to us every night."

The singer in the tunnel had almost reached them. His voice was ragged, off-key, as he continued to sing. But it was the most beautiful sound Danita had ever heard.

"Wake, my child, to his rosy dawn. Wake to his promise of love."

At first Danita whispered the words as they came to her: "Wake as God himself watches o'er thee."

Then as her mother and father stepped around the corner, she sang with all her heart. "Wake in his strong and gentle arms."

By now she was crying so hard she could barely utter the words. Suddenly her father stepped to the iron gate and looked into her eyes. She reached for his hand.

"My child, you're home. You're home!"

Across from them, her mother had taken both Raúl's hands in hers. "Oh, my son! You have your father's eyes. I would have known you anywhere."

Danita met Raúl's gaze, his shock and joy shining in his eyes.

Here, in this dank and dismal dungeon, in this place where so many had suffered and died…here, where sorrow and grief had reigned supreme, rejoicing and restoration had finally arrived.

Joy bubbled up inside her as she turned to look into her father's face.

Here, in this place of evil, God had overcome. And at long last, they had come home.

EPILOGUE

Cloister gardens of Teresa of Ávila Convent

K.C. STOOD BENEATH THE SECOND-STORY ARCHED GALLERY AS Sister Calandria and Sister Josefina, one standing, one kneeling, tugged at her hem and told her to turn slowly.

She giggled as she turned. Never in her wildest dreams had she thought she would marry Gav in an outfit pulled together by two nuns who had bartered for it at a street fair, piece by secondhand piece. Even the white straw hat, with its froth of pale ivory and sunny yellow daffodils at the crown, somehow worked.

She looked down at the wonderful dress of lace and linen so patiently stitched together by these godly women who loved her. Tears filled her eyes as she watched them put the finishing touch on a hem that Sister Josefina had insisted was uneven.

Sister Josefina stood and brushed her hands. Then she

stood back with a scowl and shook her head slowly. "It will never hang correctly." She let out an impatient sigh, then looked at Sister Calandria. "I still think the ivory knit would have worked better for the skirt. It would have given it a much softer look."

K.C. giggled again and held up her hand. "It's perfect! I have never seen a more beautiful dress in my life!" She clapped her hands together in delight and turned another circle to prove her point, unable to resist adding a little jig at the end.

They stood back to admire her, the scowl still on Sister Josefina's face, a wide grin on Sister Calandria's.

K.C. was suddenly filled with an overwhelming love for the women. She knew it was against their rules—and that they would probably have to go to confession tonight for her brash action—but she couldn't resist. Before they could back away, she grabbed them both, giving them a collective, arms-wide-open hug.

"Oh, my!" Sister Calandria said, stepping back in surprise.

"Oh, dear!" Sister Josefina frowned. "Oh, dear!"

The sisters' eyes welled with tears.

"You have been so good to me," K.C. whispered, unable to keep her own tears from spilling. "I will never forget you."

Just then Duncan strode toward her. "Gav is ready. Are you?"

"Never readier!" She pushed her glasses up on her nose and gave him a nod. "We'd better do it before one of us disappears!"

Duncan laughed. "I just came from the foyer. I saw Dani and Raúl arrive with Marta and Alfredo. They make quite a family. The resemblance is astounding."

She turned as they entered the lower gallery and made their way to the courtyard garden. As soon as they were seated, she nodded. "Our guests are here. Let's begin."

Sister Calandria and Sister Josefina took their places with some of the other nuns near the fountain.

Duncan left for a few minutes, then returned with Gav. The two men walked to the circular terrace around the fountain and turned as K.C. moved to the entrance of the garden.

She paused for a moment, looking at the faces that were turned toward her. The Aznar family, newly reunited—oh, how she lifted a heart of praise for the answers to prayer, the miracle that had happened in their lives!

And her precious friends, Sister Calandria and Sister Josefina. She breathed another word of praise for their lives…for their love of helping others…for their laughter and tears. She would never forget them.

Finally, she turned to Gav.

Looking into his beloved face, she thought she couldn't contain the joy that filled her so completely.

I am my beloved's, and he is mine!

Yes, Lord! Oh yes!

Gav's tender gaze met hers, and she blinked away the quick tears that stung her eyes.

A shimmering whirl of memories danced in her mind. Gav, when they were childhood sweethearts and pledged their love would last forever. Gav, when he stepped into her life at Sugar Loaf Mountain after their long separation. Gav, when he returned to Salamanca and opened his arms for her to step into the safety of his embrace…in this very garden.

He smiled into her eyes, and it was as if the sun had risen after a very long night.

Clutching her nosegay of spring flowers, she stepped slowly toward him, her gaze never leaving his.

It was perfectly quiet except for the song of one small bird perched on a leafy twig and the trickle of water in the fountain.

And, just as Gav reached out to catch her hands in his, the joyous tolling of distant bells.